Refiguring
ENGLISH
STUDIES

Refiguring English Studies provides a forum for scholarship on English Studies as a discipline, a profession, and a vocation. To that end, the series publishes historical work that considers the ways in which English Studies has constructed itself and its objects of study; investigations of the relationships among its constituent parts as conceived in both disciplinary and institutional terms; and examinations of the role the discipline has played or should play in the larger society and public policy. In addition, the series seeks to feature studies that, by their form or focus, challenge our notions about how the written "work" of English can or should be done and to feature writings that represent the professional lives of the discipline's members in both traditional and nontraditional settings. The series also includes scholarship that considers the discipline's possible futures or that draws upon work in other disciplines to shed light on developments in English Studies.

Volumes in the Series

David B. Downing, editor, *Changing Classroom Practices: Resources for Literary and Cultural Studies* (1994)

Jed Rasula, *The American Poetry Wax Museum: Reality Effects, 1940–1990* (1995)

James A. Berlin, *Rhetorics, Poetics, and Cultures: Refiguring College English Studies* (1996)

Robin Varnum, *Fencing with Words: A History of Writing Instruction at Amherst College during the Era of Theodore Baird, 1938–1966* (1996)

Jane Maher, *Mina P. Shaughnessy: Her Life and Work* (1997)

Michael Blitz and C. Mark Hurlbert, *Letters for the Living: Teaching Writing in a Violent Age* (1998)

Bruce Horner and Min-Zhan Lu, *Representing the "Other": Basic Writers and the Teaching of Basic Writing* (1999)

Stephen M. North, with Barbara A. Chepaitis, David Coogan, Lâle Davidson, Ron MacLean, Cindy L. Parrish, Jonathan Post, and Beth Weatherby, *Refiguring the Ph.D. in English Studies: Writing, Doctoral Education, and the Fusion-Based Curriculum* (2000)

Composing Critical Pedagogies

Teaching Writing as Revision

AMY LEE

University of Minnesota

National Council of Teachers of English
1111 W. Kenyon Road, Urbana, Illinois 61801-1096

Staff Editor: Rita D. Disroe
Cover Design: Carlton Bruett
Interior Design: Jenny Jensen Greenleaf

NCTE Stock Number: 30402-3050
ISSN 1073-9637

It is the policy of NCTE in its journals and other publications to provide a forum for the open discussion of ideas concerning the content and the teaching of English and the language arts. Publicity accorded to any particular point of view does not imply endorsement by the Executive Committee, the Board of Directors, or the membership at large, except in announcements of policy, where such endorsement is clearly specified.

Library of Congress Cataloging-in-Publication Data

Lee, Amy, 1967–
    Composing critical pedagogies: teaching writing as revision/Amy Lee.
        p. cm.—(Refiguring English studies, ISSN 1073-9637)
    Includes bibliographical references and index.
    "NCTE stock number: 30402-3050"—T.p. verso.
    ISBN 0-8141-3040-2 (pbk.)
    1. English language—Rhetoric—Study and teaching. 2. Report writing—Study and teaching. I. Title. II. Series.
PE1404.L435 2000
808'.042'071—dc21
                                                        00-027466

In memory of my grandmothers, Lucy and Gerry,
My uncle Jack,
And for my parents, Tom and Mary Gerry Lee

CONTENTS

ACKNOWLEDGMENTS

The best thing I learned while writing this book was that writing—as I tell my students but had to learn for myself—really isn't an isolating or isolated activity. This book represents a collective endeavor on many levels because all along the way, readers, students, and friends challenged, supported, and extended my thinking by taking the time to read and listen to my words. Without Anne Herrington, this book wouldn't be; and even if I didn't appreciate it at the time, thanks for all the revisioning you nudged and challenged me into doing.

My colleagues at SUNY Albany provided essential support in various forms. Steve North, thanks for the curmudgeonly goading, the willingness to entertain a social vision, and mostly for just telling me to WRITE. Shari Stenberg and Chris Gallagher, well, you guys were the first to provide me with the sense of writing into an existing community of readers. For the many times you read certain sections, over and over, and talked with me about the project, infusing my enthusiasm and recharging my excitement, thank you.

Thanks also to Harriet Malinowitz, whose supportive and critical feedback on the earliest draft gave me ideas to work with and a reason to keep working. Michael Greer—thanks for pushing and prodding me along consistently and patiently. And thanks to Rita D. Disroe for her very necessary and actually educational editing. Thanks to James Stemper, a librarian-detective.

Cinthia, Yomika, and Ahrmand made my life, and writing, in Albany richer and more fun. Martha "Mommy" Bennett, you fed me well and gave me a little piece of family in the East.

Of course, without the many students I have been blessed to learn with and from, there would be no book whatsoever. Your generosity of intellectual energy, time, and enthusiastic responsiveness undergird the entire project. Thank you.

To Lisa Viola for all the times you let me call you and tell you I couldn't write anymore. To Mach Arom, the first person who *wanted* to (and didn't have to) read the entire manuscript cover-to-cover. To my brothers, Mike, Jack, and Dan—you'd never want *me* as a teacher, but you have never doubted the value of teachers' work. To my sisters, Laura and Cathy, because you've taught me a lot. And most of all, to my parents because you believe so unequivocally in the possibilities of education and because you taught me to value revision even when we saw things differently. You were my first teachers; you're still my best. Most of all, thanks to the newest eyes in our family: my beloved Elisabeth Lucile, Catherine Eldredge, and Jackson Thomas Lee. Learning from you renews my hope and faith. By the time you're able to read this, I hope some revisions have taken hold, beyond our imagination, not only in how we see but also in how we live with one another.

CHAPTER ONE

Visions, Versions, and Composing Pedagogies

Originally, I set out to write an argument about how writing and teaching writing can change the world. For me and for others I knew, "writing" (which to me includes reading both language and texts, not only making them work but also studying the work they do) had changed our understanding of the world and hence given us a starting point to act differently in the world. Not, perhaps, in sweeping revolutionary ways, but in steady and, nonetheless, important ways. Many of us read and teach particular texts because we believe they make an impact on the world; they work in and on the world. For some, it is a religious text; for others, political texts; for still others, a novel or poem. "Diving into the Wreck," *Narrative of the Life of Frederick Douglass,* "A Room of One's Own," *Beloved, Borderlands.* I have read student texts just as powerful. I have observed students write their way—even if for only the space of a text—out of their silence as the objects of systemic and individual violence, abuse, discrimination. I have also read texts in which students have come to a recognition and sense of accountability for the ways in which they have named "others" and represented them as objects. Some students have been able to name themselves in ways other than they have been named by and as others (whether this renaming is done by those who occupy positions of power or disempowerment vis-à-vis the normative subject position at hand). Don't we want our understanding of "better writers" to encompass such possibilities? Isn't this a reason to teach writing? Not only does language give voice to experience, to insight, but it also gives shape to that experience, allowing people the space for recording, reflecting on and revising their identities, relationships, and values. This, to me, is the best of what we do.

We are in the discipline of composition, the discipline of teaching writing. Our work, therefore, takes place in academic contexts and within existing curricula. I suggest, then, that we also teach forms and processes of writing, with acute attention to the specific conditions that inform how texts are read in particular contexts. We help students envision themselves as writers so that they might recognize and question the different constructions of "authority," textual logic, and structure that are normative in specific contexts. We can identify the forms sanctioned in particular discourse communities, with their attendant logics, subject-positions, and standpoints. We can help them identify the conventions that characterize particular forms and rhetorical contexts. We can also learn—from and with them—about the choices we have for not accommodating those conventions, for being authorized to object to them, to produce alternative possibilities for our versions and visions. As writers, we will find ourselves operating from within or attempting to enter into contexts that deny our authority, devalue our ideas and experiences, or reject our forms for representing them. Our conception of "better writers" surely includes these possibilities for revision as well. Recognizing and making choices about how, why, and to and/or for whom we write is also the best of what we do.

In this book, I assume that our pedagogy, how and why we teach writing, has to be informed by both our ideal visions of the function and possibilities of teaching writing, and by attention to the conditions within which we teach writing. Conditions name the local factors at play in a specific classroom, as well as the institutional, social, and political factors that inform and pervade our classes. My opening paragraph describes a vision of writing pedagogy, while the second moves from that generalized vision to a version that attends to the specific context in which many of us teach writing. The second is neither a compromise version of nor the application of the first. Rather, these two—our idealized and generalized visions of writing pedagogy and our (reflections on) attempts to enact those visions within local and specific sites—are the mutually necessary, interdependent components of pedagogy.

Composing Pedagogies

At a summer orientation for new graduate students, we went around the room and took turns talking about our present and particular areas of scholarly interest and inquiry. At the time, I recall thinking it's funny how we think first to ask about and explain our research agenda and second, if even at all, to discuss our teaching work. I was surprised, however, when more than half of the students present claimed "pedagogy" or "critical pedagogy" as an intended area of study. How much things have changed over recent years. Not long ago, "pedagogy," at least in English departments, was rarely mentioned let alone considered a legitimate area of scholarly investment. When I asked follow-up questions of these students, they talked about social justice, critical theory, feminism, social transformation, cultural studies; but—with one exception—no one talked about teaching. What, then, is pedagogy?

Pedagogy, as Chris Gallagher suggests, is always preceded by a qualifier. There is feminist, critical, oppositional, traditional, humanist, process, radical pedagogy. There is oppressive pedagogy (pedagogy of the oppressed). But what is pedagogy—unqualified, unmarked? This is a question it has taken me many years and revisions to even ask. Somehow, I took for granted that "we" shared a working definition of what pedagogy implies, that is, what it entails. For the purposes of a book with "pedagogy" in its title, I would like to suggest a working definition of the term.

Perhaps a useful analogy can be made between pedagogy/teaching and composition/writing, between the relationships of these two fields and their respective subjects and practices. Similar to composition, pedagogy centers on questions of teaching and learning, insisting that the study of these processes (like the study of the teaching and learning of writing) is a legitimate and crucial area for inquiry. Further, pedagogy also proposes that how and why we teach—the potential use, effect, impact of education—is as important as what we teach. That is, pedagogy, like composition, does not understand its subject as a body of knowledge one transmits to students; the study of pedagogy is not an attempt to produce prescriptive, procedural texts on the "craft" or the "how-to" of teaching, planning, and executing a class. Most obviously, the subject of study in both composition and pedagogy studies is not only a subject but also an action; in other words, each field studies an object and means of inquiry. Perhaps this best explains why each has been marginalized within English departments and academic institutions. They have been constructed as largely concerned with practice and therefore as atheoretical or unintellectual.

In each case, both pedagogy and writing, we put various qualifiers before the term to specify and signify particular investments, commitments, and assumptions that exceed a general commitment to teaching, learning, and writing. Bennett, D'Souza, and Hirsch have pedagogies; that is, they understand that education, as an institution and as an action, influences social, economic, and cultural contexts and conditions outside the classroom or the school. They argue that, more than simply transmitting knowledge; the study of specific literary, philosophical, and historical texts can affect cultural values, attitudes, and beliefs. But we would qualify their pedagogy differently, perhaps, than our own. We would preface it with *humanist* or *conservative* or *oppressive,* depending on our standpoints. This underscores the importance of the qualifying term that precedes pedagogy; much pressure, it seems, is exerted on and by this signifier.

When we refer to the pedagogy forwarded by John Dewey, we evoke educational progressivism, attributing a coherent and discernable framework to the methods he advocated and to the educational movement we identify with his work. In our own historical moment, there is not a coherent movement so much as there is a proliferation of progressive pedagogies. It becomes difficult to distinguish the shared vision of these frameworks, as well as to clearly articulate the different emphases and aims they foreground. Self-identified "progressive" pedagogies might now include cultural, critical, radical, oppositional, feminist, Marxist, postmodern, poststructural, postcolonial pedagogies. As Gallagher observes:

> As the prominence of "post-"s in this partial list suggests, we tend to use these modifiers to distinguish "our" visions of peda-

gogy and literacy from those who have come before us and those who surround us. But although this terminology is of late vintage, this endless proliferation of pedagogies and literacies suggests less a boom in innovation—the opening of some theoretical seventh seal—than a seemingly ever-increasing willingness to mark one's "turf" as unique, distinct, impermeable. (1998, 4)

In this book, I do not aim to present the new and improved vision of critical pedagogy so much as I aim to provide a reflexive, critical portfolio of one teacher's (ongoing) process of coming to a specific version of critical pedagogy in the teaching of writing. Much of the scholarship presents critical pedagogy as a complete and contained vision, a nexus of commitments and goals one is encouraged to adopt. There is, however, little examination or reflection of how one moves from staking a position, from naming one's self as a progressive educator, to enacting that in tangible and material ways in the day-to-day work of teaching. There is little available research that actually takes pedagogy as a process of (re)learning to teach, rather than as an argument about teaching or a theory of education. Even if one is immediately supportive of and invested in the possibilities of progressive or critical pedagogies, there is much work to do in enacting these ideas and values in the classroom, in our relations with our students, in their relations with one another and with the subject of study. So I do not begin (and end) by declaring myself to be a critical educator and exhorting like-minded writing teachers to do the same. Instead, I assume here that such a declaration is merely the starting-point of work in critical pedagogy. From claiming a pedagogy, we must move to reflecting on the challenges and possibilities of actualizing it. For it is not enough to *have* visions, we need also to consider the contexts and conditions that foster or constrain our efforts to *realize* them.

My project, then, is to consider what it means not only to claim but also to enact a pedagogy. (And I am not here evoking a distinction between "theorizing" and "practicing" pedagogy. In fact, this is a conceptual distinction I problematize throughout the book, arguing that our efforts to enact pedagogy must exert revisionary pressure on our theoretical visions.) How does working within a particular pedagogical framework affect the microlevel choices one makes as a teacher? How does it reenvision the roles and relations of students, teachers, and the subject of study? In turn, how are our frameworks revised in light of our experiences in particular sites, working with engaged participants? In discussing the question of pedagogy with new teachers, I always start by asking what it is they believe they are teaching in a given course. Are they teaching a text, knowledge of a period, a specific reading or reading practices, a particular form of writing, academic discourse, collective learning, civic responsibility, critical consciousness, social relations? Do they envision the function of their work to be intellectual, political, social, aesthetic? To whom or what is their responsibility? To the students? Society? A particular political agenda? The discipline? The institution? While these questions might seem obvious, while we might take for granted that we know what we are teaching, the answers are often surprising and complicated. They lead, of course, to questions about why we are teaching with those aims in mind, how we work to produce those results, and whom we think we are teaching, that is, who we understand our students to be. Obviously, current-traditional pedagogy will take up, emphasize, and respond to these questions differently than either process or critical pedagogy; this is precisely the function of a theoretical framework, after all.

So, for instance, expressivist pedagogy, as I am constructing it based on my experience of being trained in a process-oriented writing program and on my reading in composition studies, suggests that specific teaching practices will necessarily result in "better" writing and "better" writers. Here, "better" is understood as empowered writers, confident writing with a "voice," successful academic discourse that does not necessitate the total erasure or silencing of the individual author. Critical pedagogy, as I am constructing it on the basis of my reading in the field, as well as on my classroom research, suggests that having a political, critical conception of one's teaching will necessarily produce liberatory effects in the classroom that, in turn, will produce better citizens. Here, "better" is understood as capable of critically reading dominant discourses of identity and socioeconomic relations, recognizing that we are shaped by these discourses and are capable of resisting and revising them, and working toward a radical democracy.

Expressivist pedagogy emphasizes practices, offering teaching methods that promote better writing and better writers; both, in turn, result in better people. The primary focus is on individual classrooms and students, while the teacher's role, largely implied, emerges indirectly. Teachers are perhaps best characterized as coaches, working on the sidelines to improve the performance of each student. Critical pedagogy emphasizes a theoretical and political framework within which teachers can understand what and why they are teaching. It emphasizes the institution's (and by extension the classroom's) relationship to social, economic, and political conditions—that what takes place in a classroom is informed by and informs what takes places in simultaneous spheres. Critical pedagogy foregrounds the teacher or educator, providing her a context for understanding her work as well as a set of aims that will result in radical, political effects. The students' role is largely ignored, so that while they are described—invested with specific qualities and capabilities—they are not actively represented in the discourse of critical pedagogy. Teachers are centered in this framework, while students are presented as subjects of and subject to critical pedagogy.

Both pedagogies share a commitment to writing as transformation; composition pedagogy articulates a wide array of possible effects of this transformation, while critical pedagogy generally claims a transformation to critical consciousness. Both frameworks demonstrate and assume the dynamic potential of writing (and reading) to shape and reshape writers/"selves"/citizens in relation to readers/"others"/citizenry. Empowerment, power, authority, and transformation are central terms in each pedagogy I take up throughout the book, considering the relationship between the ways we define these terms and how we understand and teach writing.

Pedagogy as Reflection and Action

Each of these pedagogical frameworks provides a writing teacher with a foundation for understanding her teaching in a broader social, institutional, and political context. But a central argument throughout this book is that a viable pedagogy cannot exist only in the abstract, but must be conceptualized in relation to the real contexts, to the complex and dynamic sites in which our teaching takes place. We need to define pedagogy in relation to the real stories of our teaching, and not only according to what we hope can, or ideally will, happen in our classrooms. In other words, practice must be a central concern in our research on pedagogies; not practice understood as the "natural" or simple application of theory or ideas, but practice understood as the complicated and uncertain process of working to enact the pedagogies we claim to espouse. How can one proclaim a "student-centered" or "liberatory" pedagogy and then proceed to invent an entire course plan, complete with assumed or imposed student-student, student-teacher relations and dynamics before one has begun working with students? Such a vision of one's class assumes that students are an afterthought, that they will come in and occupy the necessary and idealized personae and positions we declare for them. What would it mean not only to imagine or advocate more substantively democratic classroom relations but also to work with our students to foster the conditions necessary to achieve such relations? This book is concerned not with proving my pedagogy to merit a particular qualifier, but rather with demonstrating the ongoing process of reflexive critique through which I am attempting to enact my pedagogical goals in my teaching work. Being "critical," this book argues and illustrates, is a process in which one must consistently (re-) engage. It must be realized, both conceptually and actually, over and over again—in word and action, in deed and in mind.

Traditionally, pedagogy is understood as theories and practices of teaching. At one moment, we think about teaching writing (or we think about teaching writing "critically" or so as to empower students as writers) and in the next, we go and do it. Such a conception is deeply problematic, similar to suggesting that composition or writing is only the final product, the finished version. What about all the time spent thinking about writing before we actually begin; what about drafts, revisions, readers' comments, reflective notes? "Writing," as we generally understand in the discipline of composition and are often trying to teach those outside of our field, is a process. It consists of reflection and action, doing something that results in a "product" but that necessitates thinking about what we're doing, how we're doing it and why. Often times, this reflexive thinking can occur only after we have done some writing. It is not a sequential or linear process of thinking and then doing, but rather a recursive one. I would like to suggest that pedagogy is also constituted by reflection and action. That pedagogy takes place in multiple and sometimes simultaneous spheres of action in the "classroom" (whether that's a public meeting, a committee, a place of worship, a workplace) and outside of it. That pedagogy is teaching, working with students, committee members, colleagues, citizens, and parishioners in specific contexts. And that pedagogy is also thinking about what, how, who and why we are teaching in those specific sites.

Gramsci, Foucault, and feminists such as Harding and Phelan show how politics and ideology operate in important ways in the everyday, in our concepts of self, in common sense. Hegemony is working best precisely where we begin to perceive the world as given, natural, or just common sense. I would argue that this happens in our pedagogies as well. Once we teach or understand our teaching in certain ways, or once we consciously adopt and enact a specific pedagogy, it becomes difficult to critique our assumptions and practices. They come to seem inalterable, given, unchallengeable. Several of the graduate student teachers I have worked with talk often about "making our pedagogies visible." In our classes, they claim, we should make explicit to students how we are teaching and why, we should articulate our commitments and assumptions, inviting collective reflection on our choices and their effects. It seems possible and perhaps important to do this in our writing as well, to consider, as Jennifer Gore suggests, not only the pedagogy we argue *for* but also the pedagogy *of* our arguments.

I have come to be convinced, again through reflexive inquiry into my teaching and into the scholarship, that writing is one of our most powerful and effective processes for unpacking and rearticulating this "common sense" as a social construction, as "the political." This is also a central argument throughout the book. In writing, we set down and are made to represent many of the assumptions, values, ideas that inform our everyday thinking about the world, but that might otherwise go un-noted, unacknowledged. In reading these texts critically, the writer and readers can make visible the unspoken, the invisible—as they impact the form of the text as well as the ideas and relations represented by it. A writing class, then, might aim to make visible the cultural and political work of our reading and writing practices. Ideally, we are working toward revision.

Writing Pedagogy as Revisioning

I have structured this book in such a way to consider what can happen in the teaching of writing when we work from a pedagogy that centers around reflection and action, both inside and outside the classroom. Throughout, I am attempting to demonstrate these two processes to enact them and not merely to argue for or articulate them. Representing our pedagogy is difficult; turning the text of our teaching into something more complicated than the familiar genres of classroom narrative—heroic quest story or confessional narrative—requires not only new forms for representing our work in the classroom but also new ways of reading. It is not only in writing but also in reading that we reproduce and reexert the functional pressure of traditional distinctions and binaries (theory-practice, teacher-student, reading-writing, rigor-nurture, scholar-teacher). When I present student texts here or conversations from our classroom, I am not using those simply as the example of pedagogy in action, nor am I hoping they will serve as prescriptive models for other teachers. Instead, the classroom, along with the scholarship, is offered as a site for research, a specific context in which our theories are enacted, critiqued, expanded, and revised. In this process of revision, students are coinquirers, not the objects of an already existing pedagogy nor are they subject to my pedagogy.

Such a conception of representing and theorizing pedagogy is different from the dominant forms with which I am familiar. It is firmly grounded in composition research where students figure prominently and are, through texts or reflective comments, immediately present in the research. Many early readers of this manuscript have commented that they read the book differently when they read as teachers than when they read as scholars. This may have been a shortcoming in the earlier text, indicating the inadequacy of my struggle to insist we should not make such distinctions if our work is pedagogy. We should not, without acknowledging and accounting for the choice, at one moment theorize about teaching or education, and at the next describe or prescribe practices for achieving those theoretical visions. But I would also suggest that readers who find themselves reading as teachers and then as scholars should consider why they ask different questions or use different lenses if the subject at hand is pedagogy. Why is it so difficult to read or to write as both teacher and theorist, as scholar and as educator? I would suggest it goes back to the normative binaries that inform our professional identities, our intellectual practices and the discursive forms for our scholarship. These binaries are so thoroughly entrenched that they often operate invisibly and need to be continually exposed and questioned. In *Left Margins*, a recent collection on composition and critical pedagogy, the editors sought to resist traditional reading and writing practices by contesting the binary relationship that typically adheres between teaching/research and pedagogical theories/practices. According to the editors, Fitts and France, the book was conceived of as "a practical pedagogical companion" that engages "day-to-day classroom exchanges" and focuses on "the actualization of theory in practice" (1995, x). Many of the essays collected here, however, reproduce normative pedagogical discourse by either describing what they, as teachers, do to or for students, or by prescribing theoretical visions for our teaching work.

These essays are valuable in that they point to the challenge of representing our teaching while also achieving some distance for critical reflection. They demonstrate the difficulty of representing students as centered in, central to our pedagogies and not simply present as we practice them. We are familiar with pedagogical discourse that theorizes *onto* the classroom; finding a way to theorize *out* of the classroom is more challenging. According to Fitts and France, their central objective for this collection was to reverse the invidious hierarchy that locates theory as an elite (read "masculine") prerogative and classroom practice as private (read "feminine") sphere. . . . [W]e hope to intervene in the tendency to reduce teaching to a set of "implications" that anyone can "apply" to the classroom or conference. Instead, we assume that . . . in this instance at least, we can reverse the polarity of the privileged practice theory binary. (1995, xi)

This notion of reversal, of exchanging one term of the binary for another, is precisely what is problematic about our ways of representing and discussing pedagogy. Because, finally, it leaves in place the assumption that pedagogy consists of theory and of practice, one of which must be privileged, and that these occur in distinct spheres, at separate moments. Instead, as the most useful articles in *Left Margins* insist and attempt, we might more productively question the conditions that sustain the oppositional relationship between theory and practice. And rather than attempt to overturn the conventional hierarchy, we might then seek ways to revision and represent pedagogy as necessitating reflection and action both in and outside the classroom.

One of the central objectives of this book is to foreground students as active participants in and cocreators of our pedagogies. In order to intervene in the familiar discourses of education, of teaching, we need to find ways to more actively represent students' roles in our classrooms and texts. Throughout this manuscript, I foreground the reflections and texts of specific students. I do not aim to recuperate a humanist, pre-Habermasian Individual as the seat and site of knowledge, autonomy, self-determination, and power; rather, I wish to understand the individual in Gramscian terms, as in specific and often competing relationships to various discourses and relations of institutional location, class, race, ethnicity, gender, and sexuality. I am attentive as well to factors that figure into our composite identities but that normally elude theoretical attention in our race to identify and thus somehow "know" our students on the basis of their physical bodies or their textual productions. Students who have been raped or molested, for instance, occupy yet another configuration in the pool of locations that come to inform one's self-conception and relation to other positions. One might argue that these "local" experiences can be understood by an analysis of one or another category; you could suggest, for instance, that class is the primary determining factor in identity. Violence of women, however, transcends class boundaries. To then move to understand it strictly as a woman's situatedness, as a violent manifestation of her location and experience in patriarchy, doesn't seem sufficient for representing or accounting for that experience of being beaten, of one's reaction and response, of the years of figuring and refiguring such an experience. To ignore this experience, not only its impact upon that composite individual but also its relation to the systems that entitle other individuals to perpetrate these acts of violence, is to ignore the complexity of the individual student we seek to understand.

Reflections on Enacting Critical Writing, Critical Pedagogy

My younger brother recently told me that the "cool" thing about my writing is that he, and therefore anyone, can read it. I presume his reaction is a result not only of the language I use but also of the decision to focus on teaching, classrooms, students, and their texts. Such a choice grounds ideas in accessible, familiar contexts. Indeed, this was one of my goals in writing this book, and yet I have found myself struggling to realize that goal (both in terms of actualizing or enacting it, and in terms of continuously re-affirming why it's so crucial to this project) time and time again. In fact, when my brother told me this, I was certain there was something missing from my text; surely an accountant should not find it such an easy read.

When an early reader commented that this text offers no "new" theoretical insights but is useful for people who teach writing, I presume he was responding to the same textual qualities as my brother, but from a different set of assumptions. For instance, people who teach writing are distinct from, are looking for something different from, people who make or seek new theoretical contributions. I have read over and over again the insistence by scholars such as Henry Giroux that the choice not to speak in a highly specialized discourse is also a decision to dumb down one's ideas, to speak down to one's audiences; it is, therefore, a sign of intellectual arrogance, as it disrespects readers. These moments lead me to question my decision and to wonder whether this text would be taken more seriously—perceived as more rigorously intellectual, more radical even—had I made the decision to write in a different discourse. Of course, I would then have to consider whether I should be focusing on students, their texts and comments, and our classroom as well.

At the center of this project, however, is a belief that scholars and teachers and students from a variety of disciplines, from a variety of frameworks and positions, need to be able to access one another's ideas and contributions in order to engage with them fully, whether to reject, resist, corroborate, or confirm. I very much wanted the students who contributed to this project to be able to read it without feeling frustrated or excluded. The fundamental question thus becomes whether one sacrifices intellectual rigor or complexity in making the decision to translate. This is an important aspect of a critical writing course—students do not simply learn to produce "better" academic discourse. They inquire into the conditions and contexts (historical, social, cultural, institutional) that lend legitimacy to certain texts, while silencing or dismissing others. They investigate not only their own processes of writing and reading but also the normative, institutionalized process of academic reading and writing, considering how each is informed by specific contexts and relations of power and authority. They might then realize and make choices about whether and how to disrupt, participate, or intervene in the rhetorical context at hand.

I have no doubt that the students who are present in this book are quite capable of comprehending and responding to the ideas presented here. However, I am also aware that the decision to write in a specialized discourse immediately distances certain readers who might not have access to generally agreed upon meanings, much less evaluations, of specific terminology. I am not, that is, suggesting that a "regular, real" teacher or student can't comprehend this and a scholar can. It is not a matter of our profession, but of our familiarity with specific discourses. Consider these terms: freewriting, process, peer review, alienation, hegemony, agent, ideology, pedagogy, discourse, deconstruction, critique-al, fragmented subject. Although these terms might be meaningful for all readers, they take on specific and specialized meanings within a (sub-)disciplinary discourse. This is an obvious point.

To be aware that readers and writers will not share specialized discourses is not to say that they are incapable of comprehending the ideas. Rather, we are motivated to speak in specific discourses to certain readers in certain contexts. In writing, we inevitably make decisions about how to engage readers and which readers we hope to engage; we might, however, usefully aim to make those decisions critically and self-reflexively. Indeed, this is a central goal I work toward in my writing courses: to foster a consciousness about how readers are addressed by and represented in a text, so that we might consciously make those inevitable decisions, instead of falling into default mode.

I also wonder at the work we fail to do when we refuse to speak across and among, when we insist that all readers meet us where we are. Reading Hurston is not necessarily easier or harder than reading Stein, which is not necessarily easier or more difficult than reading Fitzgerald or Anzaldúa or Wideman or Milton; it all depends on what a reader brings to the text: training, experience, history, discourses. To put too much absolutely into the discourse is to mask the transactional nature of texts, to assume (implicitly) that reading is a process of nonactive absorption. Here is a second foundational assumption that informs my writing courses: readers play a role in the production of a text's meaning, bringing their specific situatedness and investments to a textual product just as writers bring them to the textual process. The processes of reading and writing, then, are not dissimilar, except insofar as we usually expect one to result in a written, tangible product.

To suggest that there is only one way to write a book on pedagogy (or anything else for that matter), or one discourse to write in, or only one word which means absolutely this, is to assign meaning as inherent in the language itself, to assume that texts are—to some degree—transparent, and a reader needs only the proper training or initiation into the text's discourse in order to "get it right." I would like to suggest that we need to learn how to read pedagogy differently. Instead of demanding that it satisfy theoretical and/or practical concerns, we might challenge how (and whether) a pedagogical text engages the relationship between theory and praxis, and how it represents this relationship. I aim, then, not to provide an unshakable defense of this text. Rather, I want to raise the possibility that, just as I have experienced difficulty writing a text that enacts reflection and action, engages classrooms and scholarship, one that represents a different understanding of the nature and relationship between theory and practice, so also might we have difficulty reading such texts because they elude our dominant categories for classifying texts as either theoretical or practical. How do we read a text that is pedagogical both in its focus and in its process?

I might suggest, for instance, that the reader I mentioned earlier could usefully consider why he expects theoretical breakthroughs in order for a book on pedagogy to be useful to an audience beyond teachers. I might ask him in what form and sites he expects or allows such breakthroughs to occur; can they develop in classrooms, from students, while teaching? Clearly, his expectations and assumptions about what constitutes theory and how it is distinct from practice, and how innovations or insights are different from usefulness, inform his reading of this text, and preclude other possible responses. Very much at the heart of this book is the belief, which I also attempt to enact, that we need to learn how to read and write pedagogy differently, that we need to learn how to think about and represent the work of our classrooms not simply as the application of or experimentation with "theory"; our classrooms are not merely the places where we "practice" what we already know. Rather, our classrooms should be sites for research, sites for negotiating, talking back to, and revising our theory. How do we represent our teaching and classrooms as active sites for, and not simply the products of, theoretical inquiry? Here, then, is another parallel between the foundational assumptions in this text and those that inform my teaching. A first draft is not the representation of what a writer already knows; otherwise, we would believe (and teach) that a single draft or version is sufficient, is the appropriate and acceptable encoding of what we know. I aim to foster in students an understanding that writing and reading are both means (processes) and objects of inquiry. We can critically engage our readings and writings of texts; in this way, the textual products of our inquiry become sites of future inquiry. This is not an endless process of playing with construction, signification, interpretation, but rather the chance to make evident or somewhat tangible the processes by which we engage texts and then to study those processes—not to take them for granted but to become critical of them.

Chapter Previews

In Chapter 2, I consider the politics of pedagogy, specifically how "the political" is constituted and deployed within composition and critical pedagogy. I demonstrate that all pedagogies are political in that they represent and imply, like rhetorical forms and discourses, specific normative truths, identities, and relations. In Chapter 3, I move on to consider my training in teaching writing. As a new teacher, this training was important in developing my understanding of what it means to center a course around student texts, and to generate active learning, as well as to teach writing. However, this training in teaching writing left me without a larger framework within which to question and consider what I was doing, how and why I was teaching in particular ways. I believe it is important to provide new teachers with strategies and ideas for how to teach, and, eight years later, I still use many of the practices I learned from our orientation and teaching meetings. The problem is that these methods are presented, in the literature and in our orientation, as universal and unpositioned "tools" for teaching writing, as the natural way to teach writing. In exerting the pressure of context on these methods, I hope to open up the possibilities for more reflection on our actions, those in which we engage and those in which we ask our students to engage.

In Chapter 4, I examine the discourse of critical pedagogy, and argue that conceptualizing and articulating a critical pedagogy in the abstract, without attention to contexts, classrooms, students, and institutions, is very different from enacting critical teaching in our classrooms. Some of us become incapable of working within the central contradiction of the dominant discourse of traditional American critical pedagogy, which situates the teacher as an already liberated, already "critical" agent, while students are largely represented as those to be acted upon by pedagogues, as subject to pedagogy. Some of us have rejected the romantic concepts of "critical consciousness," "empowerment" and "liberation," which pervade the literature on critical pedagogy. The deployment of these terms within the discourse of critical pedagogy often reminds me of romantic ideals of "love," envisioned as a state one falls into and never leaves, as though it is not a series of choices, an ongoing negotiation, but a state in which one comfortably remains. I would suggest, instead, that we emphasize these terms not as products, but as processes, requiring ongoing self-reflexive critique and negotiation. Being radical is not a state one finally achieves, but a framework, with organizing assumptions and aims, through which one responds to and interprets daily life. Declaring one's self to "be radical" or to "be critical" seems a starting point not a guarantee. Similarly, declaring one's pedagogy to be radical, feminist, humanist, or critical is a starting point.

In Chapter 5, I begin articulating a pedagogy of revision, one that seeks not to reform process or critical pedagogy, but to take seriously the commitments of each—to students, to the value of the subject, to the civic and social world. Here I explicitly consider the pressure exerted on composition and critical pedagogies when we assume a poststructural concept of discourse, power, and authority. What happens to the subject in a critical classroom (both the writing subject and the subject of writing)? What methods might we engage in a writing class that assumes that authority and identity are not coherent or unified, and that discourse is contingent and determining, rather than stable and reflective? How do we teach a writing class in which students are simultaneously subject to and subjects of language? While Lester Faigley recently described composition studies as being resistant to postmodern theory, an increasing number of composition scholars are writing about revisioning their classrooms according to critical concept of the nature of language, the function of literacy, and the role of education. Perhaps composition is moving toward "surrendering its belief in the writer as an autonomous self, . . . in the stability of the self and the attendant beliefs that writing can be a means of self-discovery and intellectual self-realization" (Faigley 1992, 15). While the belief that writing is a means of coming to "know oneself" has not been entirely abandoned, these texts I examine rely on a poststructural understanding of the self as constructed, in-process—a temporary "self" that we may represent and interrogate through writing.

In Chapter 6, I foreground the specific processes through which I have attempted to teach writing while fostering critical revision as it is elaborated in the previous chapter. I consider not only the processes but also their effects as my students and I experienced and understood them. In Chapter 7, I represent and reflect on specific moments that challenged my concept of what, how, and why I was teaching. This chapter attests to how my pedagogy has undergone revision as a result of reflection and action in specific sites of engagement. Informing the whole project is my conceptual and strategic understanding of revision. I understand this not simply as a literal term—of teaching students to revise papers so that they more successfully communicate to a specific readership. Though important, this is only one point of access to the concept of revision. Revision informs my teaching on every level, from my own attempt to examine and understand my practices—within the context of a given course, the institution, the discipline, various communities—to my belief that, finally, revision is what I am teaching my students. Revision as an ongoing process of recognizing one's "self" and one's text as in specific relations to others; revision as the ability to enact alternative relations within texts, classrooms, and beyond.

Further Reflections on Composing Critical Writing Pedagogy

In the scope of this book, I endeavor to engage and revise pedagogy through inquiry into two sites of research—scholarship and teaching. It is important to emphasize both sites because the book not only argues for but also demonstrates a pedagogy that attends to the relationship between these sites, rather than foregrounding one or the other. Critical reflection on the texts of our scholarship and our-classrooms-as-texts are both central to work in pedagogy and we need to move beyond describing their mutual interdependence to representing it in our research. I am committed to attending to both the pedagogy I argue for and the pedagogy of my argument. This articulation, which I take from Jennifer Gore and elaborate on throughout the book, has been a foundational principle in my development as a teacher and writer. Whether in the classroom or in my text, I am interested in how and whether we can enact and engage ideas, not simply espouse or enforce them. This informs my attempt to center my research in both the scholarship and the classroom; claims for liberatory political or textual effects are not made at the level of theoretical discourse, but are located in specific writing and reading practices. I consider my writing to be a site of pedagogy, so I have attempted not only to critique particular versions of composition and critical pedagogy but also to reflect on and critique the choices I am making, the version I am advocating. Throughout the book, I look at students as specific and concrete writers who work within histories and contexts; this very much contests the generic "student writers" or "students" as these terms and constructions figure so powerfully in the discourses of composition and critical pedagogy.

Initially, when I decided to do this project, I looked more closely at the scholarship, attempting to test out and apply its aims and assumptions in my classroom. What I came to discover, however, is that the classroom was not a site for transposing or applying or even practicing pedagogical theory, at least not if I was committed to a central tenet of both process and critical pedagogy—that students need to be engaged, accountable, and active coinquirers. This conception removes the possibility for understanding my job as exposing them to alternative knowledges or enforcing those knowledges. Rather, my role was to promote the conditions necessary for those knowledges; I could not create them nor simply impose them. Instead, I used my authority to advocate for these alternatives, to acknowledge them and articulate why they were valuable, but we could only enact them together. I could enter my classroom and "order" students to critique their identities, their concepts of the world, their relations to others. However, such a critique would likely be a performance by students, it would not necessarily engage them in substantive processes of inquiry and reflection. We can, rather, work together to shape the class as an ongoing process into reading, writing, and revisioning as cultural work.

In Chapters 2–4, I focus on written reflections on pedagogy, on our research into teaching. I am considering writing and Critical Pedagogy, drawing secondarily on the classroom as a site for research and reflexive inquiry on the scholarship, on these discourses of pedagogy. In Chapters 5–7, I foreground the classroom, attempt to demonstrate how I read the classroom as a site for inquiry, as an integral source of research for my written reflections on writing pedagogy. Students, their texts and narratives about our class, are present throughout this book. But they take center stage in the final chapters. In this way, the structure of the book is intended to enact my own process of defining, reflecting on, and enacting a pedagogy of revision.

I have not abandoned the belief that teaching in general, and teaching writing in particular, are political activities with important possibilities for effecting change both within and beyond our classrooms. I believe, further, that regardless of our pedagogical choices, we have a responsibility for reflecting on the implications and assumptions of our methods and frameworks. This book is based on the notion that it is important to teach students to engage in reading and writing as critical processes that are effected by and might also effect their actions, relations, and conceptions outside the classroom, beyond the text. Ultimately, revision is the only reason worth teaching—learning with my students to see ourselves, authority, meaning, and texts as ongoing processes of construction, and writing as a means of reflecting on and participating in these processes.

Notes on Research Methods

My reflections on practice and enactment are drawn from two Basic Writing courses I taught in fall 1993 and 1994 and three College Writing courses I taught in fall 1992 and spring 1993 and 1995. Over that time, I kept a teaching journal in which I recorded and reflected on specific classroom interactions and scenes. Further, because of my interest in studying my teaching, I have consciously taken notes during class discussions (student comments, when in quotations but not marked as Interchange excerpts, are transcriptions from notes taken during discussion with students' permission to quote them directly), and—with their permission—solicited samples of student essays, peer reviews, self-assessments, and process writings. Finally, in 1995, ten former and current students met with me to discuss questions specifically related to this project. These conversations were held on-line, using the Daedalus asynchronous conversation program known as "Interchange." I chose to use Interchange, instead of an oral, non-electronic mode as a means of engaging the participants in reflective conversations with one another, and to avoid a one-on-one, question-and-answer format. While I initially posed questions, I was also interested in letting the agenda shift according to students' interests, reactions, and ideas.[1] So, for example, the first session began with the following questions:

> Amy: What do you think is the point of "becoming educated?" To what end do you hope to use your education? As product? As process? Also, what do you recall from our writing class, what still stands out in your memory in terms of specific moments, feelings, issues, etc.

In each session, student participants spoke to one another, as well as to me, and, rather than reining in the conversations, we let them move and shift spontaneously. The Interchange sessions took place between November 1994 and April 1995; Andalib, Joshua, Beth Anne, and Karen S. met three times; Paul attended two sessions; and Kafui, Karen F., Patrick, Fred, and Mariam came to the final session, at which point they had been in my writing course for two-thirds of a semester. These students were not chosen as a representative sampling. I cast a wide net in seeking volunteers and, out of forty, I chose these ten as they seemed to present a range in terms of their initial attitude about being in Basic Writing or College Writing, their image of themselves as writers, learners, and thinkers, their individual histories and subjectivities. All of them define their experience in the course as successful, but for a variety of reasons and toward an array of ends.

Before turning to Chapter 1, I would like to introduce (and thank) the student-writers who participated in the Interchange sessions. They have written their own introductions, and I present them here in the order in which we were in class together. The voices of Karen S., Paul, Beth Anne, Andalib, Joshua, Frederic, Karen F., Mariam, Patrick and Kafui are most directly present in Chapters 3, 4, and 5, but their work and thinking inform mine throughout. They gave much of their time, energy, insights, words, and ideas to the conceptualizing and revisioning of this dissertation. More important, they provided an enormous share of the inspiration.

Contributors

Karen Sutcliffe (College Writing, fall 1992): My name is Karen Sutcliffe. I was born in Bayonne, New Jersey, in 1974. I am an only child, I decided to come to UMass to escape the wrath of my parents. They were very overprotective, so I knew I had to go at least a few hours away. It was between here and Indiana University, so I chose the place with fewer cows. UMass won. I am very involved in student life here on campus. I am a resident assistant and a summer counselor for incoming students. I am a double major in Political Science and Communications, and I will graduate in the spring of 1996. I hope to go to law school and someday work for women's and children's rights in this country. I would also someday like to run for public office. Writing has become a big part of my life since I took College Writing; I typically write between ten and twenty papers a semester.

Paul Distasi (College Writing, fall 1992): Born in Massachusetts, 1974. Family supported itself through trucking/farming. Raised around nature and cycles; immersed in an unfavorable economic position and all its pleasures. Came to UMass to separate myself from family. Stake it out alone. Macho 60s thinking meets 90s expectations. I've lost my truck, jobs, wits, friends, finances yet retained my pride. I am strong-willed and opinionated, yet reserve any true effort for adventures/discoveries outside traditional productive behavior. I am a perfectionist of sorts, yet lack the focus or resolve to truly devote myself to one thing. I believe in the perfection of mind, body, and soul and the interdependent relationship between the three. I consider myself aligned neutrally, an observer willing to interfere if necessary. I hope to one day feel as if life was worth it . . . and to keep moving.

Beth Anne Manchester (College Writing, spring 1993): I am from a very small, very white town in Massachusetts. Now, as a student at UMass, I am learning to *appreciate* differences. I am an educator-advocate at the Everywoman's Center here. I want to be an educator someday but I am not sure what kind (inside or outside of a classroom). I am particularly interested in the idea of "voice" and of giving "voice" to women.

Andalib Khelghati (Basic Writing, fall 1993): My name is Andalib Khelghati. I was born in Togo, West Africa, have lived in various places, attended high school in Canada, and am presently living in Lunenburg, Massachusetts. I truly believe in the Oneness of humanity and hope that my education can contribute to fulfilling that principle. I am a double major in Education, and Social Thought and Political Economy. N'est-ce pas.

Joshua Berman (Basic Writing, fall 1993): My life turned around after a trip to Israel in high school, when I was 16. I realized then how important Judaic culture is to me. I've always been involved in helping people and I have geared my major here at UMass to allow me to contribute to sustaining a thriving Jewish community. My other dream is to open a cooperative vegetarian restaurant with a socialist mentality—where everyone is equal, does equal amounts of labor, and receives equal amount of rewards. This class was extremely important in the fact that the number one reason I dreaded coming to college was having to write papers. Now, in my liberal arts major, I find I write **many** and long papers—and I even choose writing-oriented courses. Because of my learning disability, I have the opportunity to choose the style of my exams. I have found the essay style is most beneficial (over, say, multiple choice), because now I know how to get my thoughts out on paper.

Mariam Sarkarati (College Writing, spring 1995): My goal upon graduation is simply to help kids. I really enjoy giving of myself to do for others, especially a child. There is no greater reward than to see a child look up at you and smile with appreciation for something you have done for them, no matter how minor it may seem to you. To make an impact on someone's life is a capacity we all have, though many never utilize that capacity.

Frederic Carrie (Fred) (College Writing, spring 1995): Six-feet tall, well-built, my name is Frederic Carrie. I was born somewhere in North Carolina, and I've been raised all my life in Haiti. I went to a French Catholic school from first grade to thirteenth grade. Well, the French system consists of thirteen years of school; in the American system, that last year would be considered to be the first year of college. Anyway, as you have probably guessed, I speak French, which is my first language, and then

English, which I've learned at school. I also speak Creole (Patois), which is a derivation of French, Spanish, and some African languages. I am currently living in Walpole with my uncle and attending school here, at UMass. I'm majoring in Civil Engineering and so far my academic career is going well. I consider myself to be a "B" student overall. I hope to get into graduate school and specialize in the field of transportation and construction. After grad school, I think I'm going to head South where I can get a good job and raise a family.

Kafui André (College Writing, spring 1995): My name is Kafui André, and I am an international student. I was born in Benin, a small country in west Africa, but I've lived most of my life in the Ivory Coast. I've been residing in this country for the last two years and have grown to learn more about this country and its inhabitants. I am currently a student at the University of Massachusetts at Amherst, where I study Industrial Engineering. I've spent a wonderful semester in the company of the entire College Writing class, taught by Amy Lee. I'd like to thank the Lord and my parents for this opportunity to study abroad and to develop my young mind.

Karen Foster (College Writing, spring 1995): My name is Karen Foster and I am a nineteen-year-old sophomore at the University of Massachusetts at Amherst. I am a Legal Studies major with a 3.0 average. I came to UMass for the sole purpose of receiving a fair amount of financial aid. UMass was my safety school, and the only school that offered me aid for my freshman year. The Federal and State governments say that my parents are way above the upper-middle class line. (That may be why I didn't receive either a state scholarship or a Pell Grant.) But I think that $50,000/year can be considered as nothing when have you basic bills to pay, a mortgage, water bill, furnace bill, *and* other children in college. The one thing that is most important about my college career is to graduate with honors. Not because I am concerned with which graduate schools are going to accept me, but because that's a very hard goal to achieve in *this* society when you are black and a female.

Patrick Bien Aimé (College Writing, spring 1995): Hi! My name is Patrick and I'm twenty years old. I was born in a small country named Haiti. When I was eleven years old, I moved to Boston and I've been living there ever since. My first language is Creole, my second is French, in which I forget how to say a lot of stuff, I can understand nice and clearly everything if I have a conversation. My third language is English, which I can write, read, and speak very well. My major is Mechanical Engineering—I love working with cars. Therefore, I'm trying to do my best to stick with the major even though it's a hard one. My dream is to build one of the fastest cars and to open my own business in order to help others who can't help themselves.

Note

1. Excerpts from Interchange sessions are indicated by the use of a different font (Helvetica rather than Sabon) and are set off from the regular text in the format for citations.

CHAPTER TWO

Politics and Pedagogies

Now, back to the beginning.

> I just don't see how we can change anything. I mean, I'm only 18, but even if I live until I'm 80, I feel like I can't really make a difference. Everything seems done already. Like racism, it just is—it's everywhere—inside. The same with the Gulf War, even if I disagree, I can't do anything about it, it's out of my reach. (Taylor, a student in my fall 1990 College Writing course)

The original version of this book began with this written statement by a student in the first course I ever taught. Taylor's comment, in response to a prompt presented by a classmate, stuck to me at the time, through lots of time, and formed the beginning of the first version of this manuscript. My readings of her remark provide a portfolio of sorts, representing how we might revise our concept of what, how, and why we are doing when we teach writing. My interpretations demonstrate how pedagogical frameworks exert pressures on the text of our teaching by posing specific questions, aims, and assumptions to that text, enabling (and limiting) us to narrate and interpret it through a positioned lens.

At the time Taylor wrote this, I was teaching my first class and I found her words to be deeply troubling. Only twenty-two myself, I could not imagine how a seventeen-year-old could feel so detached from, so impotent in, the world around her. But many of my students presented similar attitudes, a sense that events, relations, possibilities, and problems existed in some realm separate from them. Taylor's comment, written in response to a particularly frustrating class discussion generated by a student prompt on the imminent Gulf War, implies a distinction between herself or her sphere and a world "out there" in which she feels powerless. This sense of impotence is not unique to "students" or to Taylor; many of us, unable to envision ourselves in relation to others and to events, cannot recognize ourselves as agents beyond the context of our own lives. Even when they respond to an event with passion, anger, or hope (as did Taylor to the issue of US intervention in Kuwait), my students often remain stuck in their sense of frustration and immobility, uncertain as to how change may be effected or where to direct their energy.

This was frequently evident in their writing, which, early in the semester, seemed distanced, vacant, sometimes even mechanical. I deemed it important, then, to find ways to teach writing that would promote students' investment in their texts (my own experience as a student and my observations that first semester indicated that this intensified the process of improvement) *and* their reflection on the "worlds" (identities, relations) represented, imagined, ignored in their texts. Because they do not recognize or conceive of even having choices, they may surrender rather than choose. "When students see their lives or history as inevitable, they are not encouraged to work for change" (Christensen 1989, 14). As a result of her inability to connect herself to the world, Taylor unwittingly ensures her own powerlessness (and passive complicity) by declaring it as inevitable. I am not arguing that all students are *actually* powerless; rather, many students do not perceive themselves as actors in a public sphere. For example, while many of my students enjoy autobiographical writing, they initially perceive their lives as texts to entertain and celebrate rather than to critically reflect on and learn from. As William Bigelow writes:

> The message given (across disciplines and throughout schooling) is that great people make change, individual students do not. So it's not surprising that some students wonder what it is they have to learn from each other's stories. . . . They simply do not believe their lives have anything important to teach them. Their lives are just their lives. (1990, 439–40)

A year later, I had begun preliminary reading in the field of critical pedagogy; in light of that reading—which was helping me to articulate my aims as a writing teacher—and my increasing belief in a poststructural concept of language, discourse, power, identity[1], I interpreted Taylor's comment differently. I found Taylor's remark objectionable rather than sad; it became a reflection of a large group of people's sense that they have a choice whether to intervene in or resist a system or a set of conditions they recognize as problematic, unjust, flawed. I wanted to teach her that people who live comfortable lives in relation to normative discourses of sexuality and race, and who occupy the privileged economic situation necessary for material and social comfort, have the luxury of perceiving action as a choice. What Taylor does not seem to recognize, or at least to acknowledge, is that these cultural and economic systems also function largely to ensure her own privilege.

These two readings of Taylor, for indeed I am not simply responding to or interpreting her words, but making assumptions about the person who wrote them, lead to entirely different responses in terms of the action they provoke. My first reaction, wanting to counter Taylor's sense of uselessness and helplessness, led me to want to help her develop confidence, power and investment in her ability to write in, and by extension to act on, the world. I tried to find ways to help her perceive herself as an agent, one who can act on and who is not only acted upon by the worlds and texts she encountered and constructed. Such a response represents expressivist pedagogy's concern for individual students, for the idea that a teacher's work is to foster their sense of themselves as powerful authors of the textual realm. But what about Taylor's authority and responsibility in the cultural and material realms? My revised reading of Taylor led me to want to generate a sense of accountability, a recognition of the very privilege that underscores and allows for her sense of detachment and ennui. I wanted to engage her in a close reading of her own comment, one that reveals the assumptions about choice and privilege, detachment and impotence. Now, I am not only interested for her to feel empowered by writing but also for her to become a critical reader of texts, including those she writes.

During that first semester teaching, I encountered another type of student, seemingly the opposite of Taylor and yet limited by the same inability to see connections between self and other, between words and world. I was struck by the ease with which these students claimed authority and knowledge. Often, their essays relied on sweeping generalizations, the assumption of "rational" readers who would easily assent to their articulation of universal truths, and loud, very confident voices. While my process-oriented training did not explicitly address the necessity (or means) of critiquing or questioning students who enter our courses with an already active voice and a sense of themselves as empowered writers, I could not unequivocally praise the ability to speak from a position of presumed power and authority any more than I could simply *tell* Taylor to take power. Although process approaches aim to encourage the development of confident, empowered student writers, how might we challenge already powerful writers to interrogate the ease with which they claim authority? How might we begin to encourage them to examine the unspoken assumptions on which their claims to truth and universal interpretation rest?

As John Schilb advocates in "Pedagogy of the Oppressors?" we must articulate strategies for educating those students who occupy positions of authority and privilege, strategies that challenge them to recognize how privilege is constructed and conveyed by ideologies and economic conditions and through social and academic discourses, rather than based on an inherent right. Similarly, when it comes to writing instruction, we should engage students in recognizing how truth, textual logic, and authority are rhetorical constructions, dependent on formal choices, assumptions about audience, and so on. The privilege these students assumed as writers came largely from their familiarity and comfort with deploying the conventions of academic discourse, their lack of awareness of other possible rhetorical contexts or choices.

Having been out of college for only a year myself, I attempted to reflect on what had made classes meaningful to me. Most important, a few significant courses challenged the predominant lesson conveyed by my high school, where difference was not only literally but also ideologically and conceptually invisible. Initially women's studies courses, in which I began to recognize the role constructed for me and first acknowledged that I was not an entirely free and autonomous individual, provided a sense of the reciprocal relationship between individuals and cultural productions, personal values and ideological forces. In other classes, I began to consider myself on the other end of the construction dynamic—investigating the ways in which I envisioned others according to roles already available to me in the culture. While classes that challenged my assumptions, opinions, or values did not necessarily result in a change of mind or position, they did necessitate actively considering that which I had previously taken for granted, considered as "natural." Instead of assuming an existing, unified and receptive *audience* like me, I had to find ways to convince *readers*, who would actively engage my text and who were not like me, to share my interpretive and evaluative moves. This strategizing required a preliminary recognition of my interpretation and evaluation as one choice among many (even if I did not grant equal legitimacy to *every* position), thus pushing me to acknowledge having not chosen possible subject-positions, even if I was not yet ready to articulate why I had not chosen them. For me, college initiated the realization, and the resulting process of self-reflection and critique, that I came not only from a particular, but also a privileged, background and that with textual and social authority came responsibility—not that of making someone else's (a teacher's, a parent's) "right" choices, but of recognizing and accounting for the choices I made.

My own teaching practices, however, had inadvertently reinforced a dichotomy between self and others, between words and the world.[2] While working to change students' sense of powerlessness in their writing and struggling to find a way to challenge those students who were comfortable with their authority, I failed to make the connection between writing a text and representing a world, that is, to interrogate what is embedded in language. What I never made explicit to Taylor or my other students is that each time she speaks, writes, uses language, she enters into a process of constructing the world, not simply describing it from a distance. While I presented the text as a process of construction in which writers can actively intervene, I did not then extend this notion of construction and intervention to the ways in which writers and texts make meaning, much less to the ways in which the meaning we attempt to make is not only influenced but also constrained by the language we use.[3]

I am now able to recognize that my pedagogy, despite my process-oriented strategies, fell short because we did not move from Taylor's power to construct a text to her text's power to construct a world. She was unable to see that her own words implied a choice rather than an inevitable expression. In my teaching, I did not address that words do not simply describe a reality, but rather, that words actively construct a reality. While she may have become a more insightful peer reviewer in my course, Taylor did not become a more critical reader. While she became a more successful and confident writer in an academic context, I did not foster her awareness that she was working within a specific discursive context, nor did I foreground the effect of this context on the texts we were producing and valuing.

Implicit in both Taylor's claim of powerlessness and other students' sense of themselves as always powerful is an abdication of responsibility, a declaration of blamelessness. On the one hand, by distinguishing between herself and a world "out there," Taylor ensures her immobility and impotence in the social realm, erasing her potential agency simply by not recognizing it. On the other hand, students who unproblematically assume authority seem to be unaware of alternative possibilities for constructing a worldview and a text. In assuming an audience like themselves, such writers need not confront their investment in a specific and constructed subject-position. Again, they mitigate their responsibility for both the texts and the knowledge they produce by being unaware that a choice has been made. What Taylor does not seem to recognize, or at least to acknowledge, is that these cultural and economic systems also function largely to ensure her own privilege. After all, her description of powerlessness might be read as a declaration; she ensures her inability to act, thereby dismissing her accountability because her words attribute these problems to "the world," cast responsibility away from her to some place, some realm, over there, out there. While I certainly want to spark powerful voices, I also want to encourage active, critical thinking about and participation in the process of constructing meaning through language. One without the other seems incomplete: what good is a critical consciousness if you cannot articulate it, and of what use are empowered voices that speak in a sociopolitical, historical vacuum, unaware of the meaning in their words? I would like my students not only to feel capable of using language powerfully, toward a specific intent and to a particular audience, but also to feel responsible for the world within their words and for the readers they do (and do not) evoke—that is, represent—in their writing.

At semester's end, Taylor was—according to any definition—a better writer. She talked about her new enjoyment of and relaxed attitude toward writing and could point to her successful experiences in writing assignments for other classes. A clear trajectory was evident in her portfolio. Seemingly, we had both done our jobs satisfactorily. And yet, while these results are neither worthless nor objectionable, in light of Taylor's comment, they also *are not enough*. This recognition inspired my sense that I should promote something more through my pedagogy, something other than better writers. It also inspired me to reflect on what constitutes "better" writing or writers, and to consider how much pressure the context in which we teach or write determines what we value as good writing.

Politics and/of Pedagogy

> "Finally, in regard to those who possess the largest shares . . . of worldly goods, could there, in your opinion, be any police so vigilant and effective, for protection of all the rights of person, property, character, as such a . . . system of common schools could be made to impart. . . . Would not the payment of a sufficient tax to make such an education and training universal be the cheapest means of self-protection and insurance" (Horace Mann, in a report to Mass. Board of Education, 1844, cited in Kozol 1981, 6)

> "We want one class of people to have a liberal education, and we want one class of persons, a very much larger class of persons, of necessity, to forego the privileges of a liberal education and fit into specific manual tasks." (Woodrow Wilson, cited in Kozol 6)

These citations, in stark clarity, testify to what some teachers and scholars believe to be obvious: schooling is not a historically or inevitably neutral process designed to impartially educate a nation's population; rather, it is a motivated process aimed at certain products—training a citizenry so as to promote and maintain specific economic and social structuration. Though surely we do not all share the motivations articulated by Mann and Wilson, we cannot simply ignore or gloss over the reality that "Education" (at any level) did not originate and has not evolved in our country as a democratic, good-willed, equal access, nondiscriminatory mechanism by which to foster intellectual development for its own sake, or for "the common good." The point, put so simply, seems so obvious as to be not worth mentioning at all.

Yet in the struggle over pedagogies, the argument is often made that radical pedagogies *unnecessarily* politicize the activities of teaching and learning. The assumption underlying such an argument (an assumption readily available in textbooks, popular media, the discourse of assessment, and standards) is that teaching and learning in their natural states are benevolent enterprises. In regard to teaching writing in particular, we assume it is good for students and educational institutions to teach successful or effective writing practices and products to students; teaching writing, therefore, is or can be an apolitical practice. The "real" work of composition, so the argument goes, is to teach writing, not to indoctrinate students or disrupt the "real" work of the course in order to attend to a subsidiary political agenda. Radical pedagogies (feminist, critical, oppositional) in this framework seem unnatural and invasive to the discipline and practice of Composition, because they interrupt the teaching of a received body of disciplinary knowledge by asking questions about how that knowledge has come to be sanctioned as worth knowing. Who is authorized to make such decisions? In whose interest (*all* students? some students? teachers? those who possess the largest shares already?) is it to pass on certain knowledge, certain visions/versions of history, writing, literature, anthropology, physics, and even education itself?

Even when we allow that political *content* is appropriate in a writing class, we are cautious about the methods of such a course. Donald Lazere suggests there are important negotiations to confront—between exposing and imposing, between teaching writing and political science.

I endorse the general concept of introducing political subject matter in writing courses. . . . But I also share the concern of critics that such courses can turn into an indoctrination to the instructor's ideology or, at best, into classes in political science rather than composition. . . . I believe that college English courses have a responsibility to expose students to socialist viewpoints because those views are virtually excluded from all other realms of the American cognitive, rhetorical, semantic, and literary universe of discourse. I am firmly opposed, however, to instructors imposing socialist (or feminist, or Third-World, or gay) ideology on students as the one true faith. (1995, 189)

But the obvious point I reiterated in the opening paragraph would suggest that *every* pedagogy must recognize and contend with the fundamentally *subjective* nature not simply of teachers but of education, of teaching. As William Bigelow claims, "All teaching *is* partisan. Whether we want to be, all teachers are political agents because we help to shape our students' understandings of the larger society" (1990, 445). Education is *never* neutral because, even if we believe ourselves to be working for and with *all* students, we operate within contexts and discourses that did not evolve arbitrarily nor to serve the best interests of all students by ensuring equity, access, or inclusion. During a recent discussion in the graduate teaching practicum, a teacher repeatedly insisted, "students don't like to think too hard; they don't expect to do any work; they won't take responsibility." From earlier discussions, I know this teacher is committed, that she works hard to actively engage her students in the material, and to position them as co-inquirers, not as objects of her pedagogy. Her remarks, however, are all too familiar in their assumption that "all students" are lazy/slippery/out for the easy grade; her discourse moves to center blame on students, rather than on teachers or pedagogical practices whenever things, classes, plans do not go as the teacher intended. We might also be familiar with complaints that "students" are apathetic, acritical. Regardless of the specific terms in which we condemn them, we often represent students as needing transformation. When I objected to the implicit disrespect and condemnation of students in her remarks, she was visibly offended and surprised. She claimed repeatedly that she does not devalue students, that she likes teaching. In-

deed, I believe she does. My point, however, is that we too easily—despite our *declared* goals or identities as teachers (in this
case, "student-centered")—fall into the readily available and generally sanctioned *practice* of blaming students, lumping them
together in a group, and envisioning them as impediments to our
teaching. Is this more or less damaging than indoctrinating students or enforcing agendas on them? Does this enable or inhibit
our ability to teach the ostensible subject of our classes?

Lazere suggests that some degree or manner of politicizing
our teaching is acceptable so long as we carefully pursue exposure and not indoctrination or enforcement. I would suggest that
these are negotiations we need to consider regardless of whether
we have consciously adopted a politicized pedagogy. Indoctrinating and enforcing students are not *more* likely within a radical pedagogy; instead, radical pedagogies aim to make visible the
conditions by which knowledge is constructed, calling attention
to the relations of power and effects of authority within classrooms. I would suggest that every teacher—student-centered,
humanist, expressivist, feminist—should be reflexive about and
accountable for how she enacts her pedagogy, attentive to how
students are situated in her classroom in relation to the object of
study, one another, and the teacher. The concept that heavy-hand-
edness and the risks of silencing or indoctrination are endemic
only to certain, explicitly identified "political" pedagogies leaves
unchallenged certain normative and naturalized concepts of teachers, students, pedagogy, and education. In such a conception, only
those pedagogies defined as "other," as alternatives, are expected
to account for the implication and consequences of their methods of enactment. In a similar way, as feminist scholars and writers (Minh-ha, Anzaldúa, hooks, Woods) work in revisionary forms
so as to contest dominant academic conventions about textual
logic and the construction of authority, the burden is on them to
simultaneously account for and legitimize these alternative forms.
Those of us who write in traditional academic forms do not bother
to justify or situate that choice, taking for granted that well-trained
readers will "assume" the position, accepting the legitimacy and
value of how we write, our formal, stylistic choices, even if they
reject or wrestle with what we claim.

We cannot simply step into our teacher shoes and become ideological innocents or agenda-free, neutral coaches. Even before we step into the classroom, we have made many choices that will impact the roles and responsibilities assigned to our students and convey an attitude about the use and importance of composing—not only within but also outside the classroom. No theory or method, then, of teaching writing is politically innocent, natural, or neutral. Our local decisions of how to practice (what we do in a given class period, how we grade, assignments we invent) are determined by choices we make, consciously or not, about the role we envision for students-as-writers, the relationship we posit between writers and language and teachers and students, and how we conceive of and value both the process and product of writing. Acknowledging and accounting for these choices do not make a classroom *more* political; but rather, it allows us to be responsible for and conscious of our goals and methods. The challenge is not to shed your situatedness, but to make deliberate decisions about the methods you use and to be responsible for the world your pedagogy represents. What sort of student does a specific pedagogy envision, do particular methods reach out to? How are teachers and students constructed by a specific pedagogical discourse? Who is authorized to write and speak? Who is silenced? Who is (to be) empowered? What are our goals? What is excluded? Do we claim to be liberating students?—in the name of what? What are our concepts of self, writing, language?

To claim that all teaching is political is not simply to suggest that we should bring current events or controversial issues into our classes; such a simplistic concept of how "politics" informs the content of our classrooms ignores the broader issue that the discourses in which we teach—in which we and our students write, speak, and represent our "selves," experiences, and our teaching—are already political, already historically and socially situated. Contending with the politics of our pedagogy is to critically and self-reflexively attend to the discourses of our pedagogies, as well as the discourses that inform our classrooms and the texts composed there. Expressivist pedagogy, like various strands of radical pedagogies—feminist, critical, oppositional, multicultural—and more obviously like the conservative, "humanist" pedagogy advanced by E. D. Hirsch, William Bennett, D'Souza are *discourses* of education. Each envisions an ideal persona and a role for teacher and students, posits a relationship between participants and the subject at hand, and prescribes a function and a purpose for those who are teaching and learning that subject—whether it's writing or history or math. In the well-publicized and, within academic contexts, much criticized pedagogy of Hirsch or D'Souza, they make clear the potential causal relationship between education and normative cultural values, identities, mores, and behaviors. Exposing students to the right texts, they argue, will effect our cultural and social realms, reinforce traditional values and behaviors.

Rather than concentrating our criticism and examination solely on pedagogies we define as "other," we need to begin interrogating the pedagogies we *have* chosen to practice. Otherwise, we risk assuming that our pedagogical choices are natural, universal, or unmotivated. One might argue, further, that it is all the more dangerous and politically heavy-handed to conceal these motivations and assumptions from students. As Clifford concludes,

> A critique of writing theory and practice can only be fully understood when it is situated in a sociopolitical context. Teachers who ask students to rehearse particular composing rituals in the classroom impose an ideological agenda, admitted or not . . . of course, since ideology thrives on anonymity, we think of our appointed tasks as commonsensical, not ideological. (1991, 45–46)

The issue is not *whether* to bring politics or ideology into the classroom, but rather *to recognize and be accountable* (or not) for the ways in which our pedagogical choices and practices reflect our situated (experiential, theoretical, institutional) perspectives on writing, authority, power, and education. Those who resist or oppose critical pedagogy's foregrounding of the politics of education must define their concept of "politics," and acknowledge their own choice to place politics in the background, rather than assuming that politics should or simply can be denied entry into their teaching and classrooms.

Rearticulating the Politics of Composition

A clear indication of the political nature of our collective disci-plinary enterprise, teaching writing, is the fact that we do not solicit all kinds of texts equally, nor do we grant all discourses uniform legitimacy and acceptance. We will not find, for instance, any articles in *College English* or *CCC* that encourage the use of our writing classes as forums for encouraging students not only to voice but also to develop their identities as homophobes, rac-ists, or misogynists. If such papers remain an anomaly in our classes, surely the attitudes and ideas that inform them are present there, creeping into the margins of essays, discussions, and dy-namics. Indeed, as Richard E. Miller (1994) points out, we must be hard at work to ensure that such voices are *not* heard in our classrooms.

> If we step back . . . for a moment and consider the fact that the mixture of anger, rage, ignorance, and confusion that produced this student essay [a piece hostile towards homeless people and homosexuals] are present in varying degrees on college cam-puses across the country, what is truly significant about this event is not that it occurred, but that it occurs so rarely. (398)

It is not a question of whether such thinking occurs in school; but rather, it is a matter of where in our classrooms we relegate the discourses we prefer not to hear, those we have chosen not to value. We appear to agree, at least implicitly, that our classrooms should neither replicate nor encourage the exercise of hatred or domination against those predominantly envisioned by our eco-nomic and social systems not only as "other," but also as inferior and even inhuman. As reflected in the most widely circulated journals, our profession has conceded to the idea that prohibit-ing some discourses is valid, and perhaps even necessary. As Fou-cault notes, the attempt to elicit or to silence discourse indicates our belief (whether conscious or intuitively felt) that writing func-tions not only to *represent* but also to actively present a worldview, to confer the privileging or devaluing that inform and result from particular discourses. In other words, discourse, "far from being that transparent or neutral element in which . . . politics is pacified, is in fact one of the places where . . . politics exercise[s] in a privileged way some of [its] most formidable powers" (Foucault, 1981, 52). The decision, collectively or individually, *not* to encourage oppressive texts as ends in themselves is, inarguably, a political decision as it entails an attempt to control not simply the textual product but, moreover, the attitudes and conceptions that inform and emerge from *particular* discourse productions.

Perhaps we have, then, implicitly agreed as to what *does not* constitute an appropriate political agenda. While we may not share the poststructural conception that language, always embedded in discourse, is not simply descriptive but performative, that it not only speaks but also acts on our understanding, we do seem to accept the idea that language is not only or always a tool for empowerment but a weapon of disempowerment as well. Presumably, our decision to select certain discourses as useful, constructive, and welcome in our classrooms implies that the teaching of discursive practices is political, has consequences beyond the composition of individual texts, outside individual classrooms.

While we might agree on what *is not* an appropriate aim for composition classes, we certainly have not agreed on what *is*. In his article, R. Miller cites from a student essay entitled "Queers, Bums & Magic," a piece that supports gay-bashing and violence against economically disenfranchised people ("Fault Lines," 1994). The response at a CCCC panel to this essay ranged from suggestions to remove the student from the class to proposals that the teacher attend to the structural and stylistic elements of the piece while ignoring its content altogether. These reactions indicate that we, our profession as represented by the audience at R. Miller's panel, are unprepared to deal with what happens when the world so clearly and boldly enters our classrooms. As R. Miller points out, the production of this forbidden discourse of hate, represented by the student's essay, entitled "Queers, Bums & Magic," leaves us with "this profoundly strange state of affairs where the discipline explicitly devoted to studying and articulating the power of the written word gets thrown into a crisis when a student produces a powerful piece of writing" (394).

The unwillingness to contend with the substance of this student's piece, to engage his ideas even if (presumably) to contest them, seems largely a consequence of his being a student. I imagine many of us would find it necessary to challenge such ideas were they espoused by colleagues, politicians, friends, or family members. Were it a newspaper editorial, we might even bring it into the classroom and engage it along with our students. The notion that students are powerless, that we need to make them feel safe, is not a universal truism. In this instance, the student writes from within and into discourses (homophobia, criminalizing the poor) that empower his text and grant him authority. We need, then, to negotiate more complex possibilities for contending with his discourse beyond addressing the formal qualities of the text or banishing that which we prefer not to read.

The Power of Language and the Language of Power

Language, in its conception as discourse, is integral to how we form our identities and relations. Discourse is not signification for signification's sake, but an active form of valuing and evaluating, of naming (and renaming) in order to know (or to revision) and to not know; discourse is inextricably bound by and enabling of our economic and social relations. Giroux describes a goal of critical pedagogy as the analyses of discourse as "a continually shifting balance of resources and practices in the struggle over specific ways of naming, organizing and experiencing social reality" (1988, 60). What is important in this articulation is the explicit connection he makes between how we name, how we structure, and how we experience. We do not first *have* pure, unmediated experience and then name it with or in language. Rather, as the materialist argument goes that our economic situatedness, our objective relation to the modes of production, determines our experience, Giroux is arguing that discourse is a material praxis. Our discursive situatedness, our relation to dominant forms of representing and valuing in language, will largely impact our experiences. We name as we experience, we name before we experience, we organize and know in and through language; and language—as discourse—is regulated by cultural and material rules and relations. Discourse, then, is not simply an after-effect of experience, it is part and parcel of how our subjectivities are constructed, not simply how they are named.

"The political," therefore, is immediately present in our writing class, whether we choose to foreground or attend to it, in language itself. To engage in studying writing practices, analyzing how specific contexts (academic, popular culture, markets, nineteenth-century American culture) come to sanction normative forms and conventions (expository writing, rap music, the Nike ad slogans, personal criticism) is to engage the *politics* of form. This line of inquiry, which surely has a place in the writing course, necessitates that we acknowledge how language practices and discursive forms are constituted within historical, political, material contexts—whether they work to resist or reinforce the dominant conventions. We might also pay acute and sustained attention to how words function. Initially, most of us are introduced to language as a tool for naming what we already know; it is presented as the means for describing reality as it exists apart from the words we choose to name it in. We can, however, pose simple questions to easily demonstrate that language is not neutral nor merely creative play—nor is it arbitrary or inscrutable. Consider the following lists we have generated on various occasions when I have asked students to articulate all the words they can think of for naming (in whatever context comes to mind) occupants of the different categories. The following terms are transcribed from the lists we wrote on the board; the "+" or "–" following the terms is the consensus of the class on whether the word had immediately positive or negative connotations. A blank indicates that we decided the word's meaning depended on the context in which it was used.

> **male:** guy, man+, dude, boy, stud+, prick–
>
> **female:** chick–, woman, girl (sometimes–), babe –, broad–, bitch–, cunt–, skirt–, piece of ass
>
> **heterosexual:** straight+, het
>
> **homosexual:** gay, queer, fag–, faggot–, dyke, packer–, homo–,
>
> **white person:** caucasian, white, cracker– (but here indicates a class status) honkey

black person: African American, black (sometimes–), Afro-American, colored–, negro–, nigger–, spade–

Obviously, in reading over the words my students provided, we begin to see an ordering of the world, an encoding of a normative subject in language (discourse). The dominant subject position is marked as neutral and inscrutable; it is implied to be self-evidently "normal" or natural because it does not have to be named. A heterosexual white male is difficult to name pejoratively in the very words we use to name his race, sex, and sexuality. We would need more words to name this subject position negatively. The identifying terms themselves would not indicate judgment, hostility, dis-ease; but rather, we would have to add explicitly negative qualifying words in order to name that *individual* straight, white male derisively.

In the other categories, the words that position the body in a category, in a grouping, already resonate with negative associations and connotations. In most cases, the words devalue the body being named, but in all cases they work to separate that body out from the norm, to distinguish it from what is discursively constituted as normal and natural. To refer to a black male as "African American" does not carry the same demeaning implications as to call a homosexual man of any race or ethnicity a "faggot"; but it functions to separate him out, to call attention to his difference (from the unnamed normative position) as a defining characteristic, as one that must be acknowledged if we are to "know" him. This is not to say such a naming is always pejorative or disempowering; rather, the signification of the naming is largely context-bound, embedded in the relationship between who is speaking to whom and why, for what reasons. Our language is so familiar to us, so well-known, that we may not naturally think to scrutinize it, to attend to it as something other than inevitable. Unless we have been the object of discourse, we may not have had reason to resist or critique it. In one class, we were talking about ways of naming American citizens, new immigrants, and "illegal" immigrants. While we were discussing the significance of "illegal alien," it was clear that, although most students were familiar with what the word means, how it is used, they had not

before really noticed the words—that is, the double-edged reinforcement of other-ness, of not being invited or wanted here. As
one student asked, "Is there such a thing as legal aliens?" As
another student pointed out, surely we would understand the
literal meaning were the term *illegal residents*, so why do we
name them aliens, what is the figurative function of the term?

What also emerges in these examples is that it would be impossible, or at least ineffective, to interrogate language even on
this seemingly basic and obvious level, without attending to the
historical conditions and material relations by which these words
have emerged, taken on value and significance beyond their literal meanings, and taken on their power. The point is not to stop
at simply saying, "Well, these different words exist. They just do,
and we need to be careful now when we write." Obviously, to
stop there would be inadequate. Rather, we *begin* at the level of
words that exist not simply to name, but to inscribe and evaluate
(hierarchically) people on the basis of our bodies, our beliefs, our
situatedness. From here, we move on to consider the material
and historical contexts that have given rise to our discourse (as
well as the material effects our discourse has on the world as we
live in and conceptualize it) and the worlds we imagine and evoke
in our writing. We cannot think, know the world, name one another, outside language. We cannot use language outside the systems in which specific forms and terms of naming and encoding
arise: as in the language that evolved and took on specific meaning and power during the American antebellum era, or the discourse of late-capitalism, of Nazi Germany, or of patriarchy.
(Begin, for instance, with asking why there is no way to name a
female cuckold as the word names only a husband whose wife is
unfaithful. How do we name the wife of an unfaithful husband?
Likely, it was not necessary to name because it was not deviant; a
husband's infidelity was sanctioned and therefore not worth naming.) Language is neither slippery to the point of endlessly putting meaning off in an exchange of signifieds nor is it rooted
firmly in some "real" ground outside of very specific material,
lived relations of power. To work in and on discourse as a space
for de- and reformation might not result in tangible and immediate actions to revolutionize our collective or individual existence,
but this work is necessary and viable conceptual revisioning of

our existence. I am arguing that language itself is a material condition by which we organize, know, and are evaluated in the world. To begin to reconceptualize identities and relations in the level of language is not to engage in play for the sake of play, is not finally to teach that language is a series of endless traces always deferring a final resting place in the realm of "meaning." Nor is it to claim that language is *the* field on which social transformation—or even alteration—will be waged. It is, rather, to suggest that language is one of the primary means by which we organize and conceptualize our identities and our relationship to the world, the identities we inscribe on those we encounter and imagine. Revisioning (in) language is critical to any sort of social and material reorganization we might aim for or conceptualize. (Neither as precedent nor as antecedent, but rather as part and parcel. I am not interested in arguing for a linear developmental model in which X must come first or second. I hardly think the process of change will be so tidy that we can dictate the stages of its realization.) This assertion is not based on a belief that language "can change the world," but rather that we live in and understand the world through and in language. We cannot, therefore, "change" the world without an understanding of how our experience and conception of the world is intricately, inevitably bound up in the words we use.

Revisioning the Teaching of Writing as a Critical Process

While conceiving of writing and reading as processes is still necessary, I would like to consider what they are potentially processes *of;* that is, where such processes might lead us. Rather than supporting the discourse of expressivist pedagogy that calls on us to validate a student's sense of herself as a unified, coherent self, knowable through the use of writing as a personal medium of self-expression, I am interested in investigating the ways in which a composition class that foregrounds the composing/constructing of texts and readings might function to engage students in a self-inventory. In such a pedagogy, writing serves as the means by which we actively construct a self and a world that are, in turn, determined by the very language we have access to, the words through which we express these constructions. I will argue that a writing-centered course is an appropriate and useful arena in which to initiate the process that Antonio Gramsci deems necessary for coming to a critical consciousness:

> For his own conception of the world a man always belongs to a certain grouping . . . Criticizing one's own conception of the worlds means, therefore, to make it coherent and unified. . . . The beginning of the critical elaboration is the consciousness of what one really is, a "know thyself" as the product of the historical process which has left you an infinity of traces gathered together without the advantage of an inventory. First of all, it is necessary to compile such an inventory. (1987, 58–59)

By providing a conception of how education functions in relation to broader sociopolitical contexts outside of the classroom, and by moving beyond the scope of individual teachers and student-writers, critical pedagogy aims to help students critique and more consciously participate in their constructions of self, other, and world. While process pedagogy attempts to defamiliarize writing in order that students might take an active role in the production of their writing, critical pedagogy seeks to defamiliarize the production of meaning by presenting it as a construction, highly influenced by language, in which students can actively intervene. Both process and critical pedagogies, therefore, emphasize the importance of enabling students to recognize the potential choices they have—and the choices they may unwittingly make in their texts, as writers, and in their lives—as social agents.

Contrary to the common conception of the goal of critical educators, I neither expect my students to necessarily engage in some specific form of political action in the world as a result of the class, nor do I gauge the effectiveness of my teaching in such terms. In my experience, as both a student and a teacher, we cannot control the outcome of our teaching strategies except by enforcing and imposing *our* ends on our students. In other words, a distinction and potential conflict exist between the *enactment* of a critical pedagogy and espousing its content. Were Taylor in my class now, she probably would not rush to join an antiracism coalition or a peace group. However, I would now be better prepared to offer her the means of recognizing her potential as an active, rather than merely acted-upon, agent in the social realm. A central problem with the standard discourse of critical pedagogy is that it foregrounds *products*, while paying little if any sustained attention to processes. Here, bringing composition pedagogy—with its focus on *how* we produce, on our processes of producing—provides fruitful possibilities for revision.

I have problematized the conception of "the political" as something teachers can *choose* to bring into the classroom, as something tangible or contained within specific texts or topics. In the dominant discourse of critical pedagogy, political/politicized pedagogy is constituted by specific products. "Critical consciousness," "liberation," and "radical social transformation" are presented as the ideal *products,* which an effective radical political pedagogue will somehow produce in her classroom or will teach her students to produce. The assumption, then, is that the critical consciousness produced in the classroom will necessarily effect broader social and political change. Again, I would challenge the assumption that "actual" political work or action happens only *outside* the classroom. Further, I would suggest that we need to understand these goals as *processes* and to reflect on how to foster the conditions that allow for them in our classrooms. Though enacting a critical composition pedagogy is a slower, often less tangible, process than the transmission of its agenda through lecturing or *telling*, it provides the potential for an effective and substantive pedagogy of critical revisioning. This book will seek neither to prove nor to assert that writing (as action, as reflection, as trope) is *the* single realm in which we can work to "transform" current social and economic relations. This book does insist and assume that the *discourses* present in our classrooms—represented in students' writing and reading, in our pedagogies—might be productively engaged in our writing classes as both a means and product of critical inquiry and revision.

When critical pedagogy makes arguments about critical consciousness or radical democracy, it is hard for me to see how to make these processes visible—tangible—so that I can help students understand their purpose and possibility or grapple with the challenge of enacting them. It is also hard to understand where the teaching of writing fits in these processes. When we understand writing and reading practices to be cultural work, however, then writing itself becomes the basis of our pedagogy.

Notes

1. Here, I use *belief* intentionally. Taking up the positions, the assumptions, the telos, of any theoretical framework, is largely a matter of deciding to believe. Not at the absence of further critical investigation, revision, rejection, but as a realization that, finally, one makes a decision rather than finds enough absolute proof.

2. My concept of the dominant process pedagogy is rooted in several sources: my own teacher-training at the University of Massachusetts-Amherst; the work of Peter Elbow; the general lore of process approaches, which informs composition studies (Hairston, for example); and, finally, several critiques of process pedagogy, primarily James Berlin, Lisa Delpit, Pam Gilbert, Susan Jarratt, Harriet Malinowitz, and Myron Tuman.

3. I present a more detailed critique of the limitations of process theory in Chapter 2. See also Berlin, Christensen, Delpit, Faigley, Gilbert, Giroux (1986), Jarratt, and Tuman.

CHAPTER THREE

Embodied Processes: Composing Power and Revisioning Pedagogies

When I originally wrote this chapter, I aimed, once and for all, to expose the inadequacy of expressivist/process composition pedagogy in order to more forcefully argue for critical composition pedagogies. I realized, however, that my courses very much rely on some of the assumptions, values, and methods I have learned from my work in a process-writing program. At the same time, my courses are organized around a pedagogical framework that relies on feminist and critical educational discourses. I understand my earlier impulse as typical of the nascent critic who believes she must clear the ground before she can speak or enter into the conversation. Diagnosing the gaps and limits of a set of practices and practitioners in order to declare one's own practices and self-as-practitioner as the "cure" is a critical gesture that most of us are trained to challenge during graduate school; however, it is also a stage of intellectual and writerly development many of us must work through. Yet, there remains a tendency, in composition and critical pedagogy, to construct pedagogical *territories*, to posit pedagogical choices as either/or, us/them. To articulate pedagogy within a "my side" versus "your side" framework leaves little room for discussion and exchange. In our classrooms, most of us probably act as *bricoleurs*, deploying strategies associated with a variety of seemingly competing pedagogies depending on the situation at hand. Rather than creating pedagogical territories, we might more usefully seek to expose and work at the points of linkage and intersection in seemingly oppositional pedagogies.

Process-oriented pedagogies moved composition studies beyond a concentration on skills and product toward a fuller understanding of the composing process—from the moment at which a student begins the attempt to find and use language, to the reception of texts by an audience. Further, they emphasize the value in conceiving of composing as a process in which—rather than passively acting as the medium of already selected forms and rules for written texts—students can actively intervene to shape, critique, and revise the product. Elbow, Murray, Macrorie, and Britton have argued the importance of allowing students to write from experience, simultaneously encouraging students to envision their lives as important and enabling them to speak from positions of authority in their texts. Most important, process-oriented pedagogies emphasize the importance of respecting our students and of taking their writing seriously, displacing the focus of our pedagogy from the mastery of normative conventions or forms, to writing as an action, as a complex praxis of learning to deliberately communicate.

Clearly, then, process pedagogies have been essential in moving composition studies forward, and, while many critiques have been made of process pedagogy over the past decade, we continue to rely on the practices associated with "process" in the teaching of writing: drafting, revising, peer editing, teacher conferences, writing from and about experience, making student writing public (through peer review and class publications) so that they might write to an audience beyond the teacher. As Yagelski suggests in "Who's Afraid of Subjectivity?" there are multiple meanings circulating around the term *process*. We might use the term to refer to the pedagogical practices noted earlier; or we might use it to evoke the discourse of expressivism, a theory of writing and teaching writing; finally, the term might signify a description of how writers produce a text. Process pedagogies grow out of this third meaning, evolve from our sense of "what writers actually *do* when they write" (1994, 206). Yagelski notes that critics from a variety of theoretical perspectives understand and refer to writing as process. Cognitivists, feminists, expressivists, and social constructivists alike thus deploy some of the same methods in their teaching. The critical difference, then, lies in how we understand the aim and the means of that writing process: writing for/as self-discovery or expression, writing to effect/represent the development of critical consciousness, writing as result/sign of cognitive development, writing to enable/achieve the emergence of a public, authorized voice and perspective.

Clearly, there are multiple process pedagogies, or many theoretical frameworks that might determine particular emphases and provide particular significances to our use of process-oriented instructional strategies. All the term *process* signifies in itself is a valuing of teaching writing as a series of moments and choices, an attention to the process of composing, slowing down and paying attention to the sequencing of events that go into text making. In earlier drafts of this manuscript, I did not use the term expressivism; I chose instead to refer to process pedagogies. I found that various readers problematized that choice, wanting to separate and recuperate the methods (drafting, peer reviews, etc.) from the critique of expressivist discourse. It is my aim, however, to trouble the assumption that we can easily distinguish between methods and the discourses within which those methods are experienced and take on meaning. We cannot, that is, so easily control the effects of our pedagogies. Even if we declare ourselves to be post-process or post-expressivist, it is difficult to undermine the effects of process/expressivist discourse because our students are likely to enter our classrooms already seeped in romantic, individualist assumptions about language, authors, and "the self" that inform not only process/expressivist pedagogy but also our cultural mythology. As Giroux suggests, we need to be wary of working from a view of meaning or knowledge that assumes these to be "produced in the head of the educator or teacher/theorist and not in an interactional engagement expressed through the process of writing, talking, debating, and struggling over what counts as legitimate knowledge" (Giroux "Literacy," 71).

Despite our *disciplinary* declaration that we have moved beyond either process or expressivism, then, we continue to promote its assumptions and values in our *teaching* if we are not consciously attending to the use and effects of our practices. I return to what might be, to some, an exhaustingly familiar critique of expressivism in this chapter—not to rehearse it one more time or to point the finger, but rather to show how those critiques came to resonate differently for me when I examined them in relation to my teaching, in relation to students' work in our classes. While I had understood and joined in the post-process rhetoric of our scholarship, only after I focused on my classroom, and not simply the literature, was I able to begin to think more substantively about how my *teaching* (and not only my thinking, or my conception of my classroom) should change and develop in light of that critique.

In a writing course, we are afforded the time to slow down the writing process. We and our students take advantage of that time, using it to deliberate and reflect on the various moments and choices in the development of a text. We know they probably won't slow down the composing process to this extent *every* time they write a paper, letter, essay, or article. With various projects and priorities tugging at them in a given moment, they won't likely have the luxury of time and deliberation allowed when we can make their writing the central feature of an entire class. Our hope, then, is to provide them with a set of writerly and intellectual practices, which they can call on in future moments of composition. In a similar fashion, I am artificially slowing down the process of developing a pedagogy. This process of development includes reflecting on specific moments of teaching, and also reflecting on the debates and issues in the literature of the field. My hope in freezing particular moments in order to study them is to reveal and problematize the space that has often existed between the pedagogy I have argued for and the pedagogy of my argument. Just as I ask my students to think about what it means to write deliberately, my aim in this book is to consider what it might mean to teach writing deliberately.

So this chapter exerts pressure on the familiar pieties of process pedagogy—specifically, personal narrative, peer review, and classroom publication—in two ways. First, rather than treat them as unconditionally "good" practices abstracted from material sites ("peer review *works*!!"), it theorizes these activities from complicated and conflicted classroom sites. Second, it puts pressure on these practices, and the discourse of process pedagogy, by drawing out and drawing in some important insights from critical pedagogy that understands the nature of the individual and of power very differently. In articulating these ideas, I am also *performing* a pedagogical process of recursive critique and ongoing revision. Each time I revisit the texts and classroom moments represented here, their significance and instructional value changes. I intend, then, both to argue for the value of a critical pedagogical lens in composition classrooms, as well as to demonstrate critical pedagogy as an ongoing process of development, rather than a declaration or a state of being.

Embodied Processes: Pedagogies in Context

Perhaps it is important to attempt to pinpoint what *pedagogy* signifies here, as distinct from instructional methods, social visions, or, simply, teaching. Jennifer Gore (1993) understands "pedagogy," at least as defined within radical educational discourse, to be centrally concerned with "how and in whose interests knowledge is produced and reproduced" (5). She goes on to suggest that a given pedagogical discourse has at least two pedagogies: the pedagogy argued for and the pedagogy of the argument (5). I might, for instance, tell my students in the syllabus and on the first day, that our writing class centers around students being active in the process of writing, reading, and inquiry; this class values and relies on their perspectives even as it aims to examine and perhaps challenge those perspectives. Therefore, I have argued for a student-centered pedagogy of writing; I have declared that this pedagogy will direct our class work. It would, however, still be possible for me to dominate that space— to contradict the stated aims by telling them what "good" writing is and is not—by rejecting their inquiries and assertions in a way that neither challenges nor usefully directs, but rather dictates, thus reasserting my role and power as the institutional presence of authority and knowledge. In this way, the pedagogy I am arguing for (the making of knowledge as a collaborative process) is contradicted and undermined by the pedagogy *of* my argument (the strategies I deploy in service of that pedagogical vision).

The circular arrangement of chairs is another good example because it is familiar to writing teachers. While putting the chairs in a circle means the teacher is no longer the only person who can see everyone—while it provides a different spatial relationship among participants in a course, while it is an alternative to the conventional arrangement of the classroom and its implied power-knowledge relations between teacher and students—it is in and of itself no guarantee of anything. It is simply a starting point, the beginning of an intervention and a revision of traditional conceptions and relations of knowledge and authority. Indeed, there may be contradictory repercussions in such an arrangement. In a circle, there is no hiding from the gaze, not only of the teacher, but also of one's classmates. A student in a wheelchair once noted that she felt, for the start of the class at least, that her comments were heard and responded to in light of her being in a wheelchair because it was far more obvious and evident a presence in the circle than in rows where some students might have their backs to her.

Does this mean we should no longer use the circle? Should we give up and return to rows? Try a triangle perhaps? Or couches? I am not suggesting that, because a circle does not guarantee our goals will be realized and because it may in fact even promote conditions or relations we are attempting to circumvent or problematize, we should reject this arrangement. Rather, we should approach the circle (and broach it with our students) as a complicated choice. We cannot put the chairs in a circle and assume this spatial arrangement will unequivocally or necessarily serve our pedagogical aims, whether those are identified as critical or feminist or student-centered. As Gore (1992) reminds us, pedagogy needs to account for and work with both instructional acts and social visions; we cannot simply assume that the pedagogy of our argument is in alignment with the pedagogy we are arguing for.

The distinction I am making is more complicated than the conventional distinction we make between pedagogical theory and pedagogical practice. I am not suggesting that we can easily distinguish between theory and practice, shifting at will from one realm to another. Again, this is an issue I take up here as central to a critical writing classroom; traditionally, the theory-practice relation exists as a hierarchical and oppositional relationship, where the two are not only inherently separate and distinct, but one is always elevated above, privileged over, the other. I am, rather, suggesting we consider pedagogy as necessitating consideration and engagement of two distinct elements that we might conceptualize and rename (as Freire [1987] suggests) as "action" and "reflection." Each of these elements encompasses theory and practice; perhaps it is useful to think in terms of pedagogy as requiring both reflective action and active reflection.

What, then, might one do with the circle? In my classes, I have students move into a circle on the first day. I ask them what is different about sitting in a circle, what does it allow for or encourage? How does it affect their position in the classroom in relation to me, to one another and to the subject/object of study? Why might a teacher make this choice? Which of the effects do they perceive to be useful and which to be repressive? I then explain to them why I have made this choice because, finally, it is my choice to make (even if I allow them to vote on how to arrange the room, it is my decision to "allow" them to vote). A few weeks into the course, I leave the desks in rows and begin the class. At some point during that session, I will raise the question of what now feels differently about the rows. Many students talk about how odd the rows seem in this class because they are used to and comfortable in the circle even though rows are the dominant arrangement in most of their courses. For us to understand what the circle does, we need to get out of it for a moment. The interesting thing to note here is that, for the context of our class, rows are now unfamiliar even though many of them begin the course taking rows for granted, as the natural and apolitical, impartial spatial arrangement in which teaching and learning happen.

What I am suggesting, then, throughout this book, is that all of our instructional acts take place in specific and active contexts; it is within those contexts, and not within the generic or idealized contexts that are often the default "site" implied in our pedagogy literature, that these acts take on meaning, for us and for our students. There is the institutional context, the specific subject at hand, the dynamics of the participants, the pedagogy the teacher has identified for her work, the learning histories and social, cultural inscriptions students bring with them. Obviously, we cannot control or contain all these contexts. Rather, in being aware of them, we can attempt to work with them to recognize, interrupt, or enforce the meanings they imply for our methods. Rather than assuming or arguing for the efficacy of a given practice, we need more discussions that represent and take into account the range of subjects and subjectivities that populate any actual site of writing instruction. It is important to work both in our scholarship and our classrooms to become attentive, not to "the student writer" but to our students as writers. We need to represent not simply our pedagogical ideas but also the complex workings of specific sites of pedagogy, inviting students and one another to participate in and critically reflect on our instructional praxes, as experienced and represented, and not simply as intended. Giroux offers a useful example to illustrate how we sometimes fail, as teachers, to move beyond *espousing* radical ideas or content when we assume the self-evident nature of a social vision and of how it is made clear through our instructional practices.

> The classic example might be the middle-class teacher who is rightly horrified at the sexism exhibited by male students in her classroom. The teacher responds by presenting students with a variety of feminist articles, films, and other curriculum materials. Rather than responding with gratitude for being politically enlightened, the students respond with scorn and resistance. The teacher is baffled as the students' sexism appears to become even further entrenched. In this encounter a number of pedagogical and political errors emerge. First, rather than give any attention to how the students produce meaning, the radical teacher falsely assumes the self-evident nature of the political and ideological correctness of her position. In doing so, she assumes an authoritative discourse which disallows the possibility for the students to "tell" their own stories and to present and then question the experiences they bring into play. . . . The teacher's best intentions are thereby subverted by employing a pedagogy that is part of the very dominant logic she seeks to challenge and dismantle ("Literacy," 71).

I would like to turn now to some specific "texts" (moments, writings, responses) from my classroom and to exert the pressure of critical reflection on my pedagogy as it was enacted (and not simply imagined) in particular contexts, by students and teachers who are located not in the abstract space of conceptual possibility but in complex positions that impinge on and bounce off one another. I offer these neither as evidence of success nor as of assertions of what should be, but as texts that question and should be questioned. What I have come to question in my process-oriented training is the unintended, and so sometimes invisible, effects of our methods, the effects we do not anticipate and so do not acknowledge or register.

Composing Maria: Going Public with "Personal" Narratives

> I want this story to be a question—questioning as well as questioned. I don't mean questioned in an antagonistic sense. The pedagogy I attempt to enact is critical and dialogic. . . . I don't attempt to transmit the "truth" about [social experience] to students. Rather, I ask them to critically engage with all the texts of the classroom in order to dialogue about the limits and possibilities of their liberatory potential. (Needle 1999, 2)

Eight years ago, during my first semester teaching Basic Writing, Maria wrote an essay that was both narrative and cultural critique. In this piece, she focuses on the process of putting herself together again after being raped. Her text does not center on the moment or event of the rape itself.[1] Rather, she narrates the moments directly preceding the rape and then shifts her attention to its subsequent effects—her long, self-imposed silence and internalized shame, her mother's unsupportive response, her experience of contending with images and attitudes that circulate in our culture around rape and rape victims. In her essay, Maria shifts from creating a personal voice, an effect achieved by those moments when she presents and examines her experiences and interpretations, to a more public voice where the "I" takes on a more social authority and directly addresses her readers, posing questions to them, offering "public" evidence, calling attention to and critiquing cultural images.

Maria presented drafts of her texts for peer review, and the final draft was published in a class magazine. In each workshop moment, students left the page, moving to "read" and respond to Maria and not only to her text; the form and content of her writing produced discomfort in readers, who did not like how they were positioned or represented by/in the piece. As I attempted to facilitate responses centered around the formal and rhetorical aspects of the text, I was aware that we were not able to focus on the writing itself, the formal product, the choices Maria made as a writer (instead of as a rape victim). These were ignored or glossed over as students focused instead on her topic, on how it made them feel, how they felt the piece assumed a position for them that they did not want to occupy. Similar to Richard Miller's recounting of the discussion about "Queer, Bums, & Magic," this powerful piece of writing left us unable to talk about the power of the *writing*. We were affected not simply by the writing but by the *text*. By "text," I am referring to that intersection of writerly and readerly processes, the interchange between the rhetorical, formal features with which the writer composes her subject into a written product, and what readers bring with them to this produced version of the subject. In this case, we were situated in specific ways in relation to larger circulating cultural narratives about rape, discourses of gender, victimization, privacy, and cultural narratives about rape. It was this intersection, and not simply Maria's essay, that made the experience of responding to this text so powerful.

In composition and critical pedagogy, we talk often about the importance of writing from and out of experience. In traditional process pedagogy, developing writers are encouraged to mine their personal histories so they might feel a sense of authority and expertise in relation to the subject of their texts. In critical and feminist pedagogies, experience is understood to be socially, materially, and ideologically produced. That is, we come to understand or make sense of our experience and our "selves" according to cultural narratives that transcend "personal" or seemingly individualized histories. Writing about one's history is thus a means to understanding how we have come to be positioned and composed in the here-and-now, to recognize that experience itself is inscribed by systemic social and material conditions. Whether we subscribe to the idea that we have come to be who we are through the workings of fate and destiny or as the products of sheer individual will, dominant ideology teaches us to know our selves as natural and inevitable. Inquiring into our experiences in order to *study* how our values, identities, and relationships have come to be constructed and shaped allows us to think about the possibility of making deliberate choices about the "selves" we hope to become and the relations we aim to foster.

The assignment that prompted Maria's essay was the first project of the semester. Students were asked to inquire into an experience, value, belief, or event in order to reflect, through the writing process and within the final product, on the significance it had come to hold. They were not asked to write a "personal narrative"; we were not, that is, focusing on that particular rhetorical form, nor were we working to convey an experience or feeling. As part of the project, we talked about what it means to inquire into one's history. No rhetorical form was specified for this assignment and we read a variety of texts, from poems to personal narratives to essays to cross-genre pieces, in order to consider the various rhetorical and poetic strategies available for this kind of project. Since I had begun reading in critical and feminist pedagogies, my aim was not to use this assignment as a forum for radical self-expression, but rather as way of enacting Gramsci's call for a "self"-inventory. Again, according to Gramsci, the "beginning of the critical elaboration is the consciousness of what one really is, . . . as the product of the historical process which has left you an infinity of traces gathered together without the advantage of an inventory" (1987, 58–59).

Maria obviously felt the class, this assignment, offered her the chance to tell her story. Presumably, she could have chosen other experiences to recount and analyze; she had the right to censor her narrative. Yet, at the same time, she did not feel completely free to narrate and scrutinize this experience publicly. Instead, she was aware that, regardless of her intended aim in representing her experience and reflections textually, regardless of how she attempted to make her readers understand it, they were going to have their own responses and interpretations. She saw her peers not as a unified audience who would simply receive and absorb her piece, but as readers who occupied distinct territories, based on their gender, and who would subsequently react precisely because it was an experiential narrative to *her* and not only an essay. In the end, she did publish the essay, hoping to bring up her anxieties during our discussion of the magazine. In this way, she was attempting to modify through appropriation the role she envisioned as fixed for her in the eyes of her peers.

Whether we are privy to such dilemmas, our students are experiencing social distances, oppositions, and struggles in our classroom, even if we imagine that, as teachers and students, we can avoid such wrestling. Our classrooms, explicitly or implicitly, convey more than what constitutes a good essay or a strong voice; they also serve to condition the possibilities by which discourse constitutes and/or denies power. In my student's case, writing the essay seemed to be a powerful experience. Having chosen not to tell anyone except her mother about the rape, her decision to tell a classroom of strangers can be interpreted as her decision to refuse their inscription of her as deformed, damaged, guilty, or helpless. And yet, after the power of the composing experience, she was faced with a feeling of potential disempowerment when considering how her essay would be received. Regardless of whether we choose to explicitly address such "politics" in our teaching, I believe we have a responsibility to at least acknowledge them in our scholarship and, should we decide it imperative to ignore, contain, or circumvent them out of our classrooms, to build a case for this choice rather than to posit it as natural or easier for students. Neither pretending such social tensions and discursive conditions do not enter into our classrooms nor ignoring their powerful presence is an adequate response. Among others, Sedgwick, too, has called our critical attention to the ways in which, whether conscious or not, discursive ignorance "can bring about the revelation of a powerful unknowing *as* unknowing, not as a vacuum or as the blank it can pretend to be but as a weighty and occupied and consequential epistemological space" (77). It seems to be our responsibility, then, to contend with our own and our students' unknowing.

Maria was absent on the day our class discussed the collection of essays, which included her narrative about the ways being raped had impacted her sense of self. I note this to say that her absence likely impacted the kinds of comments some students made, as well as to account for Maria's silence throughout this section of the chapter. First, a student told the class this was her favorite essay and began to describe why it had moved her. Next, a student admitted that, while he found the piece to be well-written and gripping, he also found it to be "too personal." He had peer edited this piece and said his unspoken response at that time was to question her motives for writing it, as he felt uncomfortable while reading the piece. Three other students, all male, agreed. They did not feel it was an appropriate topic for class. Because all three of them had earlier cited their favorite essay as a piece detailing a boy's escape from Viet Nam, I asked what made the rape essay somehow more personal than the escape story. One student claimed it was because the former was a "touchy" subject, while the latter was "a success story. He made it here to America, against all those odds."

In other words, Buu's story of survival against the odds—of being beaten, hungry, lost, arrested—was somehow different from Maria's story of survival in spite of the odds, of being beaten, silenced (during the experience and afterward, in terms of not telling it), and raped. Buu's story confirms our myth that America is freedom; "making it here" (whether physically immigrating or economically ascending or educationally succeeding) is upheld in his narrative as the dream. The dream is realized, attained, and the survivor lives to tell the story, so we can all celebrate. I am not discounting or devaluing Buu's experience. Indeed, his narrative and his history were remarkable. But I wondered why we could not read Maria's story through the same lens. It seemed it took communities—a grouping with some sense of shared possible, if not lived, experiences, with shared perspectives and situatedness in the world—to read her story as she wanted it to be read (or at least, not to read it as she did not want it to be read). Buu's experiences were not shared, even potentially, by any of his readers and yet were more accessible and acceptable. Perhaps Buu's narrative was more pleasing, not only because it so forcefully sustained the myth of the American dream but also because the victim and the perpetrator were clearly "others." The class members could distance themselves on the basis of geography, ethnicity, even formal governing practices. Maria's essay did not reiterate a comforting myth, and it did not present the student with "others" from whom they could distance themselves. The rapist was a friendly acquaintance, the person who blamed and silenced Maria was her mother, the victim was an average American. It was not a story of a woman attacked by strangers lurking in the bushes. Had it been, perhaps the students would have felt more comfortable responding to it in the supportive ways Maria had hoped they might, but had believed they would not be able to; perhaps then they would have felt it possible to distance themselves more from the narrative.

Another woman in the class had written of a time when she was sitting close to a girlfriend on a park bench and was attacked by three kids who were screaming "you f*@# dykes [*sic*]!" (Although she was left bleeding and bruised, she used the story to reflect inward on her own internalized homophobia.) She claimed Maria was "brave" and asked why her story about getting beat up was "okay," but Maria's story about being raped was not acceptable. "Is it because I'm not gay, so it seems like a mistake in my case?"

I was reminded, during this discussion, of Dale Bauer's claim that students (and many instructors) often insist "that the classroom ought to be an ideologically neutral space, free from (individual) interests and concerns" (1990, 385). Our discussion reveals the confusion that arises when a student's experience or text crosses these boundaries and reminds us that many of their experiences and texts inevitably do and will cross these boundaries, as not all students have the luxury to tell stories that do not implicate or introduce the social tensions (and sometimes violence) of sexuality, race, and gender. Just what story should Maria have told instead? What would have been "appropriately personal" without raising any controversial issues? Simply arriving at competing interpretations in this discussion, allowing space for "difference" among the readers of these narratives is not enough. Concluding with, "well, that's just my opinion" is not adequate. As Ohmann cautions us, "Autonomous judgment and the individual choice are themselves ideological effects. . . . opinions come from somewhere, are socially produced, conceal deep contradictions" (328).

I am not certain we were successful in fully moving beyond individual conclusions in our discussion. I pointed out that, in the essay, we learn she did not tell anyone about the rape for a year and a half because she felt guilty and ashamed. Her mother's response, upon finally hearing of the attack, was to urge her not to tell anyone else and not to repeat "whatever she'd done to ask for it." I asked the class if there was something powerful about choosing to tell a roomful of strangers a secret that even your own mother had used against you and to which society in general cannot adequately respond. One student said he could never tell anyone and claimed, "I know if I got raped I would kill myself. Seriously. I couldn't deal." To this, another student responded, "that just shows you don't know what it's like to be a woman. . . . I've known for a long time that someone might rape me someday and I'm not going to kill myself. . . . I'd deal with it." I suggested that we consider how even the decision about whether or not we prefer to read about and confront rape needs to be recognized as a privilege we have as people who have not been raped. I also told them about a student I had the previous year who was failing out of school because she could not sleep and could not relax as a result of having been violently raped the summer before. She literally could not put the pieces back together yet. I felt reading this essay, this testimony that "In my own time and in my own way, I have dealt with my rape, recognizing that it has shaped and mis-shaped me," would have helped her, rather than threatened her as it seemed to do for members of the class.

My narrative of this discussion represents the forces at play in our classrooms, whether we invite, acknowledge, or ignore them. Our students are not reading or writing in a vacuum and they bring the cultural constructions and social myths to their readings of one another's texts. Of course, they do not have to read or engage each other's texts and it's easier to pretend that politics are elsewhere when they do not. But, when all texts and responses are praised equally *because* they are student-generated, there can be no distinguishing among texts (or readings of, responses to texts) that recount or reenact violence and oppression within the classroom. Obviously, the students responded to this as a powerful piece of writing and yet the power they identified was a slippery and confusing one, making them feel privy to matters some of them would prefer to ignore and forcing them to confront—as a real, terrifying, and painful experience—an event they know only as an abstraction. How individual students responded to this piece of writing was not simply a result of the text-as-object, of the content or quality of the writing; rather, their positions as men and women, as people who had or had not been subject to abuse or threatening situations, was a more important determinant in their decision about whether the piece was appropriate or not.

Several readers of this manuscript have remarked that this particular discussion seemed acutely gender-divided and gender-driven and that, in his or her class, he or she was quite sure this would not be the case. Somehow, he or she perceived that I had led the discussion here. Yet rape is an issue that is mostly gender-differentiated in our culture at large. Not only the act itself but also our interpretations of and responses to it are forcefully informed by our gender, by how our gender situates us to the potential act of violating, or being violated. As my student noted above, many women expect they might be raped and find ways to cope in advance; other women assume it will never happen to them if they do not walk alone in "unsafe" places after dark. Either way, it is a fact many women contemplate; whether preparing for or denying the possibility, conscious deliberation is part of the process. I expect this is not the case for most men as they can live assuming that being raped is simply not an issue. (This is *not* to claim that men are never raped but that, rather, for the most part, it is not a possibility most men deliberate over; the possibility of being raped, I would argue, is *not* a substantive factor in the constitution of male subjectivity.) When you add to the mix cultural narratives that blame the rape victim, that are largely silent on substantive measures to stop rape—beyond, that is, advising women not to dress provocatively or to walk at night alone—it is easy to see how the responsibility falls to women and situates them differently than men. I am not suggesting that I was an objective, disinterested participant in the discussion. I do, however, wonder how we could prevent a discussion (or why we should) from replicating and representing these social and material divisions. If gender largely informs our experiences and identities outside the class, even more acutely in relation to rape, why should these differentials not enter into and be played out in the classroom? I would argue that this is precisely the usefulness of such discussions.

A discussion in which students are divided along the lines of gender need not serve to create an essential and non-negotiable chasm between men and women. Rather, such discussions and the dynamics enacted during these moments allow us to consider how we are situated in specific ways, how our responses to texts and experiences are not the result of our "unique" individuality.

Obviously, this piece of writing was powerful and evoked deep and critical responses from the students in the class. While the writer's decision about whether to publish this piece was a difficult one, I do not see the need to stop publishing and discussing essays. Instead, this experience solidifies my decision to have the class act as an audience of their texts. This form of sharing generates consideration and conversation about the choices writers make in constructing texts, a survey of formal, structural elements. More important, as reflected by the above dialogue, the sharing of texts allows for an explicit discussion of the power of writing both as inscribed by the text and as conditioned by an individual reader's situatedness in the world outside the text. It is not simply the sharing of stories, the exposure to another person's experiences that matters, but the chance this provides to inquire into and reflect on how our representations and readings of experience are already socially, discursively, and politically mediated. We cannot simply assume that making the texts public will inevitably facilitate a sense of collectivity or reveal to students how much they share. In this instance, my student had to consider how her exposure as a rape victim would influence her peers' response to her and her text. But beyond disclosing this experience, she had also to consider how they would respond to her critique of our cultural images of rape and rape victims. It wasn't only her experience she expected readers to be uncomfortable with; she expected them to resist her argument about the discourse of rape as well. I asked the readers, then, to consider how their reactions to being exposed to the representation of the experience of rape varied, how these responses related to their notions of private and public narratives. I believe this discussion was important and served to establish further investigation in our class of how we determine both "good" and "acceptable" writing based on our own constructed standards, our standards not only for the form and stylistics of a text but also for our sense of what we do and do not want to read, what we will and will not know.

Reading Power

> [D]ialogue cannot occur between those who want to name the world and those who do not wish this naming—between those

who deny others the right to speak their word and those whose right to speak has been denied them. (Freire 1970, 69)

An important part of my writing classes, as conceptualized by expressivism's teacherless writing class and as mandated by the University of Massachusetts' writing program, is the sharing of texts, through peer reviewing or publication of essays. Students are aware that they are not writing simply for the teacher or themselves, but for other class members— a non-unified, complicated group of readers. The potential consequences of sharing stories—which may not be simply empowering or disempowering, but might result in feeling both simultaneously—must be considered as part of the language-power equation. As Jarratt contends, "Demanding that our female students listen openly and acceptingly to every response from a mixed class can lead to a discursive reenactment of the violence carried on daily in the maintenance of an inequitable society" (110–11). While my student was able to write her story, and to tell of her rape publicly for the first time, the experience did not leave her feeling entirely powerful.

Thinking about Maria's essay and our response to it complicated my understanding of how to foreground experience as a site for inquiry that could foster both critical and writerly development. While this moment also raised questions about how to engage these essays in class, it wasn't until a few years later, after a workshop in a subsequent class, that I began to substantively grapple with the importance of teaching reading as a critical process. Both of these moments raise questions—not simply about the texts that are produced in our classes but also about the readings that are produced and what effects they might have. While we have been intently focused, as a discipline and a curriculum, as scholars and teachers, to help students understand and experience the generative capabilities of writing, we do not emphasize the similar potential of reading. That is, we focus on ways of teaching writing as a means of reflecting on and critiquing past experiences, new or closely held ideas, social relations. We work from pedagogies that attempt to counter the idea that writing is a medium for communicating ready-made, or already-known, conclusions. But our writing courses must also represent and teach reading as a similar form of active participation in meaning-making or knowledge-production, as an active, even if seemingly natural or unconscious, role one takes on in relation to a text. This means that when we engage in peer critique, we cannot simply ask students to evaluate or objectively respond to the formal aspects of the text at hand, nor to provide neutral, impartial feedback for improving the text. Instead, it means considering reading as a site of engagement and cultural work.

The following excerpt is nearly one-third of the first draft of the first essay collectively workshopped and responded to by my most recent writing class. Rather than being the simple, contained object of our analyses, Mandy's narrative shed light on the discursive situatedness readers bring to texts. Our workshop demonstrated how a reader's decision about whether a text is meaningful and valuable may be largely informed by how he perceives the text to represent him and whether the reader believes the text values or silences or objectifies him. The assignment was to draft an autobiography of some sort, with attention to how formal poetic and rhetorical devices worked in a relationship with the content writers had in mind. Mandy was the only student in the class to explicitly and consistently ground her autobiography in a cultural, social context; she wrote not of one self—even with the centrality of the "I" in her piece—but of a self who is always a member of a larger group and a self who represents a shared, group experience. Other students in the class chose to write about themselves as "individuals" detached from cultural or social groupings (with the exception of several students who focused on their closest friends who were, largely, "like" them), to represent their histories as arbitrary unfoldings, and to foreground the experiences and qualities they believed made them different. Mandy also writes about her "difference," but a difference she claims not to have selected or invented for herself, and one whose meanings, values, and effects she does not claim to control.

> Somehow along the way someone made a remark that growing up in America would be the chance of a lifetime. I would be free to choose my religion, free to say anything and free to be me. Were they black or Latino growing up in America?

I don't want to be alone,
in the rain, in the storm,
in this world.
How do I see the world?
Everywhere I turn, they are out to get me. Where do I go, who do I turn to? From the time I could remember you, my teacher, told me, "it will be okay." You said you would be there right by my side called me (*sic*) "precious" . . . and said I was "too young to be worried about the world." I felt like an outcast an outsider and you could not understand why, or did you? . . . It was the third week of the month and the new toys came in. The dolls were all white dolls and I remember distinctly a classmate told me I could not play with any dolls because they did not have black or Indian dolls and Indians don't wear clothes anyway, so I couldn't partici-pate. . . . After graduation I approached my first grade teacher to ask her why all this had happened. I laugh now recalling her expression, and all she could say was that it happens to the best of us.

I am so hurt inside that I refuse to want to wake up
I just want to go far away in the black night,
isolated and away from all of the
ignorance, pain, hate and disgust
every morning when I wake up.
. . . . Everywhere I turn, they are out to get me. So now, you are my instructor and 90% of my classmates and you automati-cally categorize me as a thug, thief, (but you were the one who stole my culture) and a threat to your society. What have I done to scare you so? . . . You say under your breath, "ohhhhh, please, that was the past why don't you forget about it and live your life?" "It is the nineties and your people have good jobs, higher posi-tions as doctors and lawyers and judges." "Women have more rights now. . . ." "It is all good for you now." WHAT?????? (Scream-ing, under my breath) Get over my past? NEVER, I will never "get over" forget our culture, our past, our present. (Excerpt from "Untitled," by Mandy)

In writing my piece the subject "I" is taking on most of the responsibility and the effort. The way the piece was set up it was like a circle going to different parts of the "I" . . . . From what I believe, it is very "harsh," the tone is "loud" and "abrupt" some-times. What I want readers to understand—if you are a so-called minority (as they would say), you'll maybe agree with me and if you've never gone through any of this, at least it would open your eyes to the things that may have happened to many people of color. (From self-assessment for the first draft of "Untitled," by Mandy)

When Mandy distributed and then read her piece aloud, her classmates (at least those who spoke first and most often) did not remark on the formal attributes of the text. Initially, not only in response to this specific piece, but because it was our first workshop, they were quiet. When someone finally spoke, it was to say that this piece made him upset, as it seemed to be yelling at him, accusing him of something. Several other students agreed with him, calling the piece "too harsh," "too angry." Two students suggested the piece was not effective because they could not "relate" to it. Mandy told us she had consciously referred to her experiences in school because she believed all of her readers could relate to those; they had all been students for most of their lives. Yet this conscious attempt to forge a connection with her readers was glossed over.

In her reflective process note, Mandy calls readers' attention to her deliberate decision to deploy the "I" as a strategic device in the piece. She distances this narrative "I" from its seemingly literal embodiment in our classroom. That is, she is not reducible to or essentially contained or conveyed by the narrator in her piece; her reflective note foregrounds this as a literary device she has chosen deliberately, hoping it will function in particular ways for readers. She also describes the tone she was attempting to achieve ("harsh," "angry"), accounting for why she felt it was an appropriate formal choice in representing her subject. These writerly choices, however, were ignored, not commented upon as an integral factor in the reactions her text evoked. In considering the way texts work and the work texts do, we need to foreground consideration of how decisions about composition and construction impact our interaction with and interpretation of a text. In that way, we do not attribute essential meanings to the text's content, form, or "voice," but are made to reflect on our own position in relation to the text and its formal elements. This is a critical way of reading we might begin teaching our students over the course of our classes. But in this first workshop of the semester, we were reproducing the tendency to take the text at face value, to allow its power to remain mystified, while also denying our own accountability for the meaning and effect we attributed to the writing.

As readers began to take issue with specific claims, the conversation shifted from vague objections to the "tone" of the piece. Alex argued that the essay went overboard in exaggerating the experience of people of color; he noted that, after all, he and his friends were observed with suspicion in stores even though they were white. He went on to question whether this was "really" an autobiography, given that it wasn't "really about Mandy." Perhaps, Alex himself was struggling to understand the assignment, looking to fix concrete boundaries for the autobiographical form. But he does not raise these as questions. Instead, he delegitimizes her narrative by imposing decontextualized normative criteria based on genre specifications. He effectively neutralizes Mandy's text, claiming she did it "wrong," and confirms France's claim (in reference to teachers, but applicable to all readers) that we value most highly those narratives that affirm our values, our sense of ourselves and the world. Our criteria for "good student writing," or Alex's sense of "good autobiography," reflect situated extratextual values and assumptions, rather than universal elements of "style" or structure.

In this workshop, the issues stood out in stark clarity, because of the literal content and formal devices of the text: a black female narrator claiming to write for people of color, writing to and about white people's refusal to acknowledge their complicity in racism. Of course, the response in our class immediately supported the allegations made in her essay. Many students were dismissing her text for how it made them "feel"; because they felt implicated, they rejected the writing without first engaging its argument or evaluating its workings. In discussing that, we also discussed what it would take to legitimize the claim of a white reader that her piece was not effective if it made them uncomfortable; that, after all, was her purpose. But Mandy also wanted them to "like" the essay, she told the class, to acknowledge that it was successful. These are not necessarily co-operative responses, though we often assume they are interdependent. Can we "like" something, regardless of its validity, if it makes us feel uncomfortable, threatened, accused? And can we admit or acknowledge that a piece is successful when we feel uncomfortable in relation to it? Within Mandy's essay, various white people are represented who tell her narrator "not to worry," who sympathize with her over the ignorance of particular individuals. Her piece politicizes this response, refusing to see it as simple kindness. Instead, she identifies it as a racist form of tolerance that refuses to acknowledge the systemic fact of racism, insisting it is local, incidental, an individual response to be dismissed by Mandy and other people of color so that they can "get on with our lives."

Our responses to this piece in class were not reactions to structural or formal qualities of the text. In fact, it took forty-five minutes before we discussed the effectiveness of the poem interspersed throughout the prose and which she used as a device for shifting the "I" from an angry, public voice of outrage to a sad, reflective, personal voice of hopelessness. In their focus on how the former voice implicated and accused them, the students ignored this latter voice. Why were they able to overlook the moments when the essay engaged in self-reflection, when the narrator revealed her pain and confusion—those moments when "they" were not addressed or implicated? Why did they focus on the anger and on the sections where they felt white people were at stake? Doesn't our collective reading simply confirm Mandy's argument that in the desire to deny one's "own" complicity in racism, we ignore how this very act of denial necessitates (and reproduces) the silencing of the voice and experience of those who are situated as the objects of racism? In this case, Mandy and her text were ignored, glossed over. Rather than contend with the essay, rather than engage it even in order to produce a critique, students simply dismissed it out of hand—"too angry," "too harsh," "this isn't me, I am not racist." The discussion then became focused on how particular readers felt in response to her piece, and Mandy's text, her narrator's voice, was no longer heard. The issues and relations that emerged during this first workshop were not resolved or defused in seventy-five minutes. Instead, they introduced questions—about writing, reading, class dynamics, identity—that we revisited throughout the semester. Further, the discussion reinforced how complicated it can be when we ask students to read one another's writing without thinking about the need to teach reading as a process, a process that sometimes needs to be interrupted and directed.

Obviously, I was troubled by how this workshop unfolded; it made evident that I had not yet adequately wrestled with how to teach response as critical inquiry into the text. Instead, reading was performed as an act of applying universal criteria, with readers positioning the text as an objective and isolated artifact whose meaning and effectiveness could be determined without any reference to or awareness of a reader's situatedness. I had learned to teach *writing* about experience as a critical and deliberate process, but I was still failing to contend with interrupting or making visible the process of *reading* these texts.

Idealizing Pedagogies

These moments expose the space that sometimes exists between the way I intend my instructional practices to work and the effects they actually have when they take place within the complicated, multilayered context of a classroom. Clearly, process-oriented strategies (drafting, self-assessment, revision, peer response) were useful, empowering even, for Mandy and Maria as writers. They both talked about these essays as something they "needed" to write, claiming they had lacked the occasion and the confidence to do so. It is not these practices I am rejecting, but rather the common sense assumption that they inevitably produce specific effects, extra-textual results. We need to reflect on, and not simply employ, these practices.

While the literature in critical pedagogy provides useful and energizing accounts of how this theoretical framework should inform our teaching, it provides few representations of *how* our teaching might change in light of subscribing to this pedagogical vision. I found it took many "drafts," and much deliberation to begin to forge a *pedagogy* and not simply a theory about the possibilities of teaching a critically oriented writing class. As Linda Brodkey suggests, arguing for a truth, vision, or idea is different than enacting it, taking it up as a praxis.

> What Foucault and other poststructuralists have been arguing for the last fifteen or twenty years is considerably easier to state than act on: we are at once constituted by and unified as subjects in language and discourse. Among other things, this means that since writers cannot avoid constructing a social and political reality in their texts, as teachers we need to learn how to "read" the various relationships between writer, reader, and reality that language and discipline supposedly produce. (Brodkey 1989, 125)

How are our writing courses different when we aim for writers not only to make texts, but also to critically reflect on the representations they produce? How do we teach writing when we understand language as both the method and the site of critical inquiry? When we aim to foreground both reading and writing as situated processes? When we want to promote an understanding of how texts represent social, cultural, and material relationships while they might also affect those relationships? When we want students to use writing in order to understand the self as it is represented in their compositions, not to "discover" or express a singular or authentic, internal self? The question Brodkey poses for me is this: how does our teaching change if we support the argument as she presents it? If this is the truth about language and discourse that we aim to teach, how does that truth effect our pedagogical goals? And in what ways should (and can) I revision my teaching praxis so that it more adequately reflects and effects these goals? Can we simply "tweak" those methods traditionally associated with process or need our practices change entirely? The moments I represent here serve not to "reveal" the complexity of teaching writing but to reflect the challenge of enacting a pedagogy that does not reproduce the tensions and divisions so well-rehearsed and familiar in the culture at large, or the gaps and limitations already associated with process pedagogy.

How can we enact, and not simply imagine, a pedagogy that acknowledges and makes use of the ideology embedded *within* texts, whether those texts are written by Adrienne Rich, Richard Rodriguez, or one of our students? How can we contend with the fact that reading is also a situated, ideological process and engage in it constructively with our students? When we ask students to "edit" or to provide "sayback" for one another's texts, we are asking them to perform a certain kind of reading, to act as a particular sort of reader. These methods do not preclude ideology; they assume instead that the best way to contend with it in our writing classes is to ask students to ignore their situatedness from time to time.

This represents what North might refer to as practitioner "lore" in composition pedagogy—practices we rely on as central to our work, so central that their unintended effects might be invisible to us. Composition pedagogy or practitioner lore locates power within writing. (It's one of our disciplinary tenets, isn't it? A reason we offer for the importance of our work.) We need to be wary, however, of assuming an equal opportunity vision of power in which it is available to all. Maria sought an alternative to the received, normative narratives about women who are raped; she sought to resist that popular discourse. She believed that writing about the experience was important in that it allowed her to compose herself more complexly, at once a victim of rape, and the agent of how that experience would be represented to others. Maria felt written on and written about as a rape victim; her decision to write about the experience was an attempt to control its telling. Yet she knew that writing did not guarantee that she could avoid the discourse students brought with them to her text, the discourse that informed the very narratives she sought to challenge, to revision. Foucault suggests, "We must make allowances for the complex and unstable process whereby discourse can be both an instrument and effect of power, but also . . . a point of resistance and a starting point for an opposing strategy. Discourse transmits and produces power; it reinforces it, but it also undermines and exposes it, renders it fragile and makes it possible to thwart it" (1990, 101). Maria's experience of writing into an existing discourse, one that situates rape victims, rapists, men, and women in particular ways, ascribes to them specific identities, was also and simultaneously an effort to write outside that discourse, to take it up in order to deform it and reform the identity it posited for her. In or outside of school, claiming a powerful voice was a tricky process of negotiation in this instance.

Many colleagues who have heard versions of this chapter have responded similarly to Maria's classmates, similarly to those who heard "Queers, Bums, & Magic." They have responded, that is, by noting that since Maria's piece was "personal," it was not really a "critical" endeavor. Or they have pointed out that radical pedagogy is disinterested in personal experience, individual stories. But these responses evade the fundamental question this story brings to my mind: how might we effectively contend with powerful pieces of writing in our classrooms? It seems to me that no piece of writing *is* powerful if it does not appeal to, move, or touch us in some profound way that *seems* personal. That does not mean it cannot be an essay about governmental terrorism in Guatemala or about the use of capital punishment on teenaged offenders in the United States. However, it seems too simple and a willful evasion of the point to dismiss Maria's story because it is personal to the writer, or to dismiss this powerful moment in my class because I labeled her text a "personal narrative." (It clearly was a public and social issue to Maria.) Would Maria's text have been easier for us (me, her classmates, my colleagues) to respond to it if it maintained its strong condemnation of our culture's inability to substantively deal with rape but did not reveal that she had "personally experienced" rape? And if so, what does that say about us? The point is, we need to learn to read differently; I am wanting to work out the question of how *we* might learn to read our students' writing and responses differently so that we will be able to teach alternative or reflective/critical reading habits to our students.

The problem here was not how we were responding to "Maria"—either to her as a member of our class or to her textual self-construction; the challenge for me here is how we can enable critical, self-reflexive reading so that texts, and positions, are not dismissed or silenced out of hand, but engaged. This means we have to contend with what is coded—and thereby *contained*—as "the personal." Our reading and interpretive practices are informed by our educational, experiential and social histories, material situatedness, and by the dynamics and composition of the immediate context in which the reading takes place—in these instances, a classroom. It would be easy to reject or problematize the examples I draw on as simply being anomalous, atypical, or "sensationalist." However, it took these kinds of moments—not only the originary texts but also the responses they elicited—to begin to reflect on how all writing is socially mediated and to contend with that fact in my writing courses. The fact that students and teachers do not see prom or sports or research essays as "political" in the way we "naturally" read narratives about rape or race simply shows that we have learned to code the political in specific, socially authorized ways, so that we might contain and control it. Maria and Mandy's essays, as well as their classmates' readings of their texts, not only made visible, but also challenged, my implicit belief that "politics" was something I chose (or not) to bring in, through outside readings, assigned topics, or directed discussions, rather than an always present operative condition.

Perhaps it is easier to imagine our writing classrooms as places where the differences that mark us outside can be held in temporary abeyance, except as we choose to reveal them through our texts. Perhaps we prefer to envision our classrooms as places where our "differences" make us unique and are to be celebrated; maybe we aim to create classrooms where we can depoliticize diversity, without consideration of how those differences may not be individually elected, but socially inscribed on our bodies and our texts with dehumanizing or marginalizing effects. But to subscribe to the idea that classes are ideology-free in their "natural" state, is to assume that the instructor has the power to introduce or prohibit the entry of "politics" into the classroom. Giroux characterizes this pedagogy as informed by "ideology of positive thinking." In this approach, "difference no longer symbolizes the threat of disruption. On the contrary, it now signals an invitation for diverse cultural groups to join hands under the democratic banner of integrative pluralism." Further, such a pedagogy assumes that, "in spite of differences manifested around race, ethnicity, language, values, and lifestyles, there is an underlying equality among different cultural groups that allegedly disavows that any one of them is privileged" (1986, 53). Unless we restrict students not only in what they write, but also in how they write about it and in how they respond to one another's texts, I fail to see how we can invest ourselves with this kind of control or power. Nor am I clear as to why we would want to. One might here insist, but we are teaching *writing*, after all; to this I would respond that writing and reading *are* cultural practices bound up in discourse, power, and material conditions—it is not a teacher's choice to make them so. Unless we decide to stick to drills-and-skills exercises, or to turn process practices into another kind of empty drill-and-skill exercise (express, edit, revise, celebrate!), the questions and issues that emerged during our reading of Maria's and Mandy's texts are not exceptional, but to be expected.

The rhetoric of neutrality, of instructional equity and impartiality masks, but does not eliminate, the ideology at work in a given pedagogy. This is a central concern that critical, feminist, and poststructuralist teachers pose to pedagogies that claim to be simply "student-centered," neutral, or apolitical. As Gilbert suggests:

> This seemingly innocent discourse about student authorship, student literature, and student ownership of texts needs much closer scrutiny. By constructing an elaborate edifice of personal creativity over school writing, the discourse masks the ideological nature of the production of school texts. The act of creation, the individual expression of personal experience becomes the focus of attention not the efforts of [students] to construct texts from available signifying systems. (1998, 199)

In the case of Maria's essay, the immediate burden of exposure is not carried by her classmates, but rather by Maria and her text as they are turned into the object of social scrutiny (rather than the voice or product of inquiry), resisted because they challenge the narratives and values we brought to that moment of reading. Maria did not generate her essay in a vacuum. She did not anticipate unproblematic reception or celebration of her piece, and her assumptions about how others would respond to her text informed structural, stylistic, and rhetorical decisions she made as she wrote the piece. This is a political moment, a clear instance of the world—in all its ideological confusion—entering our classroom unsolicited by me. Could another teacher somehow have precluded this? Was I responsible for not having created a clearly "nurturant community" (in two weeks)? Should Maria have simply assumed that the men (and women) in the class would "appreciate her difference"? Such an assumption would require that we live in a different world, would it not, one where rape victims are not blamed, where the victims are not "shaped or misshaped" by people's reactions to their experience? (Or, ideally, a world where rape does not exist?) We cannot simply ignore or level the barriers that differentiate our students as agents and authors in the social realm when these barriers are not only theoretically inscribed, but deeply felt and materially embodied within the classroom. One might easily avoid texts like this with assignments that, while they will not keep politics out, might certainly keep rape stories out of the classroom. Such assignments, however, are not likely to foster critical interaction with experience or with language and the act and product of writing. But what if our aim is to envision and teach writing as a way of knowing, not simply as the process of composing what is already known in already sanctioned forms?

In other words, a composition pedagogy might suggest that our goal is to help writers, in this case Maria, construct an effective text. (Which begs the question: effective to what end? Effective in helping her to work out her problematic relationship to the cultural encoding of her experience? Effective in articulating a critique of the dominant narratives about sex, rape, and victims? Effective in producing a bound together, structured, coherent argument that draws on research for support and privileges experience as one site of research?) But the moment Maria and I decided to make these texts public, the moment readers were introduced into the equation, Maria and her text were opened to the effects of others' being situated differently in relation to discourse and experience. They were exposed to the effects of her readers' certainty not only about what they *knew* but also about what they refused to know or to know differently. This was not caused by the fact that Maria had written a "personal" or experience-based essay. In our writing classes and workshops, as well as in our culture at large, there is a romantic tendency to conflate the text—its voices, perspective, and characters—with the author. Hence Barthes's insistence that we work our way out of and beyond the author-myth in order to understand and make deliberate decisions about the always functioning role of the reader. For Maria's piece was precisely *not* personal in that it did not aim to simply describe or effectively render one individual's experiences and worldview. Rather, her purpose, one represented also by critical pedagogy and feminist pedagogy, was to reinsert her experience into the social realm in order to challenge how it and she were named, understood, "made sense of." She was holding the "personal" up to scrutinize its linkages to and its representation of the social.

Revisioning Critical Processes:
Learning from Our Teaching

There are a variety of reasons for exploring experience as a site for inquiry. How we use experience or the "personal"—whether we aim to politicize and problematize the myth of the Individual, to expose how social and material relations conditions seemingly individual experience, or to allow students to write about topics with which they are familiar—depends on our pedagogical framework. It is important to be mindful, though, that asking students to write about their own lives may work inadvertently to reinforce privilege, rather than to level it. As Luke contends, "To expect that women students in the university, for instance, will readily reveal their personal cultural histories . . . even when given equal opportunity and encouragement to "speak," grossly underestimates the sexual politics that structure classroom encounters" ("Feminist Politics," 37).

A student once told me, after the semester had ended, that he preferred to write research essays about topics absolutely unrelated to his experience. He claimed he could not write about himself without writing about his identity as a black person in America, about the racism, and the felt sense of difference that had played a large role in constructing his identity. As one of three black students in a class of twenty, he grew tired of feeling like a spokesperson and resented the fact that his essays automatically seemed "political" and "charged" to the other students, while theirs seemed easier to write and to respond to. While many students of color choose not to foreground race in their essays, this student believed he did not *have* a choice, because his texts would be read as racialized, *regardless* of whether he made race an explicit focus of his piece. At the time this particular student was in my course, I was not sufficiently aware that personal essays might immediately offer a different set of challenges for individual writers. Indeed, I conceived of personal essays as a means of leveling differences, allowing all students to write as authorities from their own experience. What I did not consider is that experience itself is socially determined and students do not have the opportunity of writing a self independent of the context in which that self has been valued, devalued, sanctioned, or silenced. My teaching then replicated the idea that only "difference" is remarkable and worth discussion. I could have created assignments that asked all students to foreground considerations of their social-situatedness in both the experiences they chose to recount and the way in which they narrated those experiences. Further, I had failed to recognize, much less contend with, the pressure put on these texts when they are made public.

His critique further indicates that we need to think about how essays are *read* in our writing classrooms, the ways in which reading is a process of inscription. In a classroom where writing is made public, texts are sometimes seen to stand in for the writer, or writers are seen to embody their texts. Even when the form of the writing is not autobiography or narrative, even when the subject is not experience or identity, we need to be attentive to teaching reading as a critical process, an *act* of meaning-making, filtered through our already held attitudes, beliefs, and values.

In chapter 6, I discuss some of the ways in which I use peer reviews, process writing, and personal narratives as a means of encouraging students not only to describe or express their histories but also to understand those histories within a sociopolitical framework. One goal is for all students—not only students of color, women, or non-native speakers (in other words, those categorized as "other")—to consider the ways in which their gender, sexuality, race, ethnicity, religion, and class status have determined not only what experiences they might choose to recount but also how and why those experiences have shaped their "selves." And further, they should consider how those material histories are more readily articulated and received (or not) within the bounds of particular discursive conventions and communities. Just as I asked my class to consider themselves privileged not to have even the choice to write about the experience of being raped, I have the responsibility to encourage all students to consider how even seemingly innocent or "natural" experiences and, certainly, our representations of those experiences, our decision that a given experience is worth narrating, are not individual decisions. I have heard many colleagues complain about the number of "prom date" and "football team" essays they received from students during the personal narrative section of their writing courses. Not surprisingly, the prom narratives are typically written by women, while the sports pieces are usually written by men. Here, it seems, is a perfect place for a class to begin discussing the social structuration and valuing of seemingly individual, "unique" experiences. We could ask students to consider why, out of seventeen or more years of life experience and personal history, a dance or a big game is the event most worth telling. We could find common threads among diverse narratives, whether in terms of topics, themes, conclusions drawn (the dance/ big game was a life-changing moment; being on the team/in the club/part of the fraternity has changed me, etc.) and collectively question the shared cultural myths that pervade these texts and inform the choices writers made in composing. In this way, we might ask writers not simply to generate texts, but also to critically engage the texts they compose. Similarly, readers might not only respond to an essay, but inquire into the extratextual conditions that inform and constrain that response. Rather than pretend that, as readers or writers or teachers, we can transcend our investment in a specific identity and relationship to material culture, we should deliberately investigate the intersections of personal-political, individual-ideological, particularly as they play out in our reading and writing of texts.

This does not mean we should eliminate peer response, or stop making writing public in our classes. Instead, it cautions us to be mindful of how and why we use these practices in our classroom. One semester, a student wrote an essay blaming teenage, unwed mothers for nearly all of America's problems (moral decline, economic hardship, deterioration of family values). As it turned out, the peer editor had recently supported her fifteen-year-old unmarried sister through an emotionally painful and psychologically taxing decision to keep the child she was carrying. The student came to me outraged and distressed at what she considered to be an unfeeling and uninformed analysis of teenage mothers. She could not tell, she said, whether the piece was successful; she was, she claimed, "the wrong reader." I do not see how this peer reader could have erased herself from her performance as a peer editor, could have responded to the text on its "own" terms or according to objective merits. Rather than using peer reviews simply to enable the writer to revise toward a final product, peer reviews might be a means of asking both writers and readers to tend to the ways in which language is neither neutral nor transparent, and to reflect on how readers might be positioned differently by and in relation to a given text. This peer reader was a useful and appropriate reader, someone with direct experience of and a different situatedness to the argument of the essay. What was wrong in this situation was that I had presented peer reviewing as a chance for writers to get feedback on the writing, to provide them with suggestions from readers other than the teachers. I had not considered how "the writing" was not simply an object to be improved or polished. I had not thought about how readers, depending on how the world was represented in that text, might not be able to merely or passively "review" that text, regardless of how "good" the writing was according to their training in the dominant conventions of what makes writing—in the abstract—good (clear, organized, developed, grammatically obedient, and so on).

In making texts public in this way, we need to consider how students are to negotiate the bounds of acceptability when faced with an audience they may not know, much less trust. Harriet Malinowitz articulates this gap, speaking specifically of lesbian and gay students in a composition classroom, claiming that process pedagogy

> rather glibly elides the whole question of how the material of this inner world, ostensibly so unpunctured by social complication, can be transferred to the outer sphere without dire consequences for the writer. . . . I would hold that lesbians and gay men experience this paradox in extremity. . . . Given the way that lesbians and gay men function as social signifiers and the complex systems of "editing" that are involved as they insert themselves into public discourses, their dilemmas are instructive . . . signaling the underlying hazards and concomitant limits in the usefulness of Elbowian writing pedagogy for all students. (1993, 42)

Beyond considering the setting in which writing is received, critical pedagogy emphasizes the importance of attending to how the writing-subject and the subject of the writing is constructed by dominant discourses (whether of rape, gender, race, class, sexuality, education), as this will influence her ability to take power in the process of composing. This is a critical point: not all writers will discover power through the same strategies, and not all writers can access power from within themselves. This must be a central focus of inquiry if we are to arrive at a pedagogy that accommodates and anticipates the needs of diverse students and their complex subjectivities. For instance, while the student's essay on being raped was powerful for her to write, the reception of this text was not empowering; she could not guarantee that her text would be heard or accepted by an audience. If power is only posited as residing within individuals, rather than produced materially and discursively in a social realm, we cannot help students negotiate, critique, or speak in contexts where power operates more actively and potentially in collective minds and discourses.

We need to attend more explicitly to the ways in which students positioned differently as subjects will need to confront different barriers in their attempt to develop as writers and to establish textual authority. While the writing-subject envisioned by expressivist pedagogy is impeded by an internal voice that censors his efforts to express himself through writing, this voice is not determined by or related to the felt experience of social, economic, or ideological barriers. Instead, the prohibitive voices and the means of transcending them are located within the individual writer. While many students (those both culturally and economically marked as other), may have indeed internalized this sense of difference, if they are to gain access to power as writers, they must confront not only the internal voice but also the external social inscription of themselves. Myron Tuman concludes that even pedagogies that aim at reform might "by making the entire educational enterprise seem fairer, more open, and more relevant to success outside of school, while not altering the relative disadvantage of different groups within the overall class structure . . . work to the detriment of those groups by legitimating the efforts of those best positioned to succeed" (1988, 49). Lisa Delpit echoes this critique, speaking not specifically of expressivism, but of "liberal" pedagogies in general, cautioning us to be mindful that there is no universally effective set of instructional strategies, no singularly empowering pedagogical discourse. She urges us to consider what educational, personal, and social histories are not imagined or represented by our purportedly universal, or apolitically benevolent, pedagogies.

Pedagogies in Process

Reflecting on the experience of working with powerful texts, that is, with powerful interactions between readers, writers, and writing, is an ongoing aspect of my pedagogy, not one limited to or resolved within the two moments I have recounted here. Every semester brings such unforeseen or unanticipated moments, moments that have not been represented or accounted for in the literature, moments I have not myself imagined or determined in advance how to direct and facilitate most usefully. Each such moment leads me to recursive reflection, allowing me to come to a fuller understanding of what has happened as well as to aim toward more generative and deliberate future moments. In critically reflecting on Maria's text and our responses to it, I questioned the use and valuing of experience in our writing classrooms. While I did not demand the recounting of particular experiences, I created assignments that allowed for and evoked them. On the one hand, this provided Maria with the important chance to think through some issues and events, to write a piece she felt needed to be written. On the other hand, while that moment led me to think about how we are positioned differently as rhetorical and social agents within the classroom, it did not lead me to extend this understanding to ways we read student-written essays within the classroom. It wasn't until later that I began to wrestle with what I realized is the expressivist tint informing and resulting from my teaching methods.

Later, after reading in critical pedagogy and thinking over *how* I was teaching and not only what, I returned to Mandy's piece. (And, it seems worth noting that I was not the only one still recollecting that workshop experience. Mandy came to see me recently, two years after the class. I mentioned to her that I had written about the workshop and she asked to read it. We met later, after she had read this section, and we talked again about how we understood what had happened that day. She noted that she still tells people about that day in class. She still narrates this experience of being read.) By this time, I was thinking more critically about the use and role of experience and identity in teaching writing *and* reading. Now, we were talking about form as a deliberate choice, considering what it means for experience to function in writing in ways other than as radical self-expression.

And here, people might still be criticizing my choice to use "personal" essays at all. But I can't help thinking of how useful it has been for writers to reflect in writing on their lives as lived and understood. And I can't help but think about the teacher in my program who argues that a cultural critique is somehow essentially different from an essay. Even a critique, which is not ostensibly about what the writer does, as Recchio (1994) suggests, reveals something about the writing-self as it informs that critique. So we might now code the personal essay as regressive and the cultural critique as progressive. But my point here is that we can't just keep looking for the new and critical and empowering and democratic *form*. We need instead to think about how we are teaching students to work with and within these forms (as readers and as writers), how they position specific students differently, what stories/ideas/knowledge they silence, and which ones they sanction. Maria and Mandy could have written their pieces in the form of documented research essays, eliminating the first-person pronoun, while still maintaining their central arguments and points. I do not think, however, that their peers would have responded to them more openly. And if they had, this too would be worth exploring. It was, after all, the knowledge produced in the piece with which they took issue. Calling it too personal was simply a way to avoid dealing with what really bothered them while reading the pieces.

But by the time Mandy was in my class, we were talking more specifically about the (personal) essay as a genre, as a text that is carefully composed and not simply as any piece of writing about the writer. We write about experience, then, not because the (personal) essay is a form constituted by its truth-telling, but to experiment with a form that textually—through formal choices and deliberate devices—creates the effect of believability and intimacy, a sense for readers that they know the narrator. In reading and working with this form, I emphasize that the point is not to tell "the" truth, to expose one's inner-workings, or to narrate one's life in chronological order; we talk about how a writer creates a narrator even within autobiography or personal writing. They were encouraged to play with creating narrators, cross-genre techniques and to consider the effects of their stylistic choices. But with Mandy's workshop, I realized tinkering with the way we study the form is still not enough. If I was going to continue making texts public because I valued the potential in such a practice, I needed to foreground the teaching of critical, reflective reading.

Unless we pay conscious and critical attention to the process and effects of *reading* (an activity central to peer review and publicizing students' writing), our classrooms might function to inadvertently resecure the burden on the writer who works from marginalized knowledge, subject-position, and suppressed discourses. That is, the outlier who wants to speak within and to the culture of power might indeed get her piece read but this does not ensure the kind of engagement she seeks. Attending to the role of the reader, and to the need for writing teachers to consider how we are teaching reading (as an active process and product), seems particularly necessary in classrooms that want to allow writers to write against the grain and to provide an arena in which we can, as writers and readers, represent, inquire into, and revise our assumptions and values. Asking writers and readers to critically engage the texts before them, whether those texts are personal narrative, political essays, newspaper articles, or commercials, seems a legitimate and necessary process in a critical writing class. Simply asking students to generate writing, or asking them to edit one another's work does not go far enough in exposing them to the way discourse works on and through us. We can and should question the writer-centeredness of our process pedagogies in order to find ways to ask readers not simply to express their responses to texts, but to understand, reflect on, and critique those responses in order that we have the power to reread.

No pedagogy, process-oriented or otherwise, is ideologically neutral; students in any writing class are encouraged to adopt a belief system about the nature, function, and value of writing, regardless of whether this belief-system is explicitly articulated by the teacher. Similarly, a classroom is not low-risk because the teacher declares it to be; nor is a "safe" classroom inherently less political.[2] Maria and Mandy obviously felt secure about writing their narratives. Once their texts were distributed, the only way I could have guaranteed their "safety" would have been to impose responses and evaluations onto my students. Had I employed a strategy of telling the class how to read these narratives, I would have circumvented the writers' purposes for composing these particular texts. They felt these ideas and issues were important, worth writing about, worth discussion. To preclude that possibility by providing the official reading or response would have denied these writers the chance for their texts to be taken seriously, not simply received, but engaged.

Rather than simply assume our pedagogies work to benefit and include all students, teachers might attend to their pedagogies as they are enacted within specific sites, and participated in by their students. Rather than simply claim that one environment (safe, nurturing, rigorous, critical) works best for all students or all writers, we must carefully (and in collaboration with our students) consider not only our assumed or intended aims but also the effects of our pedagogy.[3] As Ohmann suggests, echoing Gore, there is no neutral pedagogy for simply teaching writing; further, the failure to acknowledge how our pedagogies are played out leaves us unable to contend with those moments when the pedagogy of our arguments contradict the pedagogy we are arguing for.

> [T]he ways we teach have political consequences, or . . . enact a politics. There is not neutral pedagogy, any more than there can be politically neutral content. Those who profess to teach in the standard or natural way—to teach transparently—simply conceal from themselves and perhaps from their students the social relations (usually hierarchical) of their pedagogies; just as those who profess to teach objectively about economics or art mask the politics of their courses and of economics and art. It follows that one may denaturalize either pedagogy or content and not the other. Further pedagogy may contradict content. (1995, 325)

While attempting to enact a participatory, dialogic classroom is fraught with the risk of failure and abuse of power (not only by the teacher but by students as well), these are risks run by any pedagogy, rather than being endemic to critical pedagogy. Rather than arguing for the possibility of suspending social discourse and relationships by creating an autonomous, "safe" space, a critical pedagogy mandates the explicit examination of ways in which "the world" in all its chaos, confusion, and contradiction is fully present in, informing and informed by, our classrooms. Rather than attempt to empower individual students, or require that others step away and examine the power they so "naturally" exercise, critical pedagogy foregrounds an examination of power itself. Similarly, critical pedagogy constructs the classroom as a space where knowledge is not simply conveyed or passed down, but where we might teach students to pay attention to how knowledge itself is constituted, and the various conditions that determine which knowledge counts.

Giroux suggests that, "though it is difficult to contest that schools exist in a particular relationship to the industrial order, . . . teachers and students do not simply receive information; they also produce and mediate it" (1983, 58–59). It is precisely within this space of mediation—negotiation—that critical pedagogy seeks to operate. Oftentimes, critiques of critical pedagogy seem motivated by the writer's sense that we cannot help but fail in our attempts to enact it given the vastness of the critical project (social transformation) and the abstract language used to depict the means of successfully enacting this project ("transformative intellectuals," "emancipatory authority," "cultural workers"). As Malinowitz (1990), Villanueva (1991), and R. Miller (1994) have suggested, we need to do work in contextualizing the possibilities and projects of critical pedagogy within a writing class, negotiating ways to engage students in an examination of the political implications and consequences of their texts, their positions as readers, their investment in being "authors," and the relations of a given classroom.

Further, we need to make visible the continued process of learning that accompanies teaching, rather than producing pedagogical representations that present a "model"—a seemingly "finished" teacher who has "mastered" critical/feminist/process pedagogy. The assumption is similar to those often made in women's studies classrooms where the teacher is understood as already having done the work of unlearning the effects of patriarchy and is now empowered and thus capable of empowering others. As Gore argues, feminist pedagogy is often conflated with the feminist teacher who "not only holds feminist ideas or perspectives but who 'teaches' them to her students" (1993, 86). Unfortunately, she adds, these classrooms often become an ending point; the work of being a feminist stops once the students have acquired the right feminist knowledges. The work of becoming a feminist is seemingly done in one semester.

If we think instead of feminism as a commitment to a lifetime struggle of working against patriarchal culture that presents itself daily in varying and multiple ways, feminist pedagogy can no longer function through transmission. Rather, it must enable a process of learning to read and critique culture, to denaturalize it, and to reflect on the ways in which we have internalized and learned it so well. And the feminist teacher can no longer act as "model," because she, like her students, is always inundated with the workings of a patriarchal culture and thus cannot ever be "finished" with her process of feminism.

In the same way, writing teachers work within constantly changing contexts and with students who bring ever-changing ideas, interests, and issues to the classroom. To finally "master" any kind of pedagogy would require that the conditions we teach within remain stagnant, and that our instructional praxes somehow produce universal and guaranteed results, regardless of how the composition of our classrooms change. But if we understand students and teachers and texts as complex subjects always in process, and if we attend to the impact and fluctuation of the conditions we work within, then pedagogy is something we can never be "done" with. Rather than seeing critical pedagogy or teaching as a process that can be finished, we need to frame pedagogy as a developmental process that continues throughout one's teaching (and learning) career.

I want to end this chapter with the comment I recently wrote (April 1999) in response to an essay written by a Steve Westbrook, a graduate student in my Composition Theory seminar. In his paper, he grappled, as both a teacher and a poet-scholar, with many of the issues and questions raised throughout this chapter, issues that have been at the center of my work since I began teaching writing ten years ago. I offer this comment for several reasons. First, it is simply another version of how we continue wrestling with, working through, these questions—with our students and one another. Second, it demonstrates the linkages we might find and foster between our classrooms and our scholarship. Third, it makes clear the ways in which I am not "done," as a critical teacher or pedagogue, but rather how I continue to reflect and revision on the texts of my teaching so that I may better understand and enact a critical pedagogy.

Steve,

It strikes me that, in the abstract, a teacher might believe she should tread carefully in responding to your piece because of some of its subject (the healing, the discussion of representing victimization, the disclosure of having experienced victimization in the form of sexual abuse). Would it be "appropriate" or "responsible" or "nurturing" (if the latter is the teacher's aim) to question where you place these disclosures or to tell you one or another doesn't "work" in this piece? Or to pose critical questions about the understanding you have come to of how these poems functioned for you as both a writer and a person? Or to critique how you name and conceptualize the experiences (of writing and surviving and healing)? That then tells me the precise reason why I don't encourage or solicit "writing-as-healing" in my classes. Because it seems a tricky minefield to navigate. I always tell my colleague, who says his work is "teaching writing and healing," "maybe you teach healing, but you don't teach writing." Because he is adamant about not critiquing the students' writing as writing because he couldn't separate the workings of the text, the choices made by the writer, from the subject matter. It strikes me, then, that I can't teach writing if students are using it only to "heal" via "disclosure" or self-revelation. "I teach writing, not therapy."

And yet, there was the time Beth Anne wrote a piece about her uncle molesting her. She began the piece with her narrator sitting in the women's room in Herter Hall (a UMass building) reading graffiti that "outed" molesters and rapists, naming and shaming them. She sat and stared for a long time and then decided she needed to speak her shame, to disclose it in order not to be victimized by it anymore. In her self-assessment, she talked about what she was trying to do in the piece, as a person, a woman, a cultural critic, a victim, and as a writer. It was this final aspect, her sense of writing this experience, constructing it for a particular context (readers and purpose), that gave me a way in to critique and respond and not simply validate or reject her woman/victim/person-ness. I could also speak to her writer-to-writer. There are many instances in my ten years of teaching when students have written as Beth Anne did, when students have sought to challenge themselves as writers and also as knowers, and when the event or issue they seek to understand is one they have directly experienced. It isn't so simple always when students self-disclose to name it "healing" or "personal." Such a rhetorical move often reduces the complexity of those texts, the challenges they put before their readers.

And it makes me think of this too: that my own discomfort in responding to such texts is also a refusal to engage those texts, isn't it? Like Maria's (the student whose piece we spoke about) classmates, I am uncomfortable reading something I inscribe as "too personal." Unlike them, my response leads not to my rejecting the piece out of hand. Rather, my discomfort leads me to patting the writer on the head. "There, there. Nice piece. Good job. I am so sorry." A patronizing, placating reader is certainly not what Maria had in mind. She wanted her text, the representation of her experience, to be engaged—as both a formal product and a piece of writing that sought to make meaning. The crucial and qualitative difference that emerges only now with some kind of clarity as I am responding to yours is that the point of the piece, rendered by its form as well as by its lingering moments and focal points and content choices, is not simply to tell the experience, to narrate a/the self. Maria's challenged us to reread rape as a cultural experience by representing her own experience. But the use of one's own experience as subject matter or "research" does not make a text self-evident or beyond critique, just as it does not preclude the writer from making writerly choices, from engaging in text making. It is certainly inadequate to say Maria simply let the piece "come out of her." It is not a discussion of personal victimization, but a question about the power/potential/ choices in representing that and to what purpose.

I guess my long-winded point is this: in this concrete and particular instance, I don't feel particularly anxious about responding, nor do I get a sense of "writing to heal" as the purpose of this piece. Like my memories of these students and their texts over the years, your piece does not seem aimed at "self"-expression, but writing to know, to better understand your experience and cultural responses to and versions of that experience. This is part of empowering one's self isn't it? And your piece reminds me of Beth Anne's piece in that the poems seem to serve a similar purpose as others' (Paul, Mandy, Maria, Nicole, Mike . . .) writing processes and products have done for them. Of taking all kinds of experiences (of pain done to and pain inflicted by us) and taking ownership of how those stories will be told, must be told, of being the narrator of one's experiences in order to get to make choices and decisions about how they're told, from what point of view. For these students, it seems like part of writing about it is the need to revision how they are represented by normative discourse. Beth Anne didn't want to be a victim or an instigator. Both these positions were given to her by people she told or conveyed/contained within the images she saw (parents, brother, culture). She wanted to refuse those roles, hold another position in her story, to be an agent/author in its telling—the very role denied to her in its moment of happening. Your poems strike me as doing some of that. And the development from one to another version/vision of the poem and the experience, which seems enabled both by your writerly development and your person-development, is testament to this kind of refiguring we do through writing.

The backdrop of the restaurant—noises and sounds and hustle and objects. The deflection your narrator does when Alvaro asks him a question he doesn't want to answer or for which he has an answer he doesn't want to think about or say. He talks about Homer, "strategic language construction," poetry as cultural memory. What is missing is what Alvaro points to and what you have pointed to in various thinking-points this semester—the why of the writer, the scrutability of the means and motives, thoughts and passion of the person writing, that is, of the poet, not Poetry. The narrator shifts his glass, looks at his food. When he does give that blechy answer on page 3 he is seemingly disgusted with his own obfuscatory impulse and he turns to the salsa, a physical action of covering, dousing, drowning out that mirrors his verbal dousing, throwing salsa over Alvaro's real question, covering the tongue on the table so that it doesn't stick out at him.

The admission, to the reader but not to Alvaro, that you sometimes write for self-discovery (or, ok ok, healing) strikes me as similar to when you have to admit to a friend that you like Barry Manilow sometimes. In the context of being "in"/included/legitimate (in the academy, in the poet's world, in your social group or whatever), there is that which is made to feel and seem unspeakable, unworthy, illegitimate, beyond the bounds of good "taste." (In other words, your narrator's impulse to not want to "admit" or "confess" this doesn't strike me as an idiosyncratic response or as reflective of his "issues," but as reflective of how we learn which are the right/cool/within the bounds of acceptable intellectual/poetic reasons to write.) But as you note later, there are as many reasons to write as there are kinds of music to like. There is one reason to write at one moment and another to write in another ("Copa Cabana" works for some occasions and not for others). There shouldn't be a problem there, should there? But school, whether poetry workshops/schools or composition squelches out those reasons, lines them up and shoots them or ignores them altogether in favor of pursuing a particular vision. The institutionalizing of writing might allow for some possibilities but screws other possibilities up, closes them off. A class might still provide the kind of occasion it did for you in the writing and rewriting of poems about a pivotal life-moment, as it did for Mike, Mandy, Paul, Beth Anne, but that is the lucky accident in some ways, isn't it? Do those moments happen for people who don't identify already as writers, who haven't felt the power of writing?

I know in reading your piece that this is the reason I want to teach writing. Self-knowledge leads to an ability to know others better because it always means seeing the self-in-relation-to—to others, to ideas, to the world, to language. This is my faith. Not Elbow's view where it magically (naturally) happens or where just loving and celebrating the self and "other" selves is enough. Or where writing, using language to express somehow inevitably leads to self-knowledge. I hear Bartholomae as I read this and wonder when that option was lost for him. If it indeed was. Or maybe it is simply censored out of his writing because it is in-scribed as affective, un-figureable, and therefore easier to sim-ply dismiss or omit. When did discourse become something we have to "subject" ourselves to, even if through a benevolent and radically enlightened instructor? Because as I see it, the point here is that part of the power in writing is when we can subject experience (and our own and others' representation of it and its implications for our identities) to language and form, when we can re-imagine our subjectivity by rendering it differently in a text. The thing your reading of your poem's and poet's development shows the importance of moments of reflective, critical delibera-tion. Of not simply writing it down, but stepping back and thinking about how you wrote it down, why, the formal choices made, the stylistics, devices, words, structure. It shows how these impact the story told, the meaning made, the tone, the place where the reader is supposed to be, and so on. Looking critically in order to reflect on the act of representation, this gives you agency/au-thority both in relation to the text/telling and the memory (through re-memory). Even the new titles for each revised version of the poem (each of which revises your understanding and naming of the experience) tell a story about writerly distancing—from ren-dering the "real" feelings by writing them down as such to trying to enact a kind of feeling in the piece itself, using the means available not to transcribe but to actively represent and (re)create.

The place where I am uncomfortable in your piece is when you describe that workshop moment. I wonder here what I would have done as the teacher? I often tell my students not to bring in poems or pieces that can't be workshopped. I tell them to find readers, in or out of the class, me or someone else, who can read pieces they feel particularly attached to. I don't say this about "personal" pieces, it is not a matter of simply omitting certain subjects or forms, but about pieces of any kind that they don't want to have critiqued, really. And yet, I am always uncomfortable with that because it also denies them the right to be read. But I just don't know that a class is the place to take that kind of leap . Or that I want to be responsible for it. I am troubled by that. To want to keep out of my class the parts that I also think are most important for the writers. Because even if I keep focus on the text, on it as a text not an experience or a representation of the person sitting there who wrote it, I can't contain or control that completely. It is an interesting turn when you read your classmates' comment as a learning experience for you. After having to interrupt the response because that was the only way to contest what seemed to you a completely off-the-mark reading of your text. And it's interesting, too, that her comment is descriptive, not evaluative. Her calling it a poem "about love" does not judge the writing itself per se, but still signals to you that the piece has failed utterly since you didn't intend it to communicate "love." But you find value in her comment only when you are able to reflect on her remark as a writer, not as the person who had the experience. When you think about what you want your poem to do and to mean. I am still very curious though how she got "love" from that. "Cold, hard, clobbered, eluding, fading, strike, pane, grime"—I can't find much even just in the words themselves, much less their arrangement or relations, that rings a note of love. This gets to me at the importance of teaching reading in writing courses and workshops.

I found the final version of the poem you included to be haunting and intricate and lovely in a not butterflies-and-daisies way. I read it three ways—once in the order written, again with only non-italicized, and, finally, only italicized. I liked how the separation of these was more distinct at the beginning as though leading readers carefully and as though the two narratives become increasingly entangled and can't be read or written separately anymore by the end (so the space given to them individually is chunkier at start, then line by line toward end). As though we're being given clues by the narrator how to read it, and by the end he trusts us less rather than more. Or trusts his words and form less rather than more as the piece proceeds.

Amy

Notes

1. I did not save a copy of Maria's piece, though I did ask her permission to take notes and to write about her text and our class for an upcoming conference presentation. At the time Maria was in my class, however, I did not realize I would be using full texts, and Maria transferred soon after our class together. So I have to draw on my computer log of responses to students' writing, and on my teaching journal for this representation.

2. Indeed, I wonder how we, situated as teachers within our classes, can determine whether our own classrooms are actually "low-risk" or "student-centered." A primary contention of those who point to the limits of process pedagogy is the fact that process theory does not consider how the composition of a particular classroom will influence students' sense of safety and will, further, determine the bounds of acceptable discourse. In certain classes, won't some students be rendered to silence, indeed to *risk*, more than others?

3. Similarly, we cannot assume one persona or role will work for all teachers. Hairston, for instance, chooses the role of "midwife" and "nurturer" (192), positing this choice not as one that suits her conception of herself as a teacher, but rather as the clearly superior choice for helping students "grow" and discover. Personally, I do not feel comfortable envisioning myself as either a midwife or a nurturer. I am also reminded here of Elbow's suggestion in "Pedagogy of the Bamboozled" that rather than dissonance, emulation/participation teaching might serve as a model. Accordingly, teacher and students become "lovers" of one another; the force that drives this kind of learning is not the itch of a problem but the itch for the person who is the teacher. Seemingly this has incredibly different implications for men than for women. After all, this is precisely what some of us as female students and teachers have questioned—do they (students or teachers) itch for us and not the class or subject or activity? It is important to consider the metaphors we engage and to be aware of their implications for teachers (and students) who are not just like us.

CHAPTER FOUR

Making Pedagogy Visible: Critical Pedagogy in Process

Yesterday, I met with a graduate student who will be teaching for the first time this semester; we were anxious to have her teach in our undergraduate writing major. She had prepared a careful selection of readings that represented a variety of traditionally unrepresented ideas and voices and that focused on the issues and politics of writing, discourse, identity, subject-positions, and authority. Her syllabus was a thoughtful, compelling theoretical discussion of "writing." The problem was that the syllabus did not indicate that *students* would be writing, or what or why they would be writing in this course. I was pleased that writing was conceptualized in her syllabus as worthy of theoretical inquiry. I was dismayed, however, that writing had been elevated so far as to become a trope, a signifier to be studied for its material, historical, and cultural functions and implications; but the act of writing, the idea of writing as a practice, was strikingly absent from this class. When, I asked, do students write? What do they write? Why do they write? When do you engage these questions in relation to the texts they write and not only to those they read? She had, it seemed, conceptualized a course about writing, but not a writing course. The problem, she said, was that she did not know how to *teach* writing, what to *do* in a writing course.[1]

My reaction to this syllabus surprised me, left me feeling as though I had become the gatekeeper of something I vaguely understood to be Composition. I was particularly confused because my reaction felt *reactionary*. Her syllabus certainly supported composition studies' assumption that writing is a legitimate site of theoretical inquiry; but somehow it went too far. The act of writing—more specifically, of students writing—was missing from the study of "Writing." What was problematic about this syllabus was that there was nothing to distinguish this as a critical *writing* course, rather than as a course framed by critical pedagogy but in another field, another subject.

At the University of Massachusetts at Amherst, our training to teach in the Writing Program (which consisted of Basic Writing and College Writing courses) was specifically geared to the teaching of writing. We were discouraged from relying on external texts and not allowed to organize our courses around assigned readings. At the time, this seemed a bit heavy-handed, more directive than perhaps we needed. What the Writing Program forced us to do, however, was to contend with students' writing, to focus our attention there. Later, as I began to use more outside reading in my writing courses, I never had the impulse to "fill" my class time or our attention with these texts because I was already steeped in the assumption that students' writing should be the central text of a composition course. Now, I can see that what I take for granted about the teaching of writing is not an inevitable or "natural" assumption, but rather a choice—one originally made for me and one I have now chosen for myself. This leaves me, then, accountable for this choice and necessitates that I argue for it as a choice.

I am not arguing that one cannot teach writing in conjunction with disciplinary knowledge, or that one can separate writing from something called "content." Rather, I am suggesting that in a writing course there is, or should be, a different orientation to students' writing and to the work of the classroom. In a studio art course, students spend time producing, experimenting with, and making paintings or sculptures or graphic designs. I would argue that a studio art course should integrate consideration of the implications of these productions; students should reflect critically on their "creations" (problematizing that term), considering how they work in relation to existing forms, considering how they are produced out of the artists' specific situatedness to social relations and material conditions. "Art" and "artists" do not transcend or escape material reality or cultural discourses; rather, they re-present them, are simultaneously enabled and constrained by their situatedness. It seems more viable and effective to study the processes and products of art-artists—and the meanings represented by or attributed to them—when students are actually engaged in *making* art.

My suggestion to the new teacher, then, was not that she should eliminate the theoretical inquiry emphasized in her syllabus in order to teach students "how" to write. Instead, I urged her to engage in this inquiry with students in relation to their writing, to envision students' processes and products and their assumptions about how texts work in the world as the entry point for the questions she felt were so important to think about in a writing course. In order to develop as writers, people need to write; writing regularly may not necessarily result in "better" writing (since that depends on the specific operative criteria), but it makes writers more familiar and comfortable with the act and process of writing. Further, it is important, though not easier, to encourage students to read their own texts critically, theoretically, discursively. Grounding an analysis of discourse, authority, and identity in students' texts might *seem* to render these ideas and concepts more readily accessible but students often perceive their writing processes and products to be inscrutable, innocent, natural, whereas professional writing is professional precisely because it is motivated, not an accident, and capable of sustaining theoretical scrutiny. If our aim is to foster a sense of how all writers and readers are situated—historically, discursively, socially—it is necessary to engage students in studying the texts they produce.

My concern with the syllabus the new teacher devised for her writing course was that it elevated "writing" to the point that writing was no longer something in which students could or did engage. Instead, "writing" became a subject of study relegated to select texts, texts to be critically read and written about for what they can teach us about writing and discourse. This teacher is committed to framing her course in a radical feminist pedagogy. So we work from shared central assumptions about teaching and learning, about knowledge and authority; we also agree on the specific questions, the primary line and purpose of inquiry, which should inform a critical course. But, while we shared some central ideas about teaching, about discourse and about why we should teach discourse, we did not share a fundamental sense of *how* to teach writing or discourse. This point parallels my central concern about the discourse of critical pedagogy. In the same way her syllabus theorized and therefore privileged writing to the point where it was no longer something students engaged in, but something they studied, critical pedagogy theorizes pedagogy to the point where it no longer requires the active engagement of students or teachers. I value teaching and learning as intellectual practices and our classrooms as sites for theoretical inquiry—not procedural processes of "applying" theories. And while I am drawn to the *vision* of critical pedagogy, to the possibility of seeing our work as educators to be meaningful within a broader context, I am at the same time wary of its tendency to posit vast and seemingly idealized goals for our work as teachers while ignoring the challenges present in any specific site of pedagogy. Certainly, we need not only to articulate pedagogical *visions*—theoretical pronouncements of the possibilities of teaching and learning—but also to reflect on these visions in light of our efforts to engage the ideas that animate them. Otherwise, teaching and learning are removed from pedagogy, and we are left with an idealized, but not realized, project. As Gore suggests:

> While naming a discourse "pedagogical," might have strong rhetorical value among teachers (in legitimating the academic and her/his discourse to other teachers) this approach could both deny and mystify the experiences of teachers, rather than affirm or interpret them. Attention to politics and pedagogy does not necessarily arrive at the politics *of* pedagogy. (1993, 8)

In the discourse of critical pedagogy, there is a lack of substantive attention to the *act* of instruction as a critical element in pedagogy. This leaves in place the traditional definitions and oppositional relationships in the academy, which privilege scholars over teachers, teachers over students, and theory over practice. Teaching and classroom relations are largely subsumed by the focus on conceptual apparatuses such as radical democracy and social transformation. The emphasis on *the* teacher-pedagogue (an image that levels the differences among teachers) as the *agent* of liberation and critical consciousness fails to contest the normative assumption that students are subject to our teaching, objects of our pedagogy. Finally, the lack of critical reflection on our attempts (in our classrooms, with our students) to *engage* and enact the ideas that animate critical pedagogy reinstates the all too familiar binary relationship between pedagogical theory and practice; classrooms are thus implicitly rendered as sites of application, rather than engagement—the place where we practice our pedagogy, but not where we challenge and critique its fundamental assumptions and aims.

Pedagogy as Social Visions and Instructional Acts

Representing our students, teaching, and classrooms in their complexity is difficult. Even for those who conceive of themselves as teacher-scholars, a term sometimes used in composition studies to emphasize the dialectic relationship between the two roles, the conceptualizing and organizing of events that transpire *inside* one's own classroom into texts that circulate *outside* the classroom can be more challenging and troubling than the representation of the intellectual and theoretical processes that inform the classroom. That is, writing about our teaching—representing and theorizing the space of our own classrooms—is often more difficult than theorizing about *the* composition class, *the* critical teacher, or students in general. This difficulty signifies the challenge of how to represent our classrooms, how to "turn the work of teaching into a text that can be read and criticized by others" (Harris 791). If, however, our aim is to legitimize the classroom as a site for (rather than as the product of) inquiry, a site for engaging in theoretical inquiry with (and not about) our students, then we need to resist normative pedagogical discourses that still position *teaching* (and students) as the after-thought, the by-product, of theory.

Jennifer Gore (1993) suggests that any *pedagogy* must contend with two interdependent components—social visions and instructional acts. If one's pedagogical vision is to teach in ways that inform students of the necessity for radical democracy, then one might argue that lecturing them on its possibility and urgency is an appropriate instructional act. If, however, one aims to foster this possibility within the classroom, one needs instructional acts that will work toward radical democracy. Each component, the social vision and the instructional act proposed by a given pedagogy, necessitates *action* and *reflection* to ensure they are working in a dialectic relationship. Rather than naming teaching as "practice" and research as "theory," I am suggesting we reconceptualize our work as teachers and scholars in order to prioritize action and reflection in both capacities. A renaming might work against the traditional hierarchical relationship, which adheres between theory-practice, research-teaching, so that a pedagogy necessitates not only theorizing onto, but also out of, our classrooms.

The new teacher's syllabus, then, might be understood to have emphasized the social vision of her pedagogy at the exclusion of instructional acts. While she clearly articulated the rationale and goals for the reflexive inquiry she hoped students would practice in relation to writing, she had not yet considered the process or means for generating this inquiry. She had invented an ideal critical course in many ways, albeit one that did not foreground the involvement of students, much less students' writing. A similar gap becomes evident in Giroux's representation of his classroom (below) and in the discourse of critical pedagogy. Idealized versions of how education might enable social visions of transformation, critical democracy, and empowerment abound; however, there is a prominent and problematic lack of consideration given to how specific instructional acts, operating within complex contexts, inhibit or enable these visions.

Ostensibly or intentionally radical or liberatory discourses and their practitioners might work to replicate the practices and effects they deem repressive in those discourses they seek to challenge. Poststructuralism's lesson is that *no* discourse is inherently liberated—that is, free from normative social and material relations—simply because it declares itself to be "transformative" or "liberatory." Further, no discourse or its practitioners (writers, students, or teachers) can be simply or permanently categorized as dominant or dominated, normative or marginalized, empowering or constraining, radical or traditional.[2] As Foucault describes, we should not envision clearly delineated and oppositional discourses, but rather

> a multiplicity of discursive elements that can come into play in various strategies. It is this distribution that we must reconstruct, with the things said and those concealed, the enunciations required and those forbidden, that it comprises; with the variants and different effect—according to who is speaking,

his position of power, the institutional context in which he happens to be situated—that it implies and with the shifts and utilizations of identical formulas for contrary objectives that it also includes. (Foucault 1990, 100)

The previous chapter argued that no practices, no methods of teaching writing, are inherently liberating or empowering; there is a difference between the intended aims of our pedagogies and our students' experience of our pedagogies. Liberatory possibilities cannot be declared, then, but arise in specific contexts, as a result of reflection and action by teachers and students. The same is true of discourses of pedagogy. Those of us who teach and write from positions within the academy are never entirely "free" from the institutional parameters and pressures that constrain what we produce (in the classroom and in the scholarship), even if the desire to challenge or subvert those parameters motivates our work. As Foucault points out, identical formulas might be employed for contrary purposes; discourses that appear to be oppositional might actually value identical subject-positions (the knower, truthsayer, the rationalist), means of claiming authority, or concepts of *truth, right, good*. In other words, the discourse of critical pedagogy is not radical simply because it claims to be or because it is positioned against traditional discourses of education. The new teacher's syllabus, and my reactionary response to it, demonstrate how it is all too easy to reproduce familiar and readily available roles both in our classrooms and in our narratives about them. The critical teacher is not clearly marginalized in relation to students in the classroom simply because she positions herself as radical, as representing subjugated or suppressed knowledge or voices. She occupies a position of institutional authority in this context and needs to negotiate that authority with students, rather than simply claim to relinquish or share it. Seemingly, then, there is a need for advocates of critical pedagogy— particularly for those authorized as "experts" in the field—to enact the self-reflexivity they so often stress as one of the central tenets of a critical educator. Rather than assuming a discourse and its practice (or practitioners) are inherently "radical" and anti-authoritarian, we must continually critique our pedagogies for ways in which we reproduce that which we seek to challenge.

Further, as Elbow contends, we cannot expect to engage students in a critical examination of their identities and voices while refusing to participate in a similar examination ourselves. "I think any teacher-as-ally can push his conviction successfully only if he is equally intent on exploring his own life and his own perception of it in collaboration with his students. Otherwise the student [or colleague or reader] will see him as a meddler, voyeur, and manipulator" (1986, 89).

It is necessary, then, to insist that we are not finally radicalized or liberated to the point where we need no longer engage in reflexive critique. The discourse of Critical Pedagogy fails to critique the agents (liberatory teachers and scholars) centered inside its own framework, implying that they are already emancipated from discourse, normative social relations, and material culture. In this chapter, I have chosen to focus on the work of Giroux and McLaren, the foremost producers of what has come to be the authorized discourse and dominant vision of critical pedagogy as it is represented in the United States. They achieved this status in terms of the sheer amount of their work, its publication in prestigious journals and presses, the number of collections they authorize and preside over, and because they are cited more often than any other critical educators by those seeking to define, demarcate, and evoke the field of critical pedagogy. While Ira Shor is clearly more concerned with practice (and the application of Freire's work in an American context), his work is already problematized and challenged in various considerations of critical pedagogy. Further, while Freire remains a primary influence on Giroux and McLaren, they draw more on postmodern conceptions of discourse as a potential site for revisioning the ongoing dialectic by which a "self" is produced and articulated through discourse. There are specific links between Giroux and composition studies too. He was a keynote speaker at the Penn State Conference on Rhetoric and Composition; his article opens the book *Left Margins: Cultural Studies and Composition Pedagogy;* he was a keynote speaker at the 1998 NCTE Annual Convention. In my own introduction to critical pedagogy, both in seminars and in the literature, Giroux and McLaren's work was often upheld as the "master" texts one had to contend with in order to be authorized in the field. Various feminists, Jennifer Gore,

Carmen Luke, Elizabeth Ellsworth and Mimi Orner, working at the intersections between critical pedagogy and poststructuralism, have problematized the dominant discourse of critical pedagogy, seeking to provide alternative versions that are centered around reflective practice rather than theoretical visions. I work closely with these texts, not with the aim of individualizing or personalizing my critique of a field, but rather with the belief that close readings of what has come to represent the master discourse are necessary if we are to facilitate revisioning of that discourse and its effects and possibilities.

In *Border Crossings*, Giroux, reflecting on the various frameworks he draws on in his work, comes to this conclusion: "I would like to call myself a good working-class, radical American . . . a critical populist who includes some elements of the IWW, Bill Haywood, C. Wright Mills, Martin Luther King, and Michael Harrington. In other words, people who speak to people in a language that dignifies their history and experiences. I don't understand how you can speak to people if you don't celebrate their voices" (1992, 13).

Just as Giroux, I too believe it is indeed necessary not only to represent, seek out, or listen to diverse voices, but also to actively value those voices and the histories, struggles, and visions they signify. However, I also believe it is necessary to confront the limited number of voices represented in the academy, and particularly the restricted access to positions of an authoritative voice, one granted the legitimacy to speak for/as the dominant construction of a given framework, pedagogy, or critical tradition. Consider, for instance, the few "voices" that come to mind when you consider process pedagogy or feminist theory. But Giroux does not engage in a self-critical examination of his own authority, his own voice, and the means by which it is constituted or granted an elite power in the field of critical pedagogy. His demarcation of himself as "radical, working-class" is problematic because he is not *only* working class in a society in which race and gender inform the distribution of power and resources at every level. Seemingly, only a white and/or a male subject could choose to ignore the social and political inscriptions of race and gender, or feel entitled to simply transcend the racialized and gendered factors of his composite subjectivity.

The Problem of the Pedagogue
(and What Happened to Students?)

The failure to contend with the concrete conditions and relations that inform any site of pedagogy has severe and damaging consequences on a variety of levels. We must move beyond proclaiming the radical effect or potential of our teaching and find ways to represent the complexity of engaging these possibilities with our students. Henry Giroux speaks to the most obvious and immediate danger—the failure to make the translation from pedagogical ideas, to pedagogical praxis:

> I felt that the most substantive aspect of my pedagogy centered on defining my *own* goals for education along with the politics of my *own* location as a teacher. For example, my overriding pedagogical project was rooted in an . . . education whose aim was to advance the ideological and lived relations necessary for students to interrogate the possibility of addressing schooling as a site of ongoing struggle over the "social and political task of transformation, resistance, and radical democratization" (Butler 13). . . . By not paying more attention to what it meant to give students more control over the conditions of their own knowledge production, I reproduced the binarism of being politically enlightened in my theorizing and pedagogically wrong in my organization of concrete class relations. (1995, 10–11) [my emphasis]

Here, Giroux acknowledges that even as the relations of the classroom were his primary object of theoretical inquiry, even as "democratizing" that space was his primary theoretical and political goal, his pedagogy failed to engage or work to realize this vision. This is not a matter of "practicing what we preach" or "practicing our theories"; nor am I suggesting we can simply apply our ideas, that is, move unproblematically from espousing possibilities to actualizing them. Fostering a sense of education as a process of negotiation and struggle is not something we can easily or unproblematically impose on our students or achieve in our classrooms. Critical pedagogy does not propose that we *tell* students about democratic possibilities or espouse radical empowerment. Rather, it proposes that we work toward these goals with our students, reflecting on and working to alter the conditions that impede them.

Giroux goes on to describe his attempts to "overcome this binarism" through a "reorganization" of his pedagogy. But even here, despite his conscious aim of positioning students as agents rather than objects of learning, his description of this particular class centers around the teacher-pedagogue:

> *I* attempted to organize. . . . *I* introduced the course by talking about power in the classroom and how it was implicated in all aspects of teaching. . . . *I* also made clear the rationale for the authority *I* exercised. . . . *I* made the form and content of my authority visible. . . . *I* relinquished all claims to objectivity. . . . *I* attempted to refute the traditional notion that teachers were disinterested. . . . *I* argued. . . . *I* attempted to open a space. . . . *I* stressed the need for social relations in the class that would give students the opportunity to produce and appropriate knowledge. . . . *I* wanted to make clear. . . . *I* further suggested that. . . . (1995, 12) [my emphasis]

In this lengthy discussion of his attempt to counter the dissonance he recognizes between this theoretical practice and his teaching practice, there is no reference to students except as the recipients of his discourse on power and authority in the classroom. Despite his intentions, this description reinscribes students as the object of critical pedagogy, those waiting to be empowered by the critical pedagogue who is, in this instance, espousing the conditions necessary for empowered and democratic learning. Telling students that, as teachers, we "relinquish all claims to objectivity," and that we need alternative "social relations" in our classroom might be starting points, but these are processes we aim to enact in a given semester, not conditions we can create by pronouncing them or arguing for them. Giroux continues, "I suggested that as a major precondition for discussing student writing . . . it was imperative for all of us to create the conditions for a 'safe space'" (1995, 14). Again, while declaring this imperative might be one step, there is no reflection on how this particular group negotiated the obstacles to creating a "safe space." How did they work to unlearn familiar and traditional classroom relations in order to produce the necessary conditions for alternative relations?

We are told, "Writing assignments positioned students as cultural producers and enabled them to rewrite their own experience. . . . There was an ongoing attempt to get the students to learn from one another . . . to decenter power . . . to challenge disciplinary boundaries" (1995, 16). While certainly I appreciate Giroux's intention to enact a dialectic (rather than binary) relationship between his intellectual and pedagogical practices, this descriptive representation of that dialectic falls short of exposing or considering the complexity of achieving these theorized goals in a specific classroom. Did students learn from one another? Was there a process by which they learned to do so, negotiated their way out of traditional top-down classrooms? Was his intention for the writing assignments realized? What challenges arose? By what strategies were disciplinary boundaries challenged, and what was the result (in terms of processes and products)? How did he position himself as "teacher" and in what ways did he rely on his authority to enact these strategies? Such factors as the composition of the classroom, a teacher's perceived social identity (gender, age, race, etc.) and its relation to students' construction of authority play an integral role in determining both what knowledges we might challenge and produce and the strategies by which we attempt to do so.

While Giroux pays rhetorical attention to the problematic of a binarism between one's theorizing and one's praxis, there is little to suggest substantive revision has occurred anywhere outside of his theorizing. These reflections on what *he* did, said, and emphasized in his classroom position the teacher as the agent of critical pedagogy, while students are relegated to objects; the teacher works his (*sic*) liberatory magic on them, while students are left to perform as directed, awaiting emancipation and empowerment. Perhaps this is not how Giroux's classroom functioned, but his textual representation, his teaching narrative, supports this reading. It is imperative, then, that we reflect on our efforts to engage these possibilities, noting the specific challenges our classrooms pose to these visions. Further, we need more complex ways to talk about our classrooms, to represent our students as subjects of and not only subject to our pedagogies. Describing assignments, recounting our directives, is not an adequate representation of our pedagogical work and it reinscribes a linear, one-way relationship between scholarship and teaching. Research remains the site where we *think* about teaching, where we theorize and intellectualize our pedagogies; the classroom is the site of application, that is, practice. Where does this leave students, how can they be "cultural workers" or "empowered learners" in a discourse that theorizes pedagogical possibilities *around* them rather than considers students as central to the enterprise of pedagogy?

Besides reinscribing the teacher as the agent of learning and the scholar as the agent of critical pedagogy, the discourse represented by Giroux and McLaren fails to consider the complex ways in which social relationships and inscriptions determine the identities and interactions within a given classroom. There is no reflection on how students, as participatory agents of the pedagogy, negotiate instructional acts or engage the visions that inform them. The implied effect is that students remain firmly in the position of being subject to pedagogy, despite the emphasis on critical dialogue, democratic relations, and so on. Enacting these ideals is not a simple process of *telling* students to listen critically but openly to one another in a class populated by contradictory and competing (both within a single "self" and among selves) experiences, identities, and voices. I had a course with twice as many women as men in which a majority of the female students expressed discomfort in participating in discussions, particularly those focused on issues of gender and power, despite their perception of me (the individual supposedly granted the loudest voice in the room) as attentive to and supportive of their particular position—which was not even always true. In that same semester, several male students remarked that they felt disrespected and excluded from discussions about gender and power. So who was speaking during those discussions? Did anyone feel "empowered" by them? Did anyone benefit? The male students considered the female students to be granted privileged voices by virtue of their bodies, while several of the women students felt silenced by what they considered to be the men's confrontational and alienating style of speaking.

Clearly, given the reproduction of social roles and tensions, I failed to enable "liberation" from normative contructions of gender or to facilitate a critical dialogue. But the dominant discourse of critical pedagogy, as represented by Giroux and McLaren, does not consider the enactment of these concepts when real, concrete, and complex human subjects/objects of the discursive, material, and cultural systems in question are involved. We cannot simply create or impose alternative social relations in our classrooms any more than we can escape the discourses that represent and reinforce normative social relations. As Ellsworth suggests, the failure to contend with how relations in the classroom might not transcend or revise the normative construction and experience of these relationships outside of class is not necessarily the failure of individual students and teachers. Rather, it reflects the tendency of critical pedagogy discourse to espouse abstract and idealized goals with no attention to enactment.

> What got said—and how—in our class . . . was a highly complex negotiation of the politics of knowing and being known . . . . To what extent had students occupying socially constructed positions of privilege at a particular moment risked being known by students occupying socially constructed positions of subordination at the same moment? To what extent had students in those positions of privilege relinquished the security and privilege of being the knower? As long as the literature on critical pedagogy fails to come to grips with the issues of trust, risk, and the operations of fear and desire around such issues as identity and politics in the classroom, their rationalistic tools will continue to fail to loosen deep-seated, self-interested investments in unjust relations. (1989, 313)

Consequently, the possibility of a dialectic, of interchange, between our work as teachers and our work as scholars is lost. Instead, a one-way relationship is reproduced—our theoretical work informs our teaching, but our teaching does not inform our theoretical work; our classrooms are not represented as posing legitimate challenges to existing pedagogical discourse and we forfeit the potential for revisioning and critiquing that discourse on the basis of our teaching. While avoiding a prescriptive, "how-to" pedagogical discourse is important, stopping at descriptive possibilities is just as inadequate. As Luke contends, the lack of performative analyses or reflective discussions results, implicitly, in a pedagogical discourse that re-centers the male, white subject.[3]

> The critical individual (teacher and student) is radical pedagogy's centered and neutered object of study. By its failure to address female teachers and female students in terms other than the insistent reference to "gender," which skirts altogether the politics of gender that structures the possibilities (of critique) for women teachers and female students, the (textual) discourse of critical pedagogy constructs and addresses an androgynous and colorless subject. . . . Exhortations to provide equal opportunities for the expression of personal voice, to encourage dialectical thinking and to foster critical agency do not provide the conceptual tools with which to rewrite those theoretical narratives and structural conditions that historically have formed the basis of institutionalized gender [and racial] asymmetries of power. ("Feminist Politics," 39)

Reflections on Reproducing When We Aim to Revision

A College Writing course I recently taught was composed of six white Americans (including myself), four African Americans, two Asian Americans, three Latinos, two Haitians, and two Africans, nine females and ten males. I was interested to observe and anxious to reflect on the way in which such a diverse group of writers and readers might engage the early assignments that focused on stereotypes. The point of these exercises is first to analyze how our identities are formed for and about us, and second to critique the readily available identities we assign to "others." Central to these analyses is a consideration of how language is integral to these evaluative conceptions; that is, discursive expressions of identity mythicize material and social reality, providing not only images but also implying relations of power between subject and object. Somewhat naively and acting on racist assumptions that essentialize the experiences and subjectivity of individuals according to group affiliations, I assumed that because most of the students had obviously experienced the objectifying and dehumanizing discursive and material power of stereotypes, they would be more capable of leveling a sophisticated and critical articulation of those stereotypes. In other words, even as I was working through this chapter, arguing against assumptions that students excluded from dominant culture will necessarily be ready or willing to critique that culture, I was acting upon this assumption in my own classroom.

For the first assignment, students interrogated stereotypes from a personal perspective. We discussed, and they wrote about assumptions they commonly encounter about their own identity, what groups they are typically assigned to, what characteristics are attributed to them as a result of this grouping, how these assumptions vary or remain the same according to context, who was most likely to buy into and act on these stereotypes, how these assumptions function not only to affect them individually but also to produce broader social and political implications, and how and why (and whether) individuals respond when they encounter them.

For four of the white students (three males and one female), this assignment was initially difficult, though in past courses predominantly populated with white students, I have not encountered such frustration or struggle with the assignment. It seemed these students perceived the initial questions I posed to generate writing (what assumptions are commonly made about you? based on what? by whom?) as created specifically for the students of color. Trying to engage these four students in an examination of the ways in which assumptions are made about them as white people, or gendered individuals, or as members of a specific generation or according to their manner of dress was challenging. Ehren resisted actively, claiming he absolutely could not answer one question and calling the assignment itself "reverse racism," as it privileged the experience of those who were conscious of experiencing stereotyping. It is interesting to me how the composition of the class, the white students' perceptions that they were in the minority, seems to have influenced their response to the assignment. Given my experience with these assignments in predominantly white courses, I wonder if these four students would have responded with less resistance in a classroom with a different composition.

Of course, their response merely reflects and confirms what other teachers have articulated as the difficulty white students (and white people) have in recognizing themselves as a group. Typically, articulations of whiteness are made implicitly, in the uttering of what whites are not. There are not visible or conscious cultural affiliations—food, religion, music, language— shared by white Americans *as* white people. As Jay notes, "white" as a signifying marker emerged to indicate a shared political interest, a privileged relationship to resources and to the power to own and distribute them, as opposed to evolving as a cultural marker. Whiteness is bestowed the privilege of invisibility, of being uncommented upon because it is the norm, the given. Engaging white students, then, in a consideration of how their race situates them in specific relationships to material culture and normative discourses is an integral process in a critical composition class.

In reading the writing they generated in response to this assignment, students remarked on how many common stereotypes were represented and dissected, and how obviously mythical the assumptions seem when exposed collectively from the perspective of the object of the stereotype. The predominant issue that emerged during our discussion of their writings was how profoundly universal and impermeable many of the stereotypes seem to be regardless of a lack of experiential evidence to support them, and despite their sometimes blatantly ridiculous nature. (One student, from Gambia, described how he was repeatedly and earnestly asked whether or not he lived in trees before he came to the United States.)

For the second part of the assignment, I asked students to explore a particular stereotype from historical, social, economic, and political perspectives and to consider origin, implied audience, objects of empowerment and disempowerment, and the role of language in creating and sustaining it. During our preliminary discussion, I asked for an example of a particular stereotype that we could examine from these various perspectives. Joseph, a gay male who was out to the class, offered, "gay men are effeminate." I began by asking them how they would recognize this as a negative or disempowering myth if they read it alone, devoid of a context. Frederic pointed out that "men" and "effeminate" are contradictions: men are supposed to be masculine. Dionne observed that any statement that begins by distinguishing the "other"—in this case, gay men—signals that something negative will follow. As she pointed out, you rarely encounter a dominant and actively disempowering stereotype that begins, "straight men" or "white people."[4] Clearly, some of the students were critical readers of the discursive functioning of stereotypes.

They were not, however, exempt from perpetuating and acting on them, as the discussion quickly shifted focus from a discussion of the statement, to a discussion of people's responses and attitudes toward homosexuality. Students who had so movingly and vehemently argued against the stereotypes that impeded, dehumanized, and marginalized them personally, were actively supporting myths about homosexuals. Jason claimed it was "natural for straight guys to be scared of gay men. We have to unlearn this kind of thinking." Magdalana asked how he could unlearn it if it was natural and claimed the point of the first assignment was that it proved stereotypes were not natural, but learned—learned in order to "keep some people on the top and the rest of us down here kicking each other." Here, she is pointing to the distinction between natural and learned, and the slippery slope of becoming a subject in a culture without even being able to easily distinguish which is which. I asked them why the notion of an entire country of people living in trees was easily laughable to them, despite most of us not having any direct experience with citizens of Gambia, and the notion of all gay men being effeminate was realistic, was not easily dismissible.

The essays resulting from these assignments and discussions represented the confusion of engaging in critical self-examination while simultaneously attempting to hang on to a piece of the world (and the relationships and hierarchies) as one has known it. Their writing represents the struggle to preserve one's "own" identity. If we attempt to construct a unified or coherent "self"—in part by staking out territories, by drawing boundaries and by creating a corresponding concept of the "other" (that which we are not)—then a re-visioning of the "other" implies a re-visioning of the attendant conception of one's "self." Several students echoed the sentiment James expressed in his mid-semester evaluation:

> To learn how to really communicate with others and to be writers we need to learn not to judge anybody by the way they look or act on the outside. We have to learn to give people a chance to prove who they are on the inside. I don't want people to think I'm a "gangsta" just because I am black, male, and wear certain clothing and I have learned not to blame anybody for being gay or lesbian because it's not their fault. They have the right to be whatever they want and there's nothing wrong with how they choose to be. (Excerpt from mid-semester evaluation by James)

On the one hand, James is making the connection between the cultural codes that result in his being stereotyped and his own practice of acting on cultural codes that sanction prejudice against homosexuals. But he is still caught in between reproducing and critiquing these codes. He is *still* in the process of revisioning and his struggle is represented discursively: he does not "blame" homosexuals now, because he no longer conceives of it as "their fault," even though he ends by identifying homosexuality as a "choice." So even as he asserts the right of individuals to "be whatever they want," he is unable to completely surrender the idea that there must be someone at "fault" or to "blame" for homosexuality. Another student, Patrick, signifies the position of being caught between intending to critique stereotypes when his language continues to reproduce them uncritically. Patrick's essay investigates the ways in which groups who have historically been the object of stereotypes nonetheless continue to invent, transmit, and act on stereotypes about one another. His essay discusses the effects of the stereotypes that Hispanics in his neighborhood had about their African American neighbors, the myths the African American community held about Jamaican and Haitian immigrants and Chinese Americans.

> These stereotypes are not just words, they lead to tragedy, violence, killing and separation in our community. My friends don't like Chinese because they believe the myth that the Chinese take the good jobs away from the African Americans. But who is giving them these jobs? . . . They also say that Chinese never

hire any other nationality to work in their restaurants because they don't want us to learn how to cook like them. I especially think they don't want us to know what it is they are giving us to eat. We could be eating dogs for all I know. (Excerpt from "Untitled" by Patrick)

Again, there is a shift here. Patrick begins by identifying stereotypes "my friends," "they" buy into and act on; but in the second to last sentence, his language shifts from an examination of "their" assumptions to his own. Not only does the "I" enter, but the last line moves from establishing rhetorical distance by claiming the assumptions to be "myth" to presenting the assumption as possible truth. During the discussion of these essays, Patrick's was specifically pointed to as "confused and confusing"; readers had trouble determining when he was skeptically interrogating stereotypes and when he was supporting them, and this confusion was evident in the structure as well as in the substance of his piece. It is no surprise that the formal and structural aspects of his writing were underdeveloped given that he was obviously still thinking his way through the ideas as he was writing about them. Patrick responded to the discussion in a written comment, "I took a critical stance towards the myths about Haitians (my own group), but not towards those against Hispanics or Chinese. We have joked so many times about eating dog food and it seems here like I just supported this stereotype." Recognizing that stereotypes are *learned* (produced through discourse in order to sustain economic and social divisions, rather than the "natural" way of dividing the world) and acting on this recognition, acting to *unlearn* stereotypes, is a complex and ongoing process—one in which Patrick is clearly engaged. Completing this process is impossible as we are constantly being introduced to new stereotypes, new ways of maintaining a unified self and an objectionable other; but we can be committed to continuing the struggle to work through these myths and the ways in which our language reposits them even as we seek consciously to disrupt or deny them.

I cite these essays and discussions for two reasons. First, they demonstrate that the lines between oppressed and oppressor, object and agent of prejudice are often shifting and blurred. All of us—students, teachers, and scholars alike—are capable of occupying positions of social, institutional, or economic disempowerment, while simultaneously excluding, objectifying, or claiming power (in the form of superiority) over others. We can be, at once and complicatedly, both agents and objects of prejudice and oppression, contesting normative identities even as we claim authority from normative discourse to identify "others." Rather than simply assign teachers and students to fixed and oppositional subject-positions, we must be attentive to moments in which we simultaneously challenge and uphold dehumanizing, destructive constructions of one another. Second, these moments demonstrate the difficulty of somehow setting our students free, of teaching—definitively—social transformation, radical democracy. Clearly, my students and I are still negotiating identities, our own and those we ascribe to others; we are not, as a result of these writings and discussions, liberated entirely from normative concept of the Other. Yet we have also engaged the possibility and enacted the process of revisoning.

These moments also indicate how we, as teachers and students, are not finally or once and for all clearly situated in relation to the systemic principles and practices that demarcate our identities and relations with one another. We are not, that is, easily categorized into classifications as oppressed/oppressor, object/agent of inequality, liberated/constrained, and so on. Rather, we are positioned differently depending on the issue at hand. This recasts a familiar and fundamental question that composition scholars and teachers have posed to critical pedagogy.

Revisioning and Representing "Students" in Pedagogical Discourse

John Schilb, in "Pedagogy of the Oppressors?" and Lil Brannon, in "Is a Critical Pedagogy Possible?" have challenged the efficacy of radical pedagogy in educating the "oppressing class." This question presupposes a clear and fixed division between students in the oppressed and oppressing classes. It is true that critical pedagogy has more often emphasized the need for retooling our educational practices and institutions in order to grant access to those who have been marginalized by conventional practices. It is also true that this shift, as Sondra Harding emphasizes in "standpoint" theory of epistemology, is an important one. Considering the function and value of education from the perspective of those historically excluded and underserved by it changes the questions we ask, the aims we envision, and exerts pressure on our organization of class time and relations.

> The students with whom I work come primarily from the dominant culture, and thus their motive to learn the discourses of the academy is very strong . . . [and] will bring them socioeconomic privilege. A very real question facing us, then, is this: In what ways can we teach our students to resist the discourse, particularly its gender, race, and class prejudices, when these students have the most to gain by conforming to its values. (1990, 17)

The concern here is an essential one: can a critical pedagogy serve to initiate and develop a counterhegemonic impulse, a radical consciousness, not only in those we identify as the objects of oppression but also in those we deem its (potential) agents and benefactors? Any progressive pedagogy that ignores a large sector of potential agents limits its capacity to achieve social change.

In other words, what does a critical classroom have to offer to a student like Taylor, whose comments opened Chapter 2? While Taylor did not recognize herself as empowered, and in fact perceived herself to be powerless, surely she (white, heterosexual, middle-class, college-educated) will materially and immediately benefit from their remaining intact. What we need to consider is how to persuade students that ultimately "we" do not—individually or collectively—benefit from these discourses; despite the privilege and authority normative discourse grants to some, we are all damaged, endangered by oppression, injustice. We need to complicate the concern Brannon and others have articulated even further as it assumes that specific groups need to be taught to resist the dominant discourse, while other students will presumably already be motivated to resist it. How can we determine which individuals perceive themselves as standing to benefit by conforming to, or at least not challenging, the dominant discourse with its implied prejudices and relations of power?

Our students are more complex than this articulation allows for: on the one hand, a student such as Taylor, someone clearly situated advantageously in material and cultural contexts, perceives herself as powerless. On the other hand, working-class students, female students, students of color often believe the very discourse and culture that inevitably empowers Taylor over them, can also convey power to them.[5] Like Villanueva, my own experience has been that many students who do not come from the "dominant culture" believe nonetheless that, once they gain access (which they perceive as possible), they will benefit from and within the dominant culture, despite their lived experience of being marginalized, excluded, or objectified by it.

> I have seen . . . students, overtly caught in institutional and state apparatuses, not resist hegemony, despite experiences that made it apparent they were oppressed. . . . They were in school to fulfill a dream, a longtime American dream of success through education. They were not in school to have their dreams destroyed. They would naturally resist any such attempt. (1991, 251, 256–257)

We cannot, therefore, assume that students whom *we perceive* as disenfranchised, dehumanized, or exploited by the dominant culture will automatically be liberated from that culture, ready to critique it and consider alternatives such as radical collectives. The tendency to assume that particular students "have" a critical consciousness, while other students need to develop one is problematic as it implies teachers who somehow can distinguish between them. Typically, this distinction is made according to our interpretation of students' lived experience; for instance, we assume white students will resist critical knowledges, while students of color will be already supportive of, or at least open, to them. These determinations, then, imply that a critical consciousness is a "natural" development, an immediate result of lived oppression. Critical consciousness, however, is not "natural"; rather, it is a process of learning to critique existing social and economic relations, coming to see one's self as always in a specific relationship to the material and social conditions of all others.

Further, we cannot simply or finally determine which students or teachers or scholars are in the dominant culture as the definition of who is included and excluded depends on the specific aspect of normative culture that is under investigation. The pedagogical narrative of my students and me critiquing existing stereotypes demonstrated that while either students or teachers might be clearly situated as oppressed or oppressors in one context, the lines might be redrawn entirely in another.

Some discourses of radical pedagogy insist that the lines are firm and indelible. Oppositional pedagogy foregrounds and centers on class and economic relations, envisioning education as the process in which teachers expose the workings of systemic economic determinism to students. The pedagogue, because she speaks from the position of repressed knowledge, is authorized to critique students' texts, remarks, and histories in light of her specialized knowledge of how capitalism functions to code our representations of experience, "truth," opinion, and social relations. Students are not positioned to actively participate in the relations of the classroom. Instead, the teacher, because she represents radical knowledge that is marginalized in, and by, dominant culture, deploys her institutional authority to engage students in a critique of the dominant discourses and relations of racism, sexism, capitalism. The following is an excerpt from a letter written to Robert Nowlan by a student in his writing course.

> In this class many students have said some very racist things, and not only have they got away with it, but it seems to me that this class has worked to draw these kinds of statements out of them. I know from what you say . . . that you are not racist and in fact actively opposed racism, but I cannot understand why you are teaching this way, why you don't simply tell these bigots off. . . . You should lecture to us about racism and how it is wrong, and demand that students show that they have understood and accepted this is true. . . . I feel like if this is to continue that I will not be able to come to class at all. . . . I like the fact that we are talking about serious social problems and that we are learning how to argue and critique. Yet, I think this could be improved if . . . you prevented our discussions from degenerating into hostile exchanges involving outrageous positions. I really hope you do something about this right away; it will make it a lot easier for me to learn, in comfort, and I am sure the same is true of others like myself in our class. (1995, 245–46)

I would not advocate the silencing of racist discourse, or that teachers can effectively contest racism by lecturing to students about it, but Nowlan's response to this student falls short. He is forceful and articulate in explaining why her suggested strategy is an inadequate solution or resolution. "It may be tempting, artificially and temporarily, simply to silence racist attitudes in the space of a classroom taught by an antiracist White teacher, and yet to do so is not to *confront* and *contest* racism but rather to *avoid* and *evade* it" (250). However, he does not attend to the impact that she claims the class is having on her; he simply urges her to speak up in class against the positions and remarks she finds unacceptable.

> If contestation in the space of the classroom is to be effective, those such as yourself, who hold oppositional views, *must* speak out . . . . What happens with and to and in classes depends as much upon what the students in the class do and do not do as what the teacher does and does not do. . . . The goal is to make White people, at least some, at least a few, at least one, feel genuinely compelled to rethink their relationship to . . . the reproduction and maintenance of racism . . . (1995, 252–53)

I agree that it is critical for students to recognize that they are accountable and responsible for what takes place and what gets said in the classroom. However, we cannot assume that there is a level playing field within the classroom in terms of who speaks or what gets said. She indicates in her letter that this class is not an arena in which she feels authorized to speak. While Nowlan declares she *must* claim and use authority to represent her position, her letter indicates that she does not perceive this as a possibility in light of how the classroom relations are currently working. Seemingly, he might consider why she, who represents the very views he says must be represented in the class, does not feel either compelled or able or willing to participate. By not engaging her critique of his pedagogy, he inscribes the failure as her own, despite her claim in the letter that she does not perceive his pedagogy as having antiracist effects, regardless of his intentions (which she legitimizes).

As he goes on to explain his purpose in engaging in this form of "antiracist" pedagogy, it becomes clear that his pedagogy is explicitly aimed at, organized around, white people.

> White people have to be *shown* that this is true. . . Whites have
> to be shown that they *are* racist . . . (248) . . .it is necessary to
> *force* White people . . . . to *show* White people . . . Whites will
> have to give up . . . White people have to be shown the *conse-*
> *quences* . . . This is why it is necessary to show White people
> . . . (249). It must be made impossible for these same Whites
> . . . It is very important to show White people . . . Whites will
> have to be *made* willing. . . (1995, 250)

Seemingly, his pedagogy is aimed at white students, at their relationship, in this instance, to racism. They are, thus, at the center
of his classroom; even as he aims to contest racist relations, his
pedagogy as represented here seems to gloss over, if not to simply
exclude, students of color. Not only is there no consideration of
their different relation to dominant racist relations, there are no
pedagogical goals, at least not articulated here, that are not aimed
specifically at white students. While he grounds his pedagogical
strategies in his identity as "an antiracist teacher" (1995, 250),
his classroom seems oriented to what white students need to know,
need to be shown, need to be made to learn. But what about
those students who are not white? How are they ignored in the
project of an antiracist pedagogue? Nowlan's articulation of his
vision and methods lends greater urgency to the student's claim
that the conditions and relations of the classroom prevent her
from actively participating. Nowlan does not seem to take into
account the relations produced within his classroom in his concern for the dominant relations outside of it. Rather than contend with her critique of the course, he inscribes the failure as her
own, "Whenever you do not speak up in such places, you are not
representing the interests to which you profess commitment"
(253).

Oppositional pedagogies, like critical pedagogy, aim to un-
mask the workings of cultural and economic determinism. The
problem lies in assuming that the pedagogue is already critical or
radical, and is no longer in need of self-reflexive critique. In my
understanding, being antiracist, being radical or critical are ongoing processes of development rather than achieved states of
being that one finally attains once and for all.

The Pedagogy Argued For and the Pedagogy of the Argument

The notion that one learns, finally, how to be a humanist/feminist/radical/critical pedagogue, is a fundamental problematic in the discourse of any pedagogy. Presumably, critical pedagogy foregrounds self-reflexive critique precisely because we are never, finally, critical or radical teachers because we are always operating within prevailing systems (of academia, of institutions, of a racialized, gendered economy). So we should conceptualize our project as a continuous process of learning to teach against these systems in ever-changing classroom contexts. Our relation to students is not fixed; rather, it shifts as the composition of our classrooms shifts each semester. Failing to reflect on, much less to represent, our own practice (as either teachers or scholars), produces a reinscription of universal concepts of *the* critical practice, *the* critical teacher and of *the* authority to determine what/who constitutes this privileged space. Students are left out of the picture, reflecting the general tendency to represent them as *objects* of critical pedagogy.

Critical pedagogy, as envisioned by Giroux and McLaren, becomes more a theory of how pedagogies might ultimately function without the concerns and challenges posed by real and multidimensional people (teachers and students), or by fluid and indeterminate contexts. In other words, they offer theory devoid of considerations of the concerns and challenges that accompany any actual pedagogical situation. I do not seek a prescriptive set of universalized critical practices so that I might simply emulate them in my own classes. Such a reproductive process is inherently contradictory to the central premises of critical pedagogy. But I find it suspect that the individuals calling for the rest of us to join theory and praxis, to move constantly between and among the two, rarely represent their own efforts to do so. The absence of substantive considerations of classroom practice leads to a positing of vague and universal aims achieved by abstract myths of already-empowered teachers and waiting-to-be-liberated students.

The two foundational principles and practices I extract from the discourse of critical pedagogy are a dialectical relationship between pedagogical visions and actions, and the necessity of engaging in self-reflexive critique. In the discussion my students and I had about the stereotypes we actively reproduce, there was a general lack of both of these elements. On the one hand, we theoretically identified stereotypes as illegitimate, serving only those already in power, mythical strategies for subjugating and oppressing anyone deemed as "other." On the other hand, some of us—a few of these same students—were unwilling to practice this theory when it came to homosexuality. (And I contradicted it by assuming those students who had clearly been the objects of stereotypes would be "naturally" liberated from perpetuating them.) Further, they were resistant to act self-reflexively, as this would have made them accountable for their homophobia. Instead, they fell back on the same strategies used by those who stereotyped—whom they criticized in their first essay—calling their own fear "natural" and "understandable." These same tendencies are replicated in the work of the most visible and vocal authors of the discourse of critical pedagogy: the willingness to at once act out against and act to re-inscribe status quo relations of power. In other words, they are capable of envisioning the correct course of action in the abstract but are unable to enact it. Here, I am not referring to the Giroux or McLaren's teaching, to their pedagogical praxis in the classroom. There is little representation of this aspect of their work available. Rather, I am using Gore's distinction (1993) between distinguishing the pedagogy argued for and the pedagogy of their arguments.

This distinction insists that our texts about pedagogy are themselves representations of pedagogical praxis. We might, then, study these arguments in order to consider how knowledge is produced, how authority is claimed, how we position ourselves in relation to other knowledge claims and knowers. Giroux claims that a "distinguishing trait" in the definition of critical pedagogy is that radical education joins theory and praxis" (1992, 10). And also, "the principle reason why radical education as a field is so exciting [is that] we can take ideas and apply them" (10).

McLaren repeatedly articulates the need for engaging in self-reflexive critique as a means of continually questioning the connection between one's theory and practice. "We must continually ask ourselves: What diversity do we silence in the name of liberatory pedagogy?" ("Language," 9). However, instead of a dialectic between pedagogical reflection and action, a re-writing of the traditional hierarchical relationship is inscribed between those authorized to theorize and those restricted to practice. While an emphasis on practice is central to the rhetoric of Giroux and McLaren, its substantive absence leaves intact, rather than challenging or displacing, the traditional division of academia: theory is identified as the province of a select, elite few; practice is for the rest of us and remains in the classroom, excluded from the scholarship.[6]

In responding to a critique posed by Elizabeth Ellsworth, an education theorist who identifies herself as within the field of critical pedagogy, Giroux and McLaren replicate the discussion in my classroom in which individuals failed to engage in self-critique, even when their actions contradicted their proclaimed principles. Unable to enact the process of critical revision, which we had deemed necessary when it came to "stereotyping" in general, or as it affected us personally, we reproduced—in the context of homosexuality, homophobia, and heterosexism—the same objectifying, silencing, and marginalizing we sought to challenge. While Ellsworth is clearly attempting to enact the ideas that animate critical pedagogy, taking them seriously by engaging (in) them with her students, Giroux and McLaren refuse to acknowledge the serious challenges posed to the discourse by her class's collective engagement. This refusal is a further indication of the tendency to ignore students as instrumental, rather than incidental, to pedagogy—a consequence of the primacy granted to our ideas about pedagogy over its enactment in specific sites.

Reflecting on her and her students' experience of attempting to enact a radically democratic, antiauthoritative classroom, Ellsworth found herself "struggling against (struggling to unlearn) key assumptions and assertions of current literature on critical pedagogy, and straining to recognize, name, and come to grips with crucial issues of classroom practice that critical pedagogy cannot or will not address" (1989, 303). Ellsworth and the graduate students in her course had made a decision to enact a critical classroom—after reading widely in the field, they moved to practice the goals articulated by Giroux and McLaren 1994 in their own classroom. What they discovered is that concepts such as *empowerment, radical democracy, emancipated authority, liberating agents* are inspiring ideals and generative visions; they are not, however, an adequate or useful basis for practicing a pedagogy. Ellsworth specifically problematizes the notion of the teacher as already-liberated agent who is to do the act of liberation somehow upon her as-yet-unempowered students. For instance, she wonders how she is to bring the "truth" of racist oppression to students who clearly know more about the experience of racism than she does. She wonders about how we synthesize a theoretical grasp and an experiential understanding of systems of oppression and inequitable power without essentializing or privileging one *over* the other?

Moving between her reflections on theory and practice, Ellsworth engages in the sort of self-reflexive process that Giroux and McLaren repeatedly insist lies at the center of the critical project. While she does not abandon the project of critical pedagogy altogether, she arrives at a revised conception of her goal as a critical educator, one based on her experience as a practioner as well as on her students' reflections of experiencing a critical classroom.

> [I] see my task as one of redefining "critical pedagogy" so that it did not need utopian moments of "democracy," "equality," "justice" or "emancipated" teachers—moments that are unattainable (and ultimately undesirable because they are always predicated on the interests of those who are in positions to define utopian projects). A preferable goal seemed to be to become capable of a sustained encounter with currently oppressive formations and power relations that refuse to be theorized away or fully transcended in a utopian resolution—and to enter into an encounter which owned up to my own implications in those formations. (1989, 308)

Seemingly then, Ellsworth is practicing the sort of dialectical relationship between theory and practice that critical pedagogy emphasizes as one of its defining characteristics. Further, she moves from the disembodied theoretical texts to an interrogation of how various, complex identities and bodies determine and influence our collective concept and practice of pedagogy. Rather than authorize herself as the sole source of critique and evaluation, she actively invites her students to participate in both the class and its investigation of critical pedagogy scholarship.

Ellsworth repeatedly calls attention to the *potential* of critical pedagogy, claiming her purpose in engaging in critique is not to denounce or abandon this project, but rather to push it forward, to rigorously interrogate its central claims, while attempting to recuperate its overall vision. Giroux and McLaren, however, seem unwilling to allow her entry into the privileged space of critical pedagogy. Instead of acknowledging the legitimacy of these concerns and challenges, or of reflecting on their own successful practice as a means of responding to her critique, they simply move to locate the "failure" in the practitioner, in Ellsworth's inability to adequately enact or comprehend the tradition. Giroux claims that Ellsworth's article

> represents less an insight than a crippling form of disengagement. She degrades the rich complexity that characterizes the tradition of critical pedagogy. In doing so, she succumbs to the familiar academic strategy of strawman tactics and excessive simplifications. This "theorizing" is a form of bad faith, a discourse imbued with the type of careerism that has become too characteristic of left academics. (1988, 177–78)

Just how does one degrade a tradition? And how does a self-proclaimed radical, antifoundationalist fall back on the assumption that there is *one* tradition—that we can all agree not only on what constitutes this tradition but also on how to interpret and enact it? The quotation marks around the term theorizing make quite clear his refusal to take her challenges seriously, serving to delegitimize her authority as a theorist of critical pedagogy. But how has Giroux earned the authority to determine what counts as theorizing and what fails as a feeble attempt? The obvious pedagogy of Giroux's argument contradicts the pedagogy he argues for; he personalizes the critique, dismissing Ellsworth (and not her ideas) out of hand, refusing to engage in a critical dialogue with her text. The patronizing and patriarchal overtones aside, Giroux denies the collective classroom experience in which Ellsworth grounds her authority to reread the theoretical discourse of critical pedagogy. In doing so, he privileges the abstract notion of a "tradition" over reflective inquiry. His voice of authority is ungrounded, unsupported; instead, he takes on the traditional role of the teacher, advocating that "students" (in this case, Ellsworth) of critical pedagogy should reproduce and transmit the tradition.

McLaren even more explicitly locates Ellsworth's inability to comprehend or practice critical pedagogy as the result of her scholarly inadequacy or incompetence.

> Ellsworth engages in a woeful misreading of the tradition she so cavalierly indicts. Consequently, the important issue with which she struggles collapses under the weight of her own distortions, mystifications, and despair. Ellsworth's self-professed lack of pedagogical success can hardly be blamed on failed critical traditions but is rather attributable to her inability to move beyond self-doubt . . . [which] served to hold her voice hostage. In this instance, critical pedagogy becomes a case for using theory as a scapegoat for failed practice. ("Schooling," 72)

McLaren clearly indicates the existence of an inner circle in critical pedagogy, a circle from which Ellsworth is excluded. Apparently, there is a right and a wrong way to evoke and interpret this "tradition," though McLaren offers neither the correct way to understand critical theory nor gives any suggestions for enacting it successfully. His presumed ability to distinguish between someone else's "self-doubt" and self-reflexivity contradicts the principles he espouses as a theorist, particularly the notions of dialogue and resistance. Elsewhere, he repeatedly insists that teachers must not simply discount or write off student resistance, but must acknowledge it as necessary to the revisioning of one's self. Earlier in this same article, McLaren has argued that a critical class needs to construct "spaces for the constitution of difference that test the limits of existing regimes of discourse" ("Schooling," 62). Presumably, critical pedagogy as one "regime of discourse," need not allow for such spaces. If McLaren reacts to student resistance in the same way, how democratic or transformative might his own classroom be?

Their responses indicate their having taken these critiques personally, which seems to further indicate their inability to separate the discourse and project of critical pedagogy, from their concept of themselves as its representatives, authors/authorities, and creators. Rather than diffusing or contesting Ellsworth's claim that critical pedagogy posits empowerment unequivocally and universally in those authorized to practice it (as teachers or theorists), rather than countering claims that this concept of empowerment is disembodied, decontextualized, and therefore problematic, Giroux and McLaren simply position themselves as the ultimately empowered keepers of the tradition.

Whether simply unwilling or unable, Giroux and McLaren fail to address the serious and substantive critique posed to critical pedagogy (by Ellsworth, Luke, Gore, Lather) in the hopes not of destroying or disproving critical pedagogy, but rather of expanding on and contributing to its tradition, and of enacting its principles. Rather than examples of how we might negotiate the tensions all of us face in the effort to move between acting in words and acting in deeds, between writing and teaching, beyond preaching to practicing, Giroux and McLaren reinserted the existence of "truths" and foundations, the same strategies relied on by those they claim are repressive, antidemocratic, elitist, and indeed dangerous to the "liberation" of all of us, students and teachers alike. By referring to the authority and evoking the sanctity of "the tradition," they assume we all agree not only on what constitutes that tradition, but on how it is to be (correctly) interpreted. Rather than engaging in constructive theoretical debate, even if motivated by the attempt to disprove the challenges posed to them, they attribute such things as "distortion," "bad faith," "failure," and "careerism" to the *individuals* (rather than the ideas *articulated*) who offer the challenge. Indeed, they demonstrate rather than diffuse the validity of the criticisms by reinscribing a "truth" to the process and product of liberation and critical thinking; a truth that they are empowered (by whom? by the tradition itself?) to protect, promote, and interpret. As Gore concludes,

> What I find most troubling is the theoretical pronouncement of these discourses as empowering or liberatory. . . . Critical discourses are presented as liberatory because they challenge dominant discourses, not because they have been liberatory for particular groups or people. Meanwhile, the "self-critical" nature claimed for critical discourses seem more rhetorical than actual (1992, 60).

Ellsworth's critique is a useful example of how we might contest and challenge the framework we have employed, in an effort to rejuvenate and push that framework forward. Not all critique implies the necessity for rejection. Further, Ellsworth's critique is local, embodied, contextualized. She does not reproduce totalizing myths about how critical pedagogy should be practiced or what its universal goals might be. Rather, she moves toward using a specific context to challenge critical pedagogy, infusing it with the complicated lived experiences and intellectual perspectives of multiple and complex individuals.

Revisioning the Discourse of Critical Pedagogy

Seemingly, then, there is a need to get more specific in our theorizing-as-practice (and in practicing our theory), as Phelan suggests. Rather than participating in the already abundant proliferation of meta-narratives (including those that profess to challenge meta-narratives but ultimately posit new ones), and universal pedagogies, we need to test our theories in specific and identified contexts, noting what they enable as well as what they prohibit, to whom they grant voice and whom they silence. As Phelan notes, we need not *"bigger"* theory, but more modest theory; we need to make the move from "converting to conversing" (1994, 3). "More local, specific analyses offers the possibility of locating the ways in which (some) [individuals] are silenced or erased and the roles (some) [individuals] play in that. It enables us to intervene at particular points, rather than being swamped with despair at the magnitude of the task before us" (10).

Ellsworth's critique is notable in that it suggests the danger of becoming unable to step outside of one's framework and reestablishes the primary importance of the two steps so consistently advocated by Giroux and McLaren: ongoing self-reflexivity and a dialectical relationship between theory and practice. Substituting one authoritative, nonreflective, repressive model of pedagogy for another simply because the alternative professes to be liberatory, progressive, or transformative might lead us to ultimately reinscribe the same relations and structures that we sought to subvert in the first place. Rather than assuming a discourse or its practioners are "radical," we need to constantly test its premises and practices in our classrooms and our scholarship. As Foucault notes,

> To say that one discursive formation is substituted for another is not to say that a whole world of absolutely new objects, enunciations, concepts and theoretical choices has emerged fully armed and fully organized in a text that will place the world once and for all; it is to say that a general transformation of relations has occurred, but that it does not necessarily alter the elements. (1972, 173)

As Gramsci repeatedly suggests, we must continually assess our roles as intellectual practitioners against the broader context of social relations, just as we attempt to engage our students in an examination of their lives outside the classroom walls during their time inside the classroom (1987, 1988). To separate our work as scholars or teachers from our work as citizens, social actors, community members leads to the risk of ignoring other concrete and viable realms of engaging in and testing out critical practices.

Without reinscribing the binary opposition that has traditionally informed the relationship between theory and practice (consider Aristotle's notion of a realm of "theoria" as distinct from—and elevated above—a realm of "praxis"), we might usefully distinguish between theorizing-as-practice and classroom practice, just as we might distinguish between discursive, conceptual action or revision and political action in the material world when determining the goals and success of our classrooms. Indeed, I recognize and value the construction of theorizing as practice, that our efforts to theorize are themselves practices. Nonetheless, a pedagogy must attend to the distinction between the realm in which we theorize/practice in scholarship and the realm in which we theorize/practice in the classroom. Without implying a hierarchical division (as traditionally adheres) between our scholarship and our teaching, I am attempting to point to the distinct conditions (physical, social, intellectual) in which each takes place. That is, even if we consider theorizing to be a form of praxis, we cannot consider our scholarship on pedagogy and our teaching to be one and the same activity, or to occur in similar spheres of action. As Gramsci notes, "the unity of theory and practice is not a given mechanical fact but an historical process of becoming" (1987, 67).

Suppose your goal is to enact a democratic classroom. At this point, most scholarship in pedagogy will argue whether or not a democratic classroom is viable or possible or useful. But there are rarely arguments, to any end and from any position, that root their conclusions in the experiences of having participated in one or another kind of classroom, as student or teacher. The arguments are based on idealized conceptions of what is liberatory (or critical or student-centered or radical) for students and for teachers, and these arguments are grounded in a reading of other texts. I am arguing that we not only need to conceptualize but also to realize a "critical composition classroom" and to consider the different understandings and practices in our studying and teaching and studying teaching. Reading contemporary work in feminist poststructural pedagogy, for example, I came to comprehend why the classroom cannot ever finally be fully democratic (no matter how much you *want* it to be) and why it is self-serving and problematic to nevertheless continue to insist it can be. I came to this comprehension, however, not only through my studies but also through my teaching experiences, through attempts to engage these ideas and realize these possibilities along with my students. If you believe democratic classroom relations are important to critical pedagogy, then you cannot simply imagine and articulate them, you need to try to enact them with your students.

Democracy is not, finally, possible in a classroom. The point becomes, rather, to consider why. What conditions prevent the realization of democratic relations? What can we do to alter or at least acknowledge and critique those conditions? We can focus our own and our students' attention on what informs the relations in a classroom; beyond the roles and constraints supplied by the institution, our economic and social histories and positions situate us differently in relation to the subject, writing, and to one another. This means also considering the effects of our situatedness (specific knowledges articulated and sanctioned; institutional, social, discursive authority granted or denied a priori, and so on).

My evolving conception of the "critical composition classroom," then, is based on my research in scholarship and in teaching, two spheres of practice I sought to theorize in relation and in response to one another. Critical pedagogy is not the unproblematic transmitting of radical knowledge—it is the search for processes and practices by which we might reflect on and revision *how* knowledge gets made. I aim in this book, then, to provide pedagogical, not theoretical, insights; to offer reflections on and representations of efforts to engage the ideas that animate expressivist and critical pedagogies with my students. If I have come to understand some of the concepts differently over time—to challenge and reject some, to revision or recuperate others—it is based on both intellectual and pedagogical inquiry.

My aim is neither to offer *the* pedagogical alternative nor to assert a given set of practices as universally sustainable, much less successful. Instead, I hope to question the very premise (implied by various factions in composition as well as in critical pedagogy) that we must—much less can—situate ourselves exclusively within the parameters of any one model. Rather than masking the contradictions and paradoxes embedded in our positions, we need to uncover and acknowledge these tensions to be more fully cognizant of the goals and concepts we reject, assume, deny, foreground, and abandon. Articulating a universal pedagogy is impossible, but we must continue moving toward a clearer understanding of how context, subject-positions, and truths inform and determine our local pedagogies *as practiced and theorized*. Linda Hutcheon 1989 makes the argument that every theory is "entangled in its own de-doxifying logic," and yet we are not paralyzed by this inevitability itself, but rather by our refusal to acknowledge and confront it:

Is there not a center to even the most de-centered of these theories? What is power to Foucault, writing to Derrida, or class to
Marxism? Each of these theoretical perspectives can be argued
to be deeply—and knowingly—implicated in that notion of
center they attempt to subvert. It is this paradox that makes
them postmodern. . . . But complicity is not full affirmation or
strict adherence . . . [as long as] the awareness of difference
and contradiction, of being inside and outside, is never lost.
(14)

The Process of Pedagogy

I would like to return for a moment to the opening section of this
chapter where I critically reflect on Shari's (the new teacher's)
syllabus. What evolved from our discussion that day represents
how our pedagogies are operative outside of specific classrooms
and must be an explicit part of our work with other teachers. In
conceptualizing pedagogy, we must not only contend with the
question how do we learn, but how do we learn to teach? In
many ways, assumptions about teacher "training" parallel familiar (and troubling) assumptions about the teaching of writing. For instance, "Writing/Teaching cannot be *taught*, so much
as it is learned by example and by doing." Or, "if students/new
teachers just have the right practice/training/orienting in their first
semester, they will obtain the requisite skills to become good,
lifelong academic writers/teachers." "If first-year composition is
successful, they will then be ready to do (or perform) the 'real'
work of an *actual*, specific discipline." But composition special-
ists would here interject, insisting that writing courses provide a
valuable site for writing and studying writing, encouraging students to reflect on the forms and functions of texts, to critically
consider language, context, communication, and so on. Writing
courses are not the means to "correct" students or to prepare
them for more important writing; they are useful ends in themselves, allowing students to engage in a process they will inevitably and productively continue to develop as they continue to write
and to reflect on writing.

Learning to teach, in English doctoral programs, is often conceived in a way that is similar (and equally problematic) to traditional models of learning to write. Learning to teach is presented as a process of training, transmission, and imitation. One is authorized to teach (or write) because one has mastered the content, questions, or methods of a particular discipline. One teaches what one knows, and one can teach simply because one knows. In this model of professing, there is little emphasis on how to facilitate knowledge-making or active inquiry; what a new teacher requires is training (a day-long "orientation") in how to organize and conceptualize a course to ensure that the necessary content can be passed on, and that students will be able to demonstrate their mastery (or lack thereof). In order to facilitate teacher *development,* we need to actively contest this model of teacher "training." Such work must be framed by a *revisionary* (a term I borrow from Nancy Welch) assumption: teaching is not something we are once and for all trained or oriented to do. Rather, teaching is an ongoing process of experimentation, critical and collaborative reflection and inquiry, and revision. This situates all teachers as teachers-in-process, rejecting the notion that some of us are finished learning how to teach, while others must work to master teaching.

In thinking about Shari's syllabus and our ensuing discussion, I was prompted to acknowledge and reflect on what I had come to perceive as the "natural" and essential aims and assumptions about the teaching of writing. My critique of her concept of the course, and of students' roles therein, exposed my own concept as one of many choices, requiring that I engage in the same process of self-reflexive critique that I ask my students to try out, and that I am here arguing that all teachers and pedagogues should practice. Since that time, Shari and I have been working together to understand critical writing pedagogy, both as an intellectual project and as part of our daily teaching lives, in a variety of contexts: in graduate seminars, in teaching groups, in one-on-one discussions and in a collaborative writing project.[7] Since Shari and I first met to discuss that syllabus, we have developed a relationship that does not replicate the master-apprentice tradition. Instead, (as we hope to do with our students) we work together as two people interested to continue our development as teachers, and to extending our understanding of what it means to teach writing so as to foster active and ongoing revision—for students and teachers, writers and readers. When we visit one another's classrooms, we do so not to produce an official evaluative account of an individual teacher's "performance," but to represent for one another our classrooms as texts that we can read critically, with the aim of better understanding what is happening and why. When we meet to discuss our teaching, we each articulate challenges, frustrations, successes; it is not the familiar model where Shari (as teacher "in-training") describes her difficulties to me (the accomplished teacher) and I prescribe solutions.

Rather, Shari and I are committed to the central premise that teachers, even those who profess highly specialized pedagogies, are never done learning. Putting this belief into practice necessarily changes how we work with students and with other teachers by presenting learning (and teaching) as an ongoing enterprise that requires *collective* reflection, whether among teachers, or students, or students and teachers. Both of us have written about the discussion we had in response to Shari's first syllabus. In this chapter, I reflected on my "reactionary" reaction. In a seminar paper (for another teacher), Shari considers how her history as a student informed her thinking about teaching, so that, before she ever taught, she in some ways learned to devalue student (and her own) knowledge in favor of "acquiring" knowledge from more "legitimate" texts. In each of our pieces, we emphasized our developing understandings of writing and pedagogy that resulted from this conversation. We are currently collaborating on an article that examines not so much the *product* of these interactions, or what we have learned together, but rather the process by which we were able to develop a generative pedagogical relationship, accounting for the complex conditions that foster such productive coinquiry.

Learning *with* Shari as a new teacher, while positioning myself as a teacher-in-process, has allowed us to revision traditional models of teacher "training" and "orientation," enabling us to instead develop the *pedagogies* that inform how we conceptualize and engage in the teaching of writing. I am not left feeling accountable for defending my "vision" of how the composition classroom should be, nor for passing on the tradition. Shari is not situated as the novice or initiate, perceived as inadequate or lacking (or in need) on the basis of her amount of experience as a teacher. *Quantity* of experience is not privileged in this model of teacher development so much as *quality* of engagement, of one's willingness to continually study, critique, and learn about teaching. This revisioning of teacher development has not happened naturally or accidentally. Apart from our shared commitments, we must consciously reflect on and work to foster the conditions that allow us to work productively together as teachers engaged in collaborative, critical inquiry into our pedagogies—both the pedagogies we argue for and the pedagogies of our arguments.

To return to my critical reflection on Shari's syllabus at the opening of this chapter, visions and products alone cannot constitute a *pedagogy*, whether critical or expressivist. While Shari was clear about where she wanted students to end up as a result of taking her class, her syllabus and our discussion revealed her uncertainty about what students would *do* in the class, how their writing would figure into her radical composition pedagogy. Visions and aims might usefully provide a theory of education, expanding our sense of the possibilities for why we teach and learn. But if we understand pedagogy to necessitate attention to *both* the processes and products of education, and to the relationship between them, then one without the other is not enough. Giroux and McLaren insist that to provide *prescriptions* would demean and undermine the critical teacher and the project of critical pedagogy. There is a fundamental difference, however, between prescribing methods and critically reflecting on the processes by which one attempts to effect the products of critical pedagogy. The refusal to represent their pedagogy at work in specific sites is, as Orner, Miller, and Ellsworth (1996) suggest, a deflective strategy that maintains the focus on theory as distinct from the act of teaching. Despite their claims that teachers and students are "empowered" and central to critical pedagogy, their discourse focuses attention on the "testimony" of scholars, not teachers (Orner, Miller and Ellsworth 85). Further, while they resist describing or prescribing *processes* of enactment, they consistently prescribe *products* and aims for our teaching. This reinforces the traditional binary and hierarchical oppositions between theory/

practice, research/teaching, and scholars/teachers. The following chapter begins to articulate a revisioning of critical composition pedagogy, while subsequent chapters represent and reflect on attempts to enact this revisioned version. Of course, focusing reflexive inquiry on our efforts to engage this developing pedagogy in specific sites produces, in turn, further revisions.

Notes

1. I would like to note that the teacher and I have discussed these issues in depth and are continuing to do so. Because we have a shared project and commitment, we have been able to engage in generative and productive critique. My criticism does not signify that she will be a "bad" writing teacher, but rather that she lacked experience in thinking about teaching writing. But she is not the only one learning and revising in this exchange as she questions my concept of the writing course and pushes me to recognize the choices I have made.

2. I am here thinking primarily of Foucault's work that investigates the "subject" as historically and discursively contingent. If we recognize that the individual might be represented differently in one discursive system, at one historical moment, in one discipline, then we are forced to contend with subjects and subjectivity as fluid, shifting, and with the systems that produce them as both potentially liberating/enabling and constraining/disabling. We cannot determine the discursive system of critical pedagogy, for instance, to be ultimately and certainly liberating as such a position essentializes the discourse apart from the subjects it produces and who engage in (interpellate) the discourse. See Foucault, 1990, 1980; Weedon 1987; and Luke and Gore, 1992 ("Introduction").

3. Carby, hooks, McDowell, and Spelman, among others, have argued that the unwillingness to engage issues of race and gender, or the "passive" ignorance of these factors when considering identity and subjectivity results in a repositing of the implied "normative" position of whiteness and maleness, the only factors granted invisibility, deemed standard and therefore not mandating scrutiny.

4. The stereotype about white people we discussed was that they do not get cold. Several students (African and African Americans) had heard this while growing up, while none of the white students had. And, interestingly enough, the white students immediately set out to disprove this benign myth by insisting they were often cold.

COMPOSING CRITICAL PEDAGOGIES

5. Of course, students are not the only members of these groups who believe that once they gain entry, ascend economically, they will become "incorporated." I refer specifically to students here because it is in the context of a discussion of classroom contexts.

6. Freire is able to make the distinction between representing and examining his own practice and offering these as universally successful or viable strategies. He too refuses the possibility or usefulness of believing he/we can *tell* people *how* to teach but does not conflate this with the need to suppress discussion of classroom practice entirely. (See Freire and Macedo 1987, chapter 6).

7. My thinking and writing here, in this final section, is fundamentally collaborative as it comes directly from the work Shari Stenberg and I have done together. So I am indebted to our discussions—not only for the productive revisioning they have generated or for the affirmative sense of community they provide, but also for the ways I am now representing those discussions.

CHAPTER FIVE

Revisionary Pedagogy

Beth Anne: As I was thinking about coming here, I kept thinking of one particular incident in class that had to do with both the way I think and how Amy taught. We were talking I think about stereotypes and associating groups of people with negative things. [We read the essay where] someone said that if a person is attacked or robbed by a black person, isn't it natural for that person to be afraid of black people. You were (the way you do) getting people to talk about what had been said. This is when I spoke. I said I didn't think it was fair to call someone who had gone through the horrible experience of being attacked a racist person. I gave examples of women being taught from the time they are little girls to fear men on the street, especially late at night. I couldn't see the difference between the fear of men (which I feel very strongly for personal reasons) and the fear of black people. At the time, [Amy] didn't *tell* me I was wrong, but gave examples of why you didn't agree. I could tell I had frustrated [Amy] by saying something very touchy and hard to argue with. It wasn't hard to argue with because it was anywhere right, but because I was comparing something personally emotional and painful to racism. In the end, you encouraged everyone to write essays about the things that came up during that discussion. I remember very clearly [Amy] didn't make me feel like the most ignorant person on earth. I didn't feel like I had been totally wrong until I wrote the essay about growing up in a very small town with only one black friend and reflected on what my upbringing meant in the scheme of how I treat people now.

Beth Anne: I like the point Karen made about Amy's teaching style. She might have been the first person who challenged me to open and use my mind. I wouldn't trade that part of her class for the world. The reason it was effective was because she didn't have to be right, but she asked people to restate what they said, to write about it as a group, what other people in the class thought about the same thing. If she had just told us we were wrong, we might never have come to realize why.

Beth Anne: I remember a woman in class specifically asking me to read her essay about being bisexual and coming out. It made me feel very good that she felt safe about letting me read her story. And she helped me showing me part of an experience I

wasn't knowledgeable about and showing how it *shaped* her
. . . . So many people in the class were learning that they had to
defend their views and couldn't just take them for granted. And I
had misconceptions too and reading her paper helped me realize and reflect.

Different people in the class all had different things to contribute. After reading her essay and realizing she'd helped me by
trusting me to share that paper, and by contributing to my understanding how lives are shaped, I felt like I had something to contribute too, about the way my life and women's lives are shaped—in
order to help people understand this. That's when I decided to
write *the* paper. And writing that paper was a huge step for me in
the healing process, in my life-planning and philosophy-forming
processes. I had never been able to express my feelings about,
never even been able to "voice," to speak those experiences.
We talked a lot in class about how different voices are shaped
and created by experiences and now I also understand this more—
especially the need for *women* to give voice to certain experiences
which usually aren't spoken. That paper was a step to my work
now as an educator-advocate at the Everywoman's Center.

An excerpt from "Shame," an essay by Beth Anne Manchester
There are some words that are hard to say. My mouth stutters
through "rape" and can't even form "molest." If I do use one of
these words in conversation, it just falls from my mouth to the floor
with a dead silent ring. My cheeks flush, and everyone must see
my horrible reaction. But there is something empowering about
being able to say a word that describes an experience in your life
without being ashamed of something that was not your fault.

The upstairs Herter [Hall] women's bathroom is full of graffiti
written by women who don't want to be ashamed. There are also
little blurbs of thought written by narrow-minded women who believe that rape, and even child molestation, is not the sole fault of
the attacker. They are the people who make me ashamed of myself and lead others to believe sexual violation is something women
and little children ask for.

I grew up denying the fact that I was molested by my uncle. At
first, I didn't understand what was happening. Later I just wanted to
hide and pretend—pretend that he never touched me, pretend I
had no problems. I wanted to be strong.

But there is no strength in hiding from yourself or hiding from
other people. The greater strength . . . is acknowledging and cop-
ing with the past. I began when I wrote my name on the wall in the
Herter bathroom. You are reading my first step toward freeing myself from an awful secret.

I wish I could say that I foresee a change and that victimized
women will be able to stand up and not be looked down on by
society. It is true I have made a huge step forward. But the bathroom wall in Herter has already been painted over. (**Beth Anne
Manchester**)

Beth Anne's writing and reflections reveal the connection she sees between her interaction with class members, a particular essay that she regards as a "turning point," and her current work as an educator-advocate for the Everywoman's Center at the university. Because her experience is one of the few that clearly links the potential for writing to provoke action, it's important to let her speak at length. Her remarks are further notable for the way in which she links an increasing awareness of how she has been constructed with an awareness that (and how) she was constructing others. Her self-reflexivity, like Karen F.'s in "Reflections" (discussed in Chapter 6), leads her to consider not only how she has been "shaped," but how she, in turn, "shapes" others; her writing also reflects her sense that she needed to contribute toward the broader class's understanding of the forces involved in this shaping process *because* others had contributed to her own awareness. Her description of the process of becoming a discursive and social activist, then, reflects Herzberg and Spellmeyer's observation that substantive revision, meaningful critical awareness, entails a consideration of the self-in-relation, of oneself as part of a larger and ongoing *social* struggle.

> Students will not critically question a world that seems natural, inevitable, given; instead they will strategize about their own position within it. Developing a *social imagination* makes it possible not only to question and analyze the world, but to imagine transforming it. (Herzberg 1994, 317, my emphasis)

> The university fails to promote a *social imagination* [my emphasis], an awareness of the human "world" as a common historical *project*, and not simply a state of nature to which we must adjust ourselves. (Spellmeyer 1991, 73)

This notion of the *social* is important to emphasize for it consciously permeates Beth Anne's account of her own process of becoming an activist; her sense of herself as a member of various groupings, of various (potential) communities, leads her to act. Envisioning her "self" in a relation to others leads her to a sense of accountability and responsibility for contributing to the groups she identified. Her increased and intensified reflection of her relation to the social, then, prompts her to act. This is important to note because Beth Anne represents not the individual success story or the heroic individual who transcends social bonds and material constraints. Rather, as her texts make clear, she understands her agency as dependent on her membership in various groups.

Talking to Beth Anne recently, I asked her if she made a conscious link between the writing of this essay and her current goals and work as an activist. Her response was that this essay alone, while a "turning point" does not explain the trajectory. She cited her experience of being in the class overall, of recognizing the power of writing to push people to resee, its influence over how *she* now sees herself and her constructions of others, of learning that she had to defend her views and, when unable, consider discarding them. In other words, for her, reading other students' essays, participating in course discussions and composing texts herself were all determining factors in what she calls her coming to "voice." She also noted how the concept of *voice,* one she was initially exposed to in our College Writing class, continues to resonate for her today as she becomes more attuned to the imposing of voicelessness—on women in particular—by social, economic, and discursive structures. Her use of the term *voice* represents one concept that spans both critical and process pedagogies. For Beth Anne and in critical pedagogy, however, the term does not name a unique essence or persona, contained or conveyed by a text, which signifies an *individual* writer; rather, the term implies the *social* and discursive, "ideological and material forces out of which individuals and groups fashion a 'voice'" (Giroux 1986, 49). That is, *voice* signifies discourse as a means to and product of power, recognizing that the means by which a subject claims discursive power is intimately linked to the position envisioned for her by the discourse itself. *Voice,* then, is not so much a descriptive term used to mark distinctiveness, but an inscriptive term that names the writer as subject to, and not simply author/agent of, the text.[1]

While the course offered Beth Anne a chance to reflect on the means by which she and others "come to voice—" that is, arrive at a position from which to speak with authority about experience and the dominant construction of that experience—the class was only one step in a longer process in which she is yet engaged. Beth Anne's experience clearly signifies the potential of a writing class to engage students in revisioning themselves-in-relation-to a world that determines, and is determined by, them; further, Beth Anne's experience of actively claiming a "voice" in her writing led her to give voice as an educator-advocate outside the classroom. However, it would be disingenuous to claim my pedagogical strategies "empowered" Beth Anne. As her comments make clear, her comfort level in the classroom, her sense that she had an obligation to contribute to our collaborative effort to understand one another, her experience of me as challenging but not domineering, her sense of having made someone else feel "safe," her sense that the "time had come" to speak her shame in order to expose and attack the social and discursive conditions that sustained it—all of these factors (only some of which a teacher might even attempt to create or control) were crucial.

Opening this chapter with Beth Anne's reflections and her writing is important for how these texts represent the potential of a critical classroom to provide a space in which students come to revision their concepts of self, other, and world. At the same time, this is not simply a critical pedagogy "success"—Beth Anne is careful to name the class as but a single factor in a broader set of necessary conditions that prompted her revision and action. I have opened with Beth Anne's reflections, then, as an example of the possibilities for critical pedagogies as well as to provide a cautionary note about the dominant discourse of critical pedagogy, which tends to proclaim education alone is a viable means of effecting "transformation," "liberation." While these are not worthless goals, I wonder how plausible they are when one considers the specific contexts of our work: fourteen weeks, twenty or more complex and differently situated students, various material conditions informing the work and lives of each participant, institutional constraints, and so on.

Aims, Goals, Defining "Success"

> Succinctly put, it is not at all clear what [students] would gain from being exposed to the [critical] practice you describe. . . . Learning to revise in a way that entertains other possibilities and alternatives is undoubtedly important, but it does not actually guarantee that the world outside of the essay will be

changed in any way: Freire's image of rewriting the word/world requires moving outside the classroom and beyond the boundaries of the essay to actual political action. Although you are certainly aware of this distinction, your essay suggests that classroom work on gender and identity is somehow equivalent to political action. ("Reader #1's" response to a manuscript on critical pedagogy and practice that I submitted to *CCC* several years ago)

There is a great deal of division over what constitutes an appropriate agenda, a legitimate aim, for a critically oriented writing classroom. Upon receiving this response two years ago, I could understand my paper's lack of success in addressing, much less working through, the distinctions raised by this reader. However, I extended the failure of the paper to the failure of our class to enact a truly critical pedagogy. At the time, I felt I must be practicing some less radical, less liberatory version of critical pedagogy. And yet, I could not imagine a classroom that could convey a substantive critical process while simultaneously prescribing the end of that process. While I would not claim that "classroom work" on gender and identity is equivalent to political action, I would also not claim that "actual political action" must occur for a critical composition class to be judged successful. Further, I am uncertain of what constitutes "actual political action"; the reader appears uncertain as well given the insertion of "actual," which implies a distinction from some other sphere of political action. But the reader's response to my paper and my response to the reader indicate the slippery and elusive task of determining what constitutes an appropriate aim for a critical class.

The rigid distinction between "inside" and "outside" seems not so much an inarguable truth, but a concept deployed in support of specific positions. The same distinction is used by Hairston as a basis for her assertion that the classroom is not an appropriate space in which to initiate or encourage political action. Whereas Hairston claims that politicizing the classroom is too radical, this reader seems to imply it is not radical enough (unless directly linked to "political" action *outside* the classroom). As Sheila indicates in the following excerpt from a reading response, the world and the classroom *do* collide regardless of whether we choose to construct a barrier (rigid or permeable) between them and we might do better to consciously appropriate the collision, to make it generative, rather than to simply deny it or to see it as a stumbling block.

> While I was in the middle of reading Adrienne Rich's essay "Taking Women Students Seriously," the boys living next door were playing a rap song that repeatedly referred to women as "bitches, ho's, and holes." How can I now disagree with Rich's argument that women in the classroom are not taken seriously when I am *in* a class with these boys and when, while studying here in my room, I can hear them being *entertained* by women being degraded and made . . . useless as anything other than a body. Am I supposed to believe these students will forget these words in class tomorrow when they sit next to me (or my teacher for that matter who might be listening to the same song or watching the video) (From Sheila's response to "Taking Women Students Seriously")

Several students each semester do become "actually" politically active, and often they attribute this (in part) to their experience in the writing course (as Beth Anne does). Many students, however, do not move so clearly from the realm of discursive revisioning to "action." While certainly I would hope for the work in the classroom to result in clear and tangible action outside the classroom, I am wary of prescribing an end that is clearly not attainable for *all* students and thus inscribes our inevitable collective failure. Instead, we need to expand our definition of "action" or of "successful" critical practice in ways that challenge us to act, while recognizing that moving students toward reflection on *past* actions might be a necessary and equally vital step in the process of critical self-awareness.

> Requiring self-reflexivity does not, of course, guarantee that repugnant positions will be abandoned. At best, it ensures only that students' attention will be focused on the interconnections between the ways they read and write. But it does not mean that this approach wields sufficient power to transform the matrix of beliefs, values, and prejudices that students (and teachers) bring to the classroom. This kind of wholesale transformation (or, to be more precise, the appearance of this kind of wholesale transformation) is only possible in classrooms where highly asymmetrical relations of power are fully reinstated and

COMPOSING CRITICAL PEDAGOGIES

students are told either implicitly or explicitly [what is and is not allowed]. (R. Miller 407)

Conceivably, then, the course provided a place for Paul,[2] who figures in the next chapter as a writer/actor who unproblematically perceives himself a free agent, as much as for Beth Anne, to engage in a larger, longer process of "self"-examination. While the process did not result in obvious or empirical radical action, Paul's engagement in revisioning did result in unsettling his sense of himself as a free agent, increasing his awareness of the ways in which he actively constructed others, and demonstrating the potential for revisioning his atomistic independently actualizing self to a self-in-relation, which entails a recognition of the relations one constructs. In the following Interchange excerpts, Paul reflects on the connections between writing, the recognition of himself as constructing and constructed, and revisioning:

> **Paul:** The more you know about yourself and what you really stand for, the more competently and creatively you can write about issues and experiences. I personally feel . . . I have stuck my face in some really ugly corners, and this had made me realize how human I am and in turn let me see other people [differently]. These are tasks we must all contend with and because someone has a problem being honest doesn't mean they are worthless or sightless.
>
> [One] of the tools which really let me start to think was the essay on my sister. For a long time, I had blocked those scenes out and many dissatisfactions I had with me stemmed from this lack of truthfulness. From that paper, I quickly jumped onto the subject of sex, to see what I could come up with as it was a large source of grief for me. What I discovered in that paper was that I was justifying my answers instead of asking why I behaved in a certain way. I wrote two pages of lies and disclaimers instead of addressing the real matter. I wrote a cowering, juvenile essay justifying my treatment of women as not all that bad or at least acceptable.
>
> My paper was, in retrospect, fairly rude and ignorant. Amy wrote a page on the back of the rough draft explaining why the paper upset her, and I saw how I was working backwards, explaining my justifications instead of asking the almighty WHY. So I went home and proceeded to think about the topic forever. I ended up writing a ten-page inquisitory essay in which I explained why I thought/acted in a certain way and also reacted to the conclusions I reached. Again, this was a very influential point in my thinking, and it manifested itself in the writing.

Such revisioning deserves recognition as a critical success. How could Paul arrive in the same (or an equivalent) place as Beth Anne, given the different inscriptions each needed to recognize and unwrite, given their different histories and positions vis-à-vis language, authority, and power? Moreover, while Beth Anne entered the class ready to know, looking to name and reflect on the shape of what she knew (her experiential knowledge) in ways that were not disempowering, Paul entered the course with a will not to know. Though conventional wisdom assumes that knowledge equals power, ignorance is often more powerful, and with particular students, we need to contend with the will not to know. For many students (and people in general), contending with what they believe they already know—to be "true," to be "natural," to be "universal"—needs to be contested, challenged, before they can access new knowledge. Unlearning is sometimes a necessary step in the process of conceptualizing alternatives—alternative ways of knowing, alternatives to what it means to be human and in a relationship to other humans, or to be a writer situated in relation to readers, rather than an author creating for an audience.

Beth Anne and Paul do not only arrive at different ends in the same classroom, they articulate different factors as most influential in their processes of development. Beth Anne stresses the importance of peer reading, group discussions, of being exposed to the texts of others; Paul emphasizes the significance of being challenged by the teacher, of having his work critiqued by someone he invested with at least some initial (if questionable) authority.

Amy: Paul and Josh, thinking over the years I've been teaching, you still remain two of the most challenging students I have had (and yes *frustrating* at times). Challenging as in a negative, push-pull sort of way. Did you intend to challenge me, others, the class? Did you expect to hate the class and so come with a certain attitude? Did you find things useless at first?

Paul: I had thought myself a pretty good writer when I started this class, which is why I was so cocky. Then I was humbled by a few of your early comments which only served to piss me off and make me want to show you I *could* write. My first essay was a crummy page-and-a-half and you wrote me a page-and-a-half comment. It was good to see someone reviewing and *critiquing*

my work instead of . . . halfheartedly going through the correc-
tions. The constant questions and adding of angles [by you and
peer readers] . . . challenged me. I felt important and, again,
challenged. You were one of the few writing teachers who had
something negative to say about my work.

Paul's initial willingness to "listen" to my voice rather than
to his peers is informed by his strong sense of himself as a writer
and human agent, leading him to perceive that he had little to
learn from anyone who was not clearly (institutionally) "authorized." Beth Anne, on the other hand, was immediately receptive
to and actively participatory in peer reviewing and class discussions. While Paul's next comment signifies his increasing investment in and responsiveness to peer criticism, he needed to first
be made aware that he was not "finished" as a writer or thinker
and that this awareness could only come from an authority.

Paul: Letting people read my drafts made me think of my audience much more, and this in turn made me wonder "What would
Karen say to that" or "If Jeffrey were talking to me now would he
think me a moron?" Stuff like that made me see us as more of a
group and I could hear the comments ringing out as I typed. This
isn't to say I censored my ideas, but I tried to say what I felt in a
way that would be more, ahh, professional? More aware and
sensitive. Although, I suppose this could work in reverse—shock
tactics, off-beat plots, etc.

The different means by which Paul and Beth Anne became
engaged in the course signify the importance of providing various points of entry to the process of critical writing. Similar to
the danger of imposing one end, one definition of "success," there
is a potential danger in assuming a particular tool will work for
most or all students; instead, we need to offer a range of strategies. (And of course, a particular danger in assuming an assignment or line of inquiry will work similarly and for all students is
that, when it fails to do so, we blame the individual students.) It
is important to consider how students experience our pedagogies.
However, in doing so, I am aware of the tendency to assume that
talking about individual students inevitably reproduces an emphasis on "the Individual." My aim is not to hold these students
up as identifiable models or as examples of successful individual
enlightenment. Rather, I want to avoid the tendency of critical

and expressivist pedagogies to evoke "students" or "writers" as general and homogeneous categories, or to proclaim that a given pedagogy might uniformly engage, challenge, and impact *all* students.

Visions of a Critical Process

Within composition, there exists a debate about how we evaluate the achievements of the critical writing classroom. On the one hand, critical pedagogy is interpreted as mandating some immediate, tangible action that occurs outside the classroom (Elbow, North, Singleton); a critical course should result in students becoming involved in coalitions, protests, or political movements. On the other hand, others (Harris, Villanueva, Schwartz) interpret critical pedagogy as mandating active critique within the classroom and assume the critical practice developed in class will manifest itself in various ways and at various moments outside class; a critical class then initiates or continues a reflective process that will not necessarily result in immediate or tangible action. Harris problematizes the opposition set up in this debate between the space "inside" and "outside" the classroom and the distinction about *where* we are to search for evidence of success, contesting the idea that

> somehow the work inside the classroom is validated by writing or discourses taken outside the classroom . . . it seems to me that writing . . . essays . . . can have a powerful, worthwhile, and critical, liberatory effect. Part of the work students can be doing can be serious academic work. They can be learning critique and *how* you do that and *where* it's applied. . . . When my students learn to do it well, . . . I'm really pleased, and my next move is not to say, "Gee! If only this had a real-world application"—I think there's a trap there. (From Interchange transcripts in *Composition and Resistance*, 152)

While we need to question what constitutes a successful critical classroom, we cannot delimit the scope of *useful* or *meaningful* change to some standardized, decontextualized notion of *action* versus non-action. As Freire notes, "It must be emphasized that the praxis by which consciousness is changed is not only action but action *and* reflection" (1985, 124). In other words, there must be action and recognition of the context in which the action has taken place, a sense of the aim toward which it is directed.

Further, if one adheres to Foucault's claim that identity, subjection to relations of oppression, and the distribution of power are not only manifest in, but also actively maintained by, the regulation of discourse, then it would follow that a change in the discursive realm must either precede or follow change in some more tangible realm of action. That is, if we believe the nexus of power-truth-discourse produces a discourse of truth that serves to enable speakers/writers to cover up or maintain blindness to the various contradictions that structure their identities and relationships, then we cannot have material change without discursive change—the two, rather, must go hand-in-hand. While we must be conscious of not conflating the two, of not assuming they are the same or "equal," we can recognize the necessity of both spheres of action and allow that change in one will ultimately impact the other. Just as breaking down the concept of a unified self requires breaking down its attendant concepts of *the other*, or similar to the need within feminism to deconstruct and displace the term *woman* (to move from an implied standardized concept of white, heterosexual, middle-class women), we need to engage students in revisioning the concepts by which they organize their lives as well as to rethink the lived, material relations conceived of, and represented by, these words.

The writing students generated about stereotypes, discussed in Chapter 4, demonstrates how students might begin their "revision" in the realm of discourse; reconceptualization requires rearticulating, and so we might carefully consider how revision within our classrooms signifies a greater change than in writing style or structure. Surely James's recognition he has stereotyped homosexuals in the same ways he fights against being stereotyped himself *counts*. As Villanueva suggests, we cannot hope to enact radical social change in a single semester. Instead, we can hope to initiate the process that will fuel such change. While claims of transformation and radical changes of mind/consciousness are seductive, we are bound to fail to achieve them in substantive ways. Claiming we can leaves us with teacher-centered pedagogies of declaration and espousal, but with few indications and little evidence of sustained impact. Hence, my preference for the term *revisioning* as the organizing metaphor and strategy for my teaching; revisioning is more local than empowerment or "transformation" and implies the legitimacy of action within and outside the classroom, within discourse and within structural and human relationships.

I have called attention to questions of naming throughout this text, the naming of a pedagogy of revisioning is important in that it suggests an ongoing, continuous process. There is not an *end* at which one is successfully and finally anti-racist or liberated from misogyny or classism. Rather, new texts, new interactions, new contexts provide us with new challenges to our existing concepts. To be open to engaging in revision is to be prepared to understand one's critical consciousness as an ongoing development, a state of being constantly in process. Ellsworth, Orner, and R. Miller suggest a "situated pedagogy"; Jay suggests a "pedagogy of disorientation." These names are important conceptual tools. The idea of a critical or radical pedagogy suggests that the pedagogy itself (and therefore its practitioners) are radical, are liberated from dominant discourses and material culture. Seemingly, the only participants in this pedagogy who are not already liberated are students who then become the objects of the teacher's critique, her liberatory power. She seeks, that is, to empower them by tapping into their latent but "natural" critical consciousness or by giving them one.

Clifford makes clear the link between a class that integrates the processes—rather than pushing the products—of composing and becoming critical:

> [S]ince power is decentered in our culture, finding its energy in properly socialized subjects, the most ambitious undertaking is not to storm the hegemonic barricades. Instead, we should do the intellectual work we know best: helping students to read and write and think in ways that both resist domination and exploitation and encourage self-consciousness about who they are and can be in the world. (1991, 51)

Increasingly, within composition, critically-oriented teachers are articulating limited, contextualized goals that draw on the relationship between composing and critical thinking. Rather than privilege some type of "actual action," these scholars have attempted to theorize the legitimacy and necessity of taking small, but substantive, steps in order to work toward long-term and progressive, ongoing revision. The conceptualizing of these steps is rooted in discursive action in order to use the composing process (given that writing is what we are teaching) as a means of enabling a revision of language as a system of inscription that determines the "self" one composes. Berlin poses a possible set of aims as follows:

> The focus is on the relation of current signifying practices to the structuring of subjectivities—of race, class and gender formations, for example—in our students and ourselves. Our effort is to make students aware of the cultural codes—the various competing discourses—that attempt to influence who they are. Our larger purpose is to encourage students to resist and negotiate these codes—these hegemonic discourses—in order to bring about more personally human and socially equitable economic and political arrangements. . . . Language—textuality— is thus the scene where different conceptions of the economic, social and political conditions are contested. . . . We are thus committed to teaching writing as an inescapably political act, the working out of contested cultural codes that affect every feature of our experience. (1991, 50–51)

The goal, then, is not to sacrifice the teaching of writing in favor of "political indoctrination," but rather to ground the teaching of writing in intellectual and critical processes—to conceive of composition pedagogy in a way that acknowledges and uses our understanding that writing and thinking, words and world, relations of identity and discourse are in a dialectic relationship.

Berlin's definition is useful not only for its clear articulation of the relationship between writing and history, discourse and hegemony, signifying and structures, but also for its description of *processes* rather than ends. When specific ends are named as the only useful goal of a critical classroom, we run into increased difficulty when mediating the tension between espousing and enacting. While we might be able to encourage students to join an antiracist coalition, does this action in and of itself signify substantive or critical revisioning of one's own implication in racist structures of privilege and oppression? Why is action privileged *over* reflection? As Liston and Zeichner note, "radically oriented [teachers] must educate, not inculcate":

> to expect students to arrive at consensus on these matters in a noncoercive environment, and then engage in political action, seems misplaced. It seems odd to expect [students] to come to agreement in areas where teachers . . . reasonably disagree. . . . The *radical* tradition . . . encompasses only those approaches that seek to develop both reflective thought and reconstructive action. . . . Although there is not and probably should never be a uniform radical view, further discussion and debate over the conceptual foundations of a radical approach are clearly needed. To date, there has been little discussion within the tradition. Most critical comments of radically oriented teachers have been directed at advocates of other traditions. (1987, 123, 127–28)

A critical writing classroom seeks to implement processes by which students might acknowledge (and hopefully revise) their concepts of self, other, world *as* constructions, as one concept along a range of choices. The *aim* then is not a definitive end (actual action, political or otherwise), so much as the development of a critical *process*. This process, in turn, aims to enable the demystification of texts and contexts, allowing students to enter into the process of constructing meaning, rather than to believe it is done for/to them or that they might inscribe meaning unproblematically or naturally. As Miller suggests, such a pedagogy assumes "the importance of seeing composition as the institutional site reserved for investigating acts of reading and writing as evidenced in and by students texts. . . . Composition [surfaces] as the field whose expertise lies in *initiating* students into an exploration of how meaning gets made" (1994, 169).

Teaching *Writing* as a Critical Process

> We are all talking, I think, about pedagogies that challenge, from one or another radical democratic standpoint, the dominations and injustices of the present social order, and *do so in*

connection with the teaching of writing. (Ohmann 326) [my emphasis]

While conceiving of writing and reading as processes is still necessary, I would like to consider what they are potentially processes *of*, that is, where such processes might lead us. How can a composition class that foregrounds the composing/constructing of texts and readings function to engage students in a self-inventory? In such a pedagogy, writing serves as the means by which we actively construct a self and a world that are, in turn, determined by the very language we have access to, the words through which we express these constructions.

There is the concern in any discipline that taking up certain issues—foregrounding questions of how knowledge gets made in a particular classroom, discipline, institution—gets in the way of the "real" work of the class. But that concern rests on the assumption that our "real" work is not already informed by these very questions. Making these issues central to a class does not impede the "real" work of teaching writing or history or algebra, but engages students and teachers in a consideration of the processes of education, along with the production of knowledge, the acquisition of critical skills. In a history course, for instance, we might ask who has the authority to determine which histories merit or are deemed worthy of becoming history; from whose vantage point is history constructed and recounted; which cultures are mythically represented as benevolent and advanced, or savage and ill-willed, and who has been in the position of writing these myths.

If I taught history, I would have to think about certain questions, and the same is true for teaching writing. The underlying questions are the same, though they are asked in relation to a different set of texts and practices. What makes a writer an author? What are the requirements for claiming "authority" in a text, a culture, or a writing class? What subject-position are successful "student writers" expected to assume? How do ideas of "logic" and "structure" and "style" work to prohibit and enable specific forms of authority, textual products, writer-reader relations? While some teachers might suggest such questions impede or intimidate writers, I would argue that the opposite is true. The students who contest these questions and their legitimacy are typically those students who are most authorized to speak in the academy, who are privileged by academic discourse. Those students who have experienced dissonance or conflict as student writers are not frustrated by such questions because this inquiry opens up possibilities; it does not shut them down. These questions might locate the source of their felt frustrations and friction in structural contexts, in systemic criteria, rather than the result of their individual failure, their individual incompetence.

A critically oriented writing classroom attempts to engage students in intellectual processes that will help them understand, articulate, and interrogate their relationship to others and to the world, how their concept of an individual self is composed according to these relationships, and to their material situatedness in the world, and to acknowledge the role of discourse in determining—not only in representing—this self, those others, that world. A writing class might work specifically with our concepts of authority so as to trouble the dominant conventions of authorship and authority, to negotiate new ways of producing authority, and to practice the alternative ways of reading and writing necessary to such a project. Because it is a writing course, we focus on "authority"—on the textual manifestation of agency—but the textual realm is only one manifestation of the relations and conditions that situate an individual comfortably or uncomfortably as an author/agent. It is not coincidental that students who are comfortably situated as writers in the academy are most often situated comfortably outside the academy, in terms of social and material conditions.

Initially, I understood my own project as an attempt to argue for critical pedagogy as *the* alternative to process pedagogy. However, the discourse of critical pedagogy, similar to expressivist pedagogy, is subject to discovering only those results, and considering only those students and teachers, which validate its existing paradigm and methodology. So the question and the challenge: how can a pedagogy account for those not envisioned by its paradigm, or those of us unable to accommodate its construction of us as teachers and students? The lesson to be learned is not that the project of critical pedagogies must be abandoned. Rather, we need to be attentive to the tensions, problematizations, and contradictions that emerge in and between our theories and practices. We need to confront and acknowledge these challenges in order to strengthen our project, rather than repressing or denying them for fear they will entail a revisioning so critical, the project itself is no longer viable. The question—and the challenge—becomes how do we account for those of us not envisioned by the paradigm, or those of us unable to accommodate its construction of us.

> The fact that the educator is not a neutral agent does not mean, necessarily, that he is a manipulator. Manipulation is debilitating and, likewise, irresponsible. . . . The question of consistency between the declared options and practice is one of the demands critical educators make on themselves. They know quite well that it is not discourse that judges practice, but practice that judges discourse. Unfortunately, many educators who proclaim a democratic option do not always have a practice consistent with such advanced discourse. Thus their discourse, inconsistent with their practice, becomes pure rhetoric. (Freire 1987, 39)

Rather than offering *the* alternative, I aim to demonstrate that while we must recognize our complex subjectivity and the inevitability that we will validate those truths we have already determined to be worth seeking, we need not be crippled by this realization. Instead, we can take it up as a challenge worth engaging in.

Putting Poststructuralism in the Mix

Poststructuralism offers the rationale, a theory of discourse as interdependent with reality and agency, for envisioning *writing* courses as viable sites for the practice of a critical pedagogy and for reflecting on the texts of our teaching. A poststructural conception of discourse does not replace the teaching of writing, but poses questions that might challenge our roles and aims as teachers of writing, and those we envision for our students as writers. As Flannery suggests, "Foucault is not reducible to a method; he does not offer a liberatory rhetoric. . . . Rather, his work can lead

us to ask difficult questions about our practice, about its affiliations, about its institutional origins, about its transformations
into something other than what we might have hoped it could or
would be" (1990, 210). Most radical pedagogies—feminist, critical, multicultural—have focused more on the content of our classrooms, than on the practices by which we engage this "content."
Similarly, while poststructuralism has been used to revision the
texts and students we teach (*what* and *whom* we teach), there
has been little attention to poststructuralism's impact or usefulness on *how* or *why* we teach.

An immediate association with poststructuralism might be
with a body of thought that does not allow much room for agency
or resistance: the death of the author, overdetermining discourses,
produced and constrained subjectivity, and so on. Rather, my
understanding of poststructuralism is that it calls into question
the construction, function, and power of subjectivity in relation
to discourse. Here, I am evoking more recent work in
poststructuralism, which foregrounds the possibilities of resistance, and re-secures the notion of agency (not an entirely free or
liberated agent) which, while constrained and determined by
material conditions, discourse, and socio-political relationships,
is simultaneously capable of resistance and of becoming a determining subject.

> To talk of agency and choice is not to return to a fantasy in
> which the individual can be or do anything, and it is certainly
> not to forget the histories and material conditions that shape
> the context of any agent's choice. On the contrary, the notion
> of ethos demands that a person . . . know well the historical
> circumstances that shape the moment in which the person must
> respond to what is with an action aimed at what might be-
> come. (Jay 1994, 626)

Rather than disclaiming foundations or metanarratives altogether, a politics grounded in poststructural-feminist analyses
"grounds its epistemology on a foundation of difference" (Luke
48). Agency, discourse, and power exist in a mutually interdependent relationship, as do agency and structure, self and others,
imagined (ideological) and real (material). None of these terms
exists or is meaningful outside the other terms; we cannot, there-

fore, fixate on individual terms as the privileged site for revision, enlightenment, or liberation. Such a politics rejects the tendency in liberal feminist theory and process theory to envision the agent as capable of changing his or her sphere autonomously, or independently of attempting structural and discursive change. Further, a poststructural analysis and concept of politics pays critical attention to language, not only culture, recognizing the exercise of power in the struggle between and among discursive representations and material relations. [3]

Here, I understand "shift" not to imply that we ignore "society" (or material conditions) and focus solely on language, but rather that discourse is one necessary and viable site for revisioning and reconfiguring socioeconomic relations because it is through discourse that we name and organize these relations.

In Chapter 1, I claimed that writing classes were especially appropriate arenas in which to execute the self-inventory that Gramsci identifies as a step in developing critical consciousness. The main objective is not to simply create "new" knowledge or new conditions for learning, but to reflect on and critique what we think we already know about writing, about our "selves," about experience. My sense that writing classes are particularly useful in this capacity stems from a poststructural concept of discourse. I have criticized expressivism's concept of language as offering power equally to all students who engage in language practices. This concept envisions language in isolation from social practice and thus fails to account for the fact that writers will face varied challenges depending on their situatedness. Further, an audience's reception of a piece entails not only the object of reception but also the situatedness of readers in relation to the text. Readers will not, cannot, respond only to formal qualities, stylistic concerns; they will respond as well to how authority is constructed in relation to the subject of the text, and to how the text evokes, ignores, or constructs them as readers in relation to it. A poststructural understanding of discourse, and its relation to concepts of identity and relations of power, more adequately represents our students' relationship to language as practiced through the writing and reading of texts.

Most important, poststructural theory contends that discourse, rather than language, is central to the process of forming a subjectivity. Language is not understood as a formal system, regulated by internal rules and structures. Rather, to understand language as discourse is to see it as a social system, informed by and determining of power, knowledge, and identity. The individual author is not the source of meaning, because language does not simply reflect or transcribe the author's thoughts or knowledge. Similarly, the reader is not an objective arbiter of the text, capable of determining the meaning. Instead, concentrating on language as discourse means attending not merely to the structural characteristics of language practice, but to social relationships and practices, to material conditions that historically and at present have been carried out in and through discursive practices, and to ideological structures, that inform the potential meanings of the text. "[D]iscursive practice implies a play of prescriptions that designate its exclusions and choices" (Foucault 1977, 199).

Neither writers nor readers, therefore, are free agents. Their ability to access language as well as to interpret a text corresponds to their situatedness within social and material contexts and to the understanding of self and world they bring to a given text. Our reaction to the essay "Queers, Bums & Magic," discussed by Richard E. Miller, is not adequately explained by claiming that we disagree with his choice of language, style, or form, or by asserting that the writer is simply wrong. Our reaction is determined not by the formal elements of the text, but by our unwillingness to sanction hateful and exclusive attitudes, or to condone the worldview presented and represented by his essay. As Brenda K. Marshall points out, "discourse itself furnishes the very criteria by which its results are judged successful" (1991, 99). The writer did not compose this piece in a vacuum or within an autonomous framework; instead he drew on myths and stereotypes available in the culture, he drew on dominant discourse about normative class and sexual behavior, just as we draw on our professional culture, our disciplinary discourse, to interpret and legitimize our response to his essay.

The discourse community Miller engaged, the audience at the CCCC panel, determines "Queers, Bums & Magic" to be "unsuccessful," as Miller puts it, because it is unacceptable vis-à-vis the sociopolitical context within which this audience is situated; our judgment that the piece is "unsuccessful" has little to do with the formal qualities of the text. After all, it is not simply his text we are struggling against or reacting to; rather it is the community, the discourse, the context that empowers this subject-position that leave us unsettled. The writer, we know, might certainly find an audience who, supplying a different context, would judge the piece to be acceptable and even successful. The discourses that shape production and reception are at play, as in the experience of Maria writing about rape. If we adhere to the notion that language is transparent and merely reflects an already existing reality, then we are helpless to critique this essay. After all, the writer, presumably, is reflecting his reality. A Foucauldian view, however, enables us to read this text as unacceptable and oppressive by separating the source of discourse from the writer. In this way, we can identify and analyze the social context that informs the act of producing and interpreting discourse, calling into question a central idea maintained by process theory: the writer is not the source of language, nor is the writer's task simply that of articulating what the world (through her experience, reading) has revealed to her. This allows us to take issue with the text, to actively and critically engage its truths, methods, and the writerly subject-position without simply blaming, excusing, or "confronting" the writer.

> Where tradition sees the source of discourses, the principle of their swarming abundance and of their continuity, in those figures which seem to play a positive role, e.g., those of the author, the discipline, the will to truth, we must rather recognize the negative action of a cutting-up and a rarefaction of discourse . . . . We must not imagine that there is a great unsaid or a great unthought which runs throughout the world and intertwines with all its forms and all its events, and which we would have to articulate or think at last . . . . We must not resolve all discourse into a play of pre-existing significations; we must not imagine that the world turns towards us a legible face which we would have only to decipher; the world is not the accomplice of our knowledge. (Foucault 1981, 67)

While process pedagogy locates truth and the production of texts as a one-way transaction between the writer and her language, Foucault brings language itself into the transaction. The language a writer chooses in order to tell a story, to construct a world, does not only reflect or describe, but also plays an active role in determining, in *producing* and not simply reproducing, that version of the story, that world. If we shift our focus from language to discourse, we can understand that writing, the act of using discourse, is not simply a means of conveying the world as we already know it to exist within ourselves; instead, discourse itself determines the world we construct, the world we come to know. As Giroux maintains, "Language has a social foundation and must be viewed as the site of struggle implicating the production of knowledge, values and identities. . . . [A]s a social phenomenon, language cannot be abstracted from the forces and conflicts of social history" (1992, 167).

If we define discourse as a construct of ideas that implies a system of beliefs, truths, and social identities, then we can no longer only move from the text inward, to the mind or subjectivity of the writer, toward the "heart of a thought or a signification supposed to be manifested" in language. We need, instead, to also direct our attention outwards, to the "external conditions of possibility, towards what gives rise to (discourse) . . . and fixes its limits" (Foucault 1981, 67). In other words, just as expressivism is misguided in suggesting that the power to claim authority lies *within* individual writers, it is further incorrect in suggesting that writers only look *inward* in order to find a source for the truths or knowledge represented by a text.

The writer of "Queers, Bums & Magic," for instance, was not simply presenting his internal belief that homosexuals are not fully human; he was not merely encoding an isolated, self-invented judgment in his text. If this were the case, if he were writing alone, independent of a like-minded contingency, we would not feel so threatened by his essay. Instead, the power of his piece rests in the fact that we respond to him as a spokesperson and to his essay as representative of a particular discourse community with which we do not align ourselves. The conditions that produce both power and discourse need also to be located socially, in the material world and the relationships by which this world is organized (both concrete, "real" and ideological, "imagined").

Reality and language exist in a mutual, two-way relationship. Expressivist pedagogy emphasizes only one direction—that reality (primarily internal as constructed through experience in a distinct external world) gives rise to language, to the need for expression. However, language may also be said to give rise to a particular vision of reality. As Brodkey suggests, poststructural theories of language argue that "words constitute world views, and hence that any attempts to describe reality are necessarily partial accounts, that is, limited by what can be seen and understood from a particular vantage point" (1989, 598).

One simple way of illustrating this point is to look at the way in which a word's meaning changes according to the context in which it is used: who speaks the word, to what audience is the word addressed. As Gloria Naylor writes,

> [A]mong the anecdotes of the triumphs and disappointments in the various workings of [my extended family's] lives, the word nigger was used in my presence, but it was set within contexts and inflections that caused it to register in my mind as something else . . . . So there must have been dozens of times that the word "nigger" was spoken in front of me before I reached the third grade. But I didn't "hear" it until it was said by a small pair of lips that had already learned it could be a way to humiliate me. (1986, Sec. C, p. 2)

Individual words, and essays or autobiographies, take on meaning within systems of belief and interpretation, indeed within multiple systems. The situatedness of the speaker and of the receiver (in this case, their physical bodies, the historical economic relations between black and white bodies, the contemporary material and social conditions of those bodies in a racist economy), and the context in which words are exchanged largely determine the meaning a word takes on as well as how power is distributed. Hence, when "nigger" was used without the intention to hurt, Naylor barely registered the word at all. Her family's use of the word neither implied nor exercised power over her. However, when a small boy uses the word, in an entirely different context, not only does the meaning (its historical and political significations) of the term shift, but the word now wounds, it becomes a tool of power for the boy, and a weapon of disempowerment for

Naylor. It is interesting to note that the boy uses the word immediately after learning Naylor has received a better grade. How
early we learn to use language, even a single word, as a de-equal-
izer, a mechanism by which to shift the dynamics of power at
hand.

One of the biggest challenges many of my students face in
my course every semester is coming to terms with the idea that
language does not tell reality, it determines a particular and situated reality. (And isn't this the problem we run into with grades,
with wanting to believe they represent a shared, objective reality,
or can/do serve as fair criteria for measuring performance and
competence.) They expect language to work according to a tangible, concrete system of rules and this is the way language has
always been presented to them, not as an object worthy of critical inquiry, but as the medium for engaging in inquiry—with not
only the process but the product of inquiry being entirely independent of, discernable from, the language through which it is
expressed or represented. Yet the distinction is profound and crucial. If we refuse to recognize discourse as the means by which
we come not only to express but also to create ourselves and our
relation to the world, we render ourselves powerless to revision
either the self we construct or its position in and perspective on
the world. Without recognizing that language actively "orders
reality," we are less capable of reenvisioning the reality we construct.

Two of the ongoing debates among my students center around
the words *nigger* and *girl*. Male students want to know *exactly*
when using the word *girl* is appropriate and acceptable; typically, they seek an age that serves as the absolute cut-off date.
Many of them have been stung by the vehement reactions of female friends whom they have "innocently" (and, I use quotation
marks to call attention to my sense that innocence, while a ready
excuse, is hardly a valid one in a society as hierarchically gendered
and sex-differentiated as ours) called girls. When females in the
class claim that their response to girl is dependent on the speaker
and the situation, this is not tangible enough. Similarly, white
students want to know why it is acceptable for African Americans to use the word *nigger* but not okay for whites to do so.
Attempting to understand that the meaning of these words is

determined by the speaker and the context (not only as uttered at a specific, present moment but as imbricated in a history of utterances and the material relations of power that inform them) is attempting to understand that discourse positions speakers differently and that words, neither absolute nor transparent, *inscribe* reality even as they *describe* it. As Naylor concludes, "building from the meanings of what we hear, we order reality. Words themselves are innocuous; it is the consensus that gives them power" (1986, C2).

The failure to acknowledge language's role in constituting our worldview leaves us incapable of changing our understanding of the world and eliminates our accountability. Brodkey writes:

> I so regularly encounter students and colleagues who presume that, with the notable exceptions of advertising and propaganda, a spoken or written text refers to a universal reality independent of language. By their logic, speakers or writers can argue that they bear no responsibility for the consequences of racist, sexist, or homophobic language since "nigger," "bitch," and "queer" simply refer to an already given reality that language only reflects. (1989, 598)

What we choose to call someone or something implies our relationship to, as well as our understanding and evaluation of, the subject or object of description. Obviously, encouraging students to quit using words such as *faggot* does not necessarily require that they critique and alter the attitudes, or the privilege and prejudice that led them to use the word in the first place. As Naylor observes, "If the word [nigger] was to disappear totally from the mouths of even the most liberal of white society, no one in that room was naive enough to believe it would disappear from white minds."

But, words *are* a starting point for the revisioning of ourselves and our relations and valuing. According to Giroux, language, in the dominant educational discourses, is "abstracted from its political and ideological usage . . . privileged as a medium for exchanging and presenting knowledge, and . . . abstracted from its constitutive role in the struggles of various groups over different meanings, practices and readings of the world" (1986, 57).

Therefore, making language itself an object of inquiry within our writing classes, explicitly interrogating it within a political and ideological context, might be a means of reenvisioning our relationship to discourse and to the world we construct in our texts. Of course, such a goal requires working through the resistance of those who are privileged by the concept of language as a transparent medium, and reality as an objective entity undetermined and uninfluenced by discourse. But the acknowledgment of resistance and the discussion of how and why we react differently to texts and words is a way of getting at the issue of how discourse and power are related.

As Foucault defines it, power is neither a thing nor an abstract concept; instead, power exists when exercised, and it implies a relationship, not merely a subject or agent. Thus, Power is defined in the context of its exercise and is a process of ongoing struggle, an action that resists closure. "Which is to say, of course, that something called Power, with or without a capital letter, which is assumed to exist universally in a concentrated or diffused form, does not exist. Power exists only when it is out into action" (Foucault 1982, 788). We might, then, envision our classes as serving not to empower individual writers, but as forums for recognizing and analyzing when we, as writers, readers, teachers, or students, exercise power, for making power (like language) a focus of study rather than simply a commodity to be produced and/or exchanged. When teachers claim their primary goal is to "empower my students" or to "empower my students as writers," I often wonder, why. Is the end, the final hope, to produce better writers? More powerful *students*? Empower them why and for what reasons?

One of the ways in which I attempt to encourage my students to consider the ways in which language implicitly advantages certain speakers over others is to ask them to offer a word for a white, heterosexual male that carries the same potentially painful, hateful, historically-laden and powerful, negative connotations of words such as *nigger, dyke,* etc. In six different classes, we have been unable to find such a word, illustrating Brodkey's suggestion that subject-positions, normative and deviant, are actively sustained and defined by discourse itself. Upon discussing the possible significance of this absence, of our inability to come up with such a word, many students insist it's a grand accident, a meaningless happenstance. Yet, as Brodkey also suggests, we should be prepared for resistance.

> Those who occupy the best subject-positions a discourse has to offer would have a vested interest in maintaining the illusion of speaking rather than being spoken by a discourse . . . . Hence, it is at least plausible to expect most, though not all, of those individuals whose subjectivity is most positively produced by a discourse to defend its practices against change. (1989, 126–27)

Obviously, this struggle over the concept and function of discourse is played out not only in our classrooms but also in our scholarship as well, demonstrating Foucault's contention that discourse itself is "not simply that which translates struggles or systems of domination, but it is the thing for which and by which there is struggle, discourse is the power to be seized." This idea directly challenges Elbow's claim that all students have equal access to power through writing. If discourse not only envisions subjects differently, but if discourse itself constitutes power, rather than simply conferring power, we must expect that students will experience the process of composing differently as a result of the role produced for them by the discourse they engage as well as by their historical experience of being empowered or disempowered by discourse itself.

Beyond envisioning language itself differently, therefore, a poststructural concept of discourse conceives of the role and function of the student-writer differently as well. As discussed earlier, process pedagogy posits the student-writer as the site of both discourse and power. The writer is a free agent, capable of expressing internal truths independent of their source in or implications for social reality. The idea of the writer as autonomous, an agent not only of language but of truth is characteristic of, but not original to, process pedagogy. Foucault traces this notion back to the great "Platonic division." Herzberg describes the shift in the rhetoric's function from the Sophists to Plato:

> [Sophist] discourse embodies and creates truth because the truth it speaks is social, a truth of persuasion, decision, political

power, justice and cultural cohesion . . . But after Plato, after philosophy defeated sophistry, truth is "displaced" from the social to the ideal. The proper role of discourse in Plato's scheme is to represent truth. The truth is to be found, not created. (1991, 70)

Recognizing language as active in determining or constructing "truth" thus means we must alter our concept of the writer who can no longer be the knower of some preexisting truth, but becomes, simultaneously, speaker of and spoken by the truths constructed by discourse. In other words, writers are not only subjects of discourse, but *subject to* discourse. According to Althusser, the term *subject* implies not only "a free subjectivity, a centre of initiatives, author of and responsible for its actions," but also a "subjected being, who submits to a higher authority" (1991, 169). In this instance, language itself (resulting from and representative of historical and material relationships) acts as the "higher authority." As Giroux maintains,

> It is within and through language that individuals in particular historical contexts shape values into particular practices. As part of the production of meaning, language represents a central force in the struggle for voice . . . . [L]anguage is able to shape the way various individuals and groups encode and thereby engage the world . . . . In this sense, language does more than merely present "information"; in actuality, it is used both to "instruct" and to produce subjectivities. (1986, 59)

Situating Pedagogies

Clearly, neither language nor experience necessarily conveys power. Some knowledge, rooted in experience, is determined by mainstream audiences to be inadmissible, unacceptable, or even subversive. If economic and social history have constructed one's self to be not only dependent on, but empowered or disempowered according to one's sexual or racial identity, how are all students expected to welcome assignments that demand self-exposure? Conceiving of power as equally accessible to all writers ignores the fact that not all knowledges/experiences are equally valued, much less permitted. We need a theory of student-writers that does not implicitly offer power only to those already well-situated by the discourse that prevails within and without our classrooms. Rather than understanding power to be located internally, and challenging students to claim their share, we (teachers and students) need to recognize that power is linked to discourse, to one's ability to speak a self publicly. Conceiving of a pedagogy based on this recognition is the focus of the following chapters. Just as the meaning of a word is dependent on the systems of interpretation that inform the context in which it is used, so is the power to be conferred on the speaker dependent on the context in which she speaks. As Foucault claims:

> Discourses are not once and for all subservient to power or raised up against it, any more than silences are. We must make allowances for the complex and unstable process whereby discourse can be both an instrument and an effect of power, but also a hindrance, a stumbling-block, a point of resistance and a starting point for an opposing strategy. Discourse transmits and produces power; it reinforces it, but it also undermines and exposes it. (1990, 100–101)

Reconceiving of student-writers not only as agents, but as subject to and subjects of discourse means explicitly considering in our classes how various discourses envision subjects differently, according them privilege or denying them permission to speak, or even to be, to exist. If we aim to offer all students an equal opportunity to speak a self, we have to reckon with the fact that the selves they have come to construct are not uniformly valued, much less granted authority to speak or to be accepted as legitimate. We must consciously address the ways in which our students enter our classes positioned differently, not only as writers but as agents, in order to move toward an understanding and critique of how power is exercised through the process of composing.

Rather than assuming that all narratives can or will be valued, we have to interrogate the ways in which social construction and discourse value our selves and our compositions differently. Two years ago, a student wrote an essay in which he attempted to persuade his readers that homosexuals make bad parents. He claimed this was a difficult essay for him to write as he believed his classmates would reject his conclusion and take issue with his supporting arguments. He perceived himself, within the class at least, to be outside the bounds of accepted discourse. On the other hand, a year ago, a student decided to write a narrative about coming out to her mother; this was a very difficult essay to write because she was aware that her homosexuality would impede her "authority" in the minds of certain peer readers. Her position vis-à-vis the dominant discourse, which posits a normative heterosexuality, creates a space in which she feels marginalized, but it also creates the momentum for resistance. Her situation illustrates the paradox Foucault describes: what begins as an act of resisting the marginalization and objectification imposed by a normative discourse, becomes not simply an act of refusal, of negating what or who one is not, but of an act of self-declaration, of positively asserting who one is. The normative discourse itself, the mechanism of exclusion, thus gives rise to the possibility for re-visioning and speaking a new norm:

> There is no question that the appearance in nineteenth century psychiatry, jurisprudence, and literature of a whole series of discourses on the species and subspecies of homosexuality . . . made possible a strong advance of social controls into this area of "perversity"; but it also made possible the formation of a "reverse" discourse: homosexuality began to speak in its own behalf, to demand that its legitimacy or "naturality" be acknowledged, often in the same vocabulary, using the same categories by which it was medically disqualified. (Foucault 1990, 101)

If the subjectivity produced by our relation to and position in various discourses is not seamless, but produces dissonance and discomfort, we might then use discourse itself as a means of reinventing subjectivity and the self imagined therein. As Chris Weedon describes, "Where there is a space between the position of subject offered by a discourse and individual interest, a resistance to that subject position is produced" (1987, 112). In writing, in the action of writing, this student was exercising power by complicating the accepted discourse on homosexuality. So, *writing* was an action, a means by which she felt capable of revisioning the predominant construction of herself, as a lesbian.

The act of writing, however, was preceded by an acknowledgment of the possible consequences of her essay's reception by the class. Her decision to write and her strategy of writing a self was complicated, not by her own sense of inadequacy as a writer, but by her understanding of her social and political situatedness. The act of constructing an alternative subjectivity allowed the student to move from being subject to dominant discourse, to being an agent of a recuperative discourse. Conceiving of power as exercised, as a relation, and as a "dynamic of control and lack of control between discourses and the subject constituted by discourses" (113) requires a more complicated understanding of the relationship between students-writers and their texts. We cannot simply determine that writing is empowering or disempowering. Instead, we need a more complex and fluid understanding of how power might be simultaneously elusive and available in a given act of composition.

It is worth considering for a moment that both of these students, one writing about her identity as a lesbian and the other writing against homosexual parents, were concerned about how they would be "read" by their classmates; their concern was not about their identity as writers, was not anxiety about being perceived as "good" or "bad" writers. Rather, they were aware that these essays would result in specific interpretations of and consequent behavior toward *them*, not their texts, not their writing. While his essay was not directly about his identity, his lifestyle, his understanding of his "self," he nonetheless worried that the essay would jeopardize his relationships to other students in the class. Unlike the student who came at the dominant discourse from a marginalized position of disempowerment, this student's position (antihomosexuals) is imagined positively by the dominant discourse. His interpretation and judgment of gay men and lesbians is sanctioned by the discourse he evokes, thus not requiring him to interrogate or demystify his own thought processes or evaluations. The student writing about her identity as a lesbian, in order to construct a positive, nondeviant self, claimed agency by deconstructing the dominant discourse. He claims agency by *assuming* the dominant discourse and does not work to explain or support his position so much as simply to describe and recount it.

When the student wrote his essay proclaiming that homo-sexuals make bad parents, I discussed with him my resistance to his premise and problematized his thesis by pointing out that the unspoken, but dominant, thesis seemed to be his own discomfort with homosexuality, rather than any evidence that gay men or lesbians have inherently inadequate parenting skills. One of his primary contentions with homosexual parents was their frequent display of affection in public, which he felt was damaging to their children. I asked him if heterosexuals were not just as often engaged in public gestures of love, caring, and sexual attraction. At first, he resisted this possibility, but later acknowledged it was not the frequency of such displays that provoked and disturbed him, but the fact that these exchanges took place between two people of the same sex. Next I asked him if two lesbians, raising a child together, who did not engage in such public moments of affection, would be better parents than two heterosexuals who did. Once the "reasons" he articulated in support of thesis were unpacked, it was clear that a reader needed to support the *un-spoken* logic that informed his reading of these examples as "rea-sons" in order to support his thesis. If one did not enter into his essay already believing homosexuality was wrong, or at least unnatural, one could not follow the logic of his text. The ideol-ogy that served to mask his real position, offering him the pro-tection of a preexisting justification, disguised, but did not erase or resolve, the contradictions of his text. He was offended more by homosexuals than by homosexuals as parents.

Being against a group of people on the basis of an experience with a few individuals, or on the basis of stereotypes, is wrong. Judging the behavior of individuals in a particular context (as parents) on the basis of their membership in a group entirely unrelated to that context, and relying on readily available and normative myths concerning group members to support your judgment is unacceptable in any sense of useful, critical intellec-tual work. I tell this story not because I "showed" him the light, but because I did not pursue my first inclination, which was sim-ply to refuse to accept the piece, or to lecture him about how useless, mean, and objectionable it was. Harsh words these are, but they represent how I felt at the time. His essay attempted to logically and "scientifically" prove that gays and lesbians make bad parents, a ridiculous claim on the surface (whether made by a student, a politician, a clergyperson, or a friend), made all the more frustrating by the attempt to use "examples" to indisputably prove his case. I found his text unethical, in Jay's terms of ethics being the name we might give to a person's *self-conscious* negotiation with cultural and economic determinism of normative social relations. The process by which his essay attempted to stake its claim, build its argument, and the product itself, demonstrated a lack of self-consciousness, self-reflexivity, and hence I call it unethical and unacceptable.

Were I in nearly any other profession, I would not have to simply accept it. Yet in the myth of the super-teacher, there is a built-in clause that we will, with equanimity and grace, tolerate all submissions, regardless of how contemptible we find them to be. Developing an idea through examples, using specifics to build toward the general, are common strategies in essay writing. So taking up the issue of his problematic, confusing use of examples, the illogic (not as defined by some static, external conception of "logic" but in terms of the essay not sustaining or building its own logic), which informed his text, was well within the purview of my authority as his writing teacher. Had he been writing an essay on how his experience on the basketball team gave him increased confidence and motivation, I might have had similar concerns with the writing if the examples he chose and the conclusions he drew from them seemed to have no correlation, or at least a correlation never made explicit by the text, but rather relied on a reader already sharing certain unspoken assumptions. In this instance, however, the writing *and* the perspective, the argument, were problematic to me. It is only because the conclusions were "wrong" that I might now face censure from my own peers for "judging" him, for "coercing" him.

I hardly see how, if we shift our perspective to include the multiple contexts in which he and I circulated, I could coerce him altogether. He had, after all, the "right" on his side; in any broader context, the notion of homosexuality as wrong, bad, is the normative discourse. To assume we can silence all students, to assume we can permanently damage all students by speaking up and speaking against their held opinions seems at once both an under- and over-estimation of the involved participants. Here is a useful example of both Jarratt's call for conflict and Ellsworth's call for situated pedagogy. To assume that all teachers hold the power to devastate and damage all students is to ignore the fact that individual, specific students and teachers are positioned differently, even in relation to the institution. As a young female graduate student teaching a required writing course, I was hardly looked on with the same fear or awe or reverence, as some of their older professors of a subject institutionally sanctioned as intellectual. As a white, heterosexual, economically privileged male, this student had no history of feeling systemically oppressed within or outside school situations.

Jay makes an important point in declaring the difference between responding to one whose position is privileged and responding to one whose position is subordinated. He does not claim we should unproblematically, out-of-hand, accept the conclusions of a woman in matters of sexism and gender because she is a female. But rather, when a student's discourse occupies the privileged position vis-à-vis the regulatory discourses of state and institutional agencies, we might more comfortably and rigorously push them to account for their positions.

I tell this story because I feel it was a successful decision on my part to engage him in a discussion of the piece. While wanting to ignore or reject it, instead I took it up with him and we did engage in a discussion. I had to clearly separate my response to the piece from my grading him for the course, but that did not seem to be a central concern for either of us. I work hard, and I think successfully, to establish a working space in which students can write about what they choose, knowing that I will react to it and that I will try, with negotiation and discussion, to sort through reactions as a teacher, with institutional power, and as a situated reader. When I told him I wanted to talk about the piece, address my responses as a reader and as his writing teacher, he was neither surprised nor hesitant. He felt nervous and awkward, but then, so did I. During our discussion, he told me his roommate had read the essay and advised him not to turn it in. "Your teacher'll fail you," he said. The student spoke of the "pc" climate at our university and how this piece was important to him, something he had long wanted to say, and that he believed in this class, he could write what he thought and felt. I find it worth noting that, while he chose to turn it in to me, he also elected not to publish it in the class magazine. He worried his peers would be more censuring, harsher in their judgment of *him*, than I would be of his text. Because all final essays are required to be published, made public, unless the students have specific reasons for choosing not to do so, he turned the piece in late, thereby missing the publication deadline. Given the decision of Maria to publish the reflective narrative about having been raped, the decision of the student to make public her process of coming-out, given the potential consequences of these decisions to make their writing public, I have trouble understanding exactly what consequences this student so feared. He said he "believed in" this essay, in its positions and ideas. Why then the overwhelming fear of exposure? Given their decisions, I have trouble respecting his decision to hide.

> In the classroom, the authority of one person's experiences quickly runs up against that of someone else, so that the limits of such authority may be usefully marked and analyzed. Clashes of cultural identity do not always yield to a happy pluralism, however, or a cheerful tolerance. On the contrary, the differences between cultural groups are often fundamental, sometimes deadly, and are better brought out into the open than repressed . . . (Jay 1994, 620–21)

At any rate, this story, on first telling, reads like a successful example of the critical pedagogue leading her student to the truth, the light. It is not such a story. It is a story of my own learning that the super-teacher clause serves only to silence and constrain teachers (perhaps so they might continue to be "liked" by their students. So they are sure never to cross the line into intimidation and coercion). And further, that formulaic, highly structured peer response might serve not only to "protect" the writer (or to provide him with license to write, unchallenged, anything he deems powerful), but to silence readers while asking them to politely "respond" to material they might find violent, hostile, or otherwise unacceptable. I cannot sacrifice engaged response for adoration and safety. In talking with this student, our discussion was heated on both sides; it was also long and frustrating. I did not leave feeling, "Ah! I have won, changed his mind and led him aright." I left wondering if it was even worth it to have engaged. And I mostly felt uncertain about whether or not I wanted a job in which, when confronted with raw anger and the abasement of human life, I had to contend with whether or not it was "okay" to respond, to voice my objections.

The point is that there are many issues operative in this exchange and in my representation of it. It is not just a happy story. When a reader of this manuscript perceived this exchange, in its original form, as an example of teachers coercing students, using their institutional authority to sway students, at least for the moment, to the teacher's sense of right, I was frustrated—not so much at his or her reading, but by my inability to represent this moment in its full complexity. I did initially choose this example because I wanted a moment of some movement, but the movement was not only his. I came to realize in this exchange and subsequent reflection that it was fundamental to my project to create a classroom climate where such differences, between students or between student and teacher, could be taken up and discussed, need not be repressed or glossed over for fear of abuse of power. A question I had long had about peer reviews was what was at stake in asking readers to respond to a text as a piece of writing, for stylistic matters, for composition. What must a reader give up, silence, if she is not allowed or given space to *respond* to the ideas, perspective and conclusions of the text, and not only to the supposedly distinguishable formal qualities of the composition.

While our discussion did not result in his proclaiming himself rid of his discomfort with and fear of homosexuality, it did lead to his having to confront the fact that other reasonable positions exist, and that his own position is not as easily justified or inevitable, not as "natural," as he had previously imagined. The second paper he wrote for College Writing (for which I was not his teacher), after finishing my Basic Writing course, was an analysis of how particular negative images of homosexuals and homosexuality are produced and distributed by television shows and advertisements. At the center of this essay was an attempt to consider the formation of his own homophobia as determined and shaped by television. While he was still grappling with the issue and not ready to fully disclose or acknowledge his own complicity, I interpret his move as significant progress. Using writing as a means of revisioning his relationship to a social world and to the bodies that coinhabit that world, he was cognizant of not only his agency, but also his subjection to predominant discursive and social norms and relationships. As Jay suggests, it is only the beginning of what will hopefully, but not assuredly, be an ongoing process.

> While a first step towards ethical intersubjectivity may be to recognize and respect someone else's difference from me, that realization still tends to leave me in the privileged position: I have the luxury of deciding to be tolerant and liberal. The structure of superiority is left intact. The sense of my own settled and unquestioned self is also left intact, while all the otherness is projected onto someone else. . . . The next step, then, and it is an ethical as well as a political step, is to see my own subjectivity from the Other's point of view. . . it is vital to undertake a defamiliarization of one's own cultural identity and the way one has taken it personally. The exploration of otherness and cultural identity should achieve a sense of my own strangeness, my own otherness, and the history of how my assumed mode of being came into existence. I could have been someone other than I think I am. (1994, 626–27)

Thus, to return to R. Miller's question about how we might contend with hateful, divisive discourse in our classrooms, we might do well to acknowledge and engage such compositions when we encounter them, rather than to simply silence or condemn them.[4] By critique, I do not imply we should inform the writer that she is "wrong" because she is racist/homophobic/sexist. Instead, by *critiquing* (which requires *engagement*, not simply dismissal) the claims and the mysterious ways in which the contradictions embedded in these claims are made invisible, seamless, we begin to pressure writers to become more responsible for the discourse they use, and for the material and social relations embedded in and represented by that discourse, for working through—or at least recognizing—how much what is *not said* informs what is said. We might then push ourselves and our students to consider and come forth with what is not said. In responding to the student's paper about homosexuals as parents, I took up how his essay failed to make sense, how its logic broke down, how its examples and conclusions were not clearly related to one another. Because his conclusions relied on what *he already knew* to be "true," what he already knew to make sense, his essay was not making explicit this knowledge, but building out of it. So we took up what he knew to be true, and how it conflicted with what I know to be true.

It is precisely because poststructuralism locates power and subjectivity in discourse that the revisioning of selves and our relation to the world is possible. Rather than understanding the self as a fixed, unified, internal essence, poststructural theory posits subjectivity as produced by discourse (which is, always, informed by the material conditions we inhabit and the ideology produced to sustain an economic and social hierarchy of limited access and exclusion) and therefore capable of being re-produced. Rather than being in possession of a consciousness that we need only articulate, poststructural theory envisions individuals as active in constructing our consciousness in the very effort to represent it with language. A critical writing classroom, therefore, focuses not on enabling students to more freely and confidently write the world they already know or to more convincingly and firmly express a vision of "self." Instead, a critical class encourages students to "develop their power to perceive critically *the way they exist* in the world *with which* and *in which* they find themselves; they come to see the world not as a static reality, but as a reality in process, in transformation . . . [and affirms] men and women as being in the process of *becoming*" (Freire 1970, 70–71).

Concentrating not only on the revision of texts, but on the revisioning of one's "self" as produced by discourse, and considering the construction not only of an essay, but of a self and a worldview as *in process* and as *part of* the process of composing are central concerns of the critical composition class. To advocate a critical composition pedagogy is not to reject the idea that students' texts should be the central focus of the class; nor is it to dismiss the emphasis on personal narratives, on writing about experiences and one's history. The *point* of focusing on this, the purpose in doing so, and the questions asked—that is what changes. In the final chapters, I will consider more specifically how my writing courses attempt to foster revisioning processes of writing, reading, and teaching as critical and cultural work. In

Chapter 6, I focus on particular assignments and strategies for engaging and enacting the principles and ideas I have thus far been developing. In Chapter 7, I reflect on classroom moments as texts, reading them in light of the pedagogical discourse I have been elaborating throughout the text. *And*, re-reading that discourse in light of these texts.

Notes

1. See also Mimi Orner, "Interrupting the Call . . ." in *Feminisms and Critical Pedagogy*; bell hooks, *Teaching to Transgress*.

2. Chapters 6 and 7 present a more elaborated and closer examination of Paul's textual and social position in the writing class. I evoke him here as a writer/actor who entered positioned differently from Beth Anne (both discursively and socially) who also found the course provided a chance to engage in revisioning. For a more detailed description of Paul, see the section entitled "Considerations and Constructions of Students as Agents and Subjects" in Chapter 6.

3. This recuperative poststructuralism is informed by the work of hooks, Hutcheon, Mouffe, Radhakrishnan, Weedon, Gore, Luke, Gramsci, Lather, Carby, Gates, Ellsworth, Orner, and the later work of Foucault.

4. Certainly, the very encounter with such an essay (and its author) will depend upon our subject-position vis-à-vis the attitudes, ideas, and judgments presented in the piece, and on whether we are targets or subjects of the essay. A friend of mine who also teaches writing is African American and, while she does challenge and engage those essays which advocate the acceptance and legitimacy of racial prejudice and division, it takes more energy and consideration for her to respond. She knows that, ultimately, the student might write off her comments as "personal" and therefore discredit any authority she has as a teacher to push them toward self-critique. Her own subject-position in a racialized society might work to negate her credibility, or even her "right" to speak in the mind of a writer already inclined to see her as Other. Again, rather than prescribing a universal response to this category of writing, I want to call attention to the fact that the risks and rewards of a particular strategy depend upon the variables at play in a given situation: our decisions and options are context bound—who is this particular writer, this teacher, their relationship, the classroom dynamics? Nonetheless, simply ignoring or silencing such writing seems to me a futile attempt to make it "go away," while doing little to initiate substantive revision or critique.

Composing (as) a
Critical Process

Composition scholarship in the past decade has focused on how feminist, poststructural, and critical pedagogies change our understanding of our work as writing teachers. There are fewer discussions that focus on what it might *look like* to teach writing as a critical process. In light of these theoretical frameworks, shouldn't we not only reconceptualize our work but also go about it differently somehow? Can we rely on the same instructional methods but deploy them toward a different pedagogical vision? Can we reject expressivist philosophy, but recuperate process techniques? When Linda Brodkey argues

> that politics figure into literacy seems to me obvious. That we can ignore them in principle, on whatever grounds, in theory and research and practice, does not mean that we have rid ourselves of politics, but means instead that they operate covertly rather than overtly. . . . To think of literacy in terms of discursive practice means to consider the political as well as the cognitive and cultural dimensions of literacy in theory, research, and pedagogy. (1992, 295)

My response is, "yes, of course." But what kind of effect should this knowledge have on my teaching? It surely affects my understanding of my work in the writing classroom, but how does it change what we do there, how do we go about the work of writing and reading one another's texts differently? As Susan Jarratt compellingly points out, individual teachers have surely found strategies for deploying process-oriented strategies without reproducing the negative effects of expressivist pedagogy. But I share her concern that we need public representations and discussions of these redeployment strategies; such work cannot remain behind closed doors, taking place in the private sphere of our classrooms. As Jarratt suggests, "Despite the efficacy of intuitive responses, . . . we need more, especially in the area of teacher training. We need a *theory and a practice* more adequately attuned . . . to the social complexities of our classrooms and the political exigencies of our country at this historical moment" (1991, 111, my emphasis). How might critical pedagogy—a conceptual framework that makes visible how issues of difference affect the process of writing, inform the textual product and its reception, and are played out in the classroom—influence how I go about the teaching of writing?

Articulating Critical Processes

My writing courses are organized around two goals that I conceive of as mutually determining and enabling. First, the courses aim for students to generate words, ideas, and confidence as writers who conceive of writing/composing as a process in which they can and must *act*, that is, intervene. Second, the courses work to initiate a sense of language as discourse, of language as not only a *mode* of inquiry but also as an *object* worthy of inquiry. Thus, I not only expect texts to be composed but I also expect for those texts to be interrogated with special attention to the role language plays in the self we compose with its attendant conceptions, values, and beliefs. Such an interrogation seeks to convey that we are not only written by (Taylor or Beth Anne) but simultaneously writing of one another (Paul). A conception of texts *as* composed (rather than as emerging mystically in a moment of inspiration or as unfolding randomly), of selves and others as written, entails an accompanying recognition of the choices we make when writing, when taking a stand, when "coming to voice." Students should become increasingly able not only to acknowledge and articulate these choices but also to justify and account for the choices they make.

The course, then, aims for writers to expose, reflect on, and critique the workings of texts (their own and others'), based on the assumption that these processes might result in revision. Revisioning is defined not necessarily as *changing* one's mind, but recognizing that one's mind is made up along an array of choices and *why* it is made up this way. Revisioning also implies a recognition that others will occupy different spaces on the spectrum and that our location is not a matter of free-choice or arbitrary placement, but the result of discursive, political, socioeconomic structures informed by and informing of experiential knowledge.

While process pedagogy seeks to offer various strategies by which writers might actively intervene in the composing *process*, the end result—the *product* and its reception—remain ignored.

> In our concern with the making of texts as opposed to their consumption . . .we are going to remain inescapably allied to the old nuts-and-bolts discourses of composition. Or we might, alternatively, achieve a new understanding of production itself as a deeply problematic undertaking. . . . We make texts, Genette tells us, through hermeneutical struggle—through appropriations, resistances, alliances, subversions, outright mutinies. . . . But after the fact, in keeping with the oldest convention of them all, we dignify our uncertainty with the name of order . . . (Spellmeyer 1994, 92–93)

A critically oriented composition class is structured around enabling participation not only in the processes of composing (selves and texts), but in foregrounding the means by which we might control—and are denied control—over the product. The class presents identity and texts as processes that result in specific, motivated products for which individuals need to be accountable if they hope to claim authority. Further, the course seeks to consider how contexts determine individual experience and the ways in which identity might be rooted in the denial or foregrounding of that context.

> My hopes are pinned on composition courses whose instructors help their students to locate personal experiences in historical and social contexts—courses that lead students to see how differences emerging from their texts and discussions have more to do with those contexts than they do with an essential and unarguable individuality. I envision a composition course in which students argue about the ethical implications of discourses on a wide range of subjects and, in so doing, come to

identify their personal interests with others, understand those interests as implicated in a larger communal setting, and advance them in a public voice. (Jarratt 1991, 121)

Various tools enable the enacting of these processes. In this chapter, I would like to consider the primary tools by which I attempt to engage students in a critical self-inventory of the sort identified by Gramsci at the start of this book, a self-inventory grounded in an awareness that the "self" we represent is shaped, constrained, and enabled by discourse. First, several readings and writings foreground a conception of the self *as* constructed, seeking to help students consider the ways in which language determines this construction. Second, through peer critique, self-assessments and publication, the course provides moments for self-reflexivity on the process of writing, and on the process of composing oneself and others in writing. Before examining specific assignments and exercises, I would like to consider the role of conflict or dissonance in the writing course as the microlevel assignments are informed by a macro belief in the necessity for students and teachers to wrangle, contend, confront, and consider opposition in order for substantive revision to be possible.

Conflicts, Collaborations, and Contact Zones

Typically, an opposition is set up between a combative classroom and a nurturing one, between teachers concerned to create a "safe" space or community and teachers who aim to generate conflict. In practice, however, such an opposition collapses. How can *generative* conflict (that is, not only asking students to *air* opposing viewpoints also but to *listen* to and *engage* them) exist without some degree of groupness? How could we contain conflict in a room of twenty plus individuals "reading" and responding to one another, or ensure community is possible, much less attainable in such a room? If we interpret "contact" as implying both collision and collaboration, Pratt's image of the "contact zone" allows for a more fluid and context-determined conception of the classroom.

By conceiving of the classroom as a zone of contact, we allow for a range of interactions rather than having to choose one form *over* another, or having to prescribe, outside the context of a specific classroom, *the* appropriate atmosphere. Further, the metaphor of contact allows for a recognition not only of opposition but also of alignment. As Brodkey notes, a critical class needs to allow for the "*cooperative* articulation on the part of students *and* teachers who actively seek to construct and understand differences *as well as* similarities between their respective subject positions" (1989, 140, my emphasis).

Min-Zhan Lu points to the impossibility of preventing conflict from informing *any* writing class, regardless of its pedagogical orientation, whether we choose to allow it to manifest itself. As reflected in students' sense that some predetermined and universal genre exist that constitutes what Josh, in Chapter 7, refers to as "college writing" or Paul identifies as "*the* formula," student writers often perceive their task as one of inserting their ideas into some pre-existing shape, regardless of whether this shape accommodates or constrains their ideas. As a result, Lu suggests, the process of writing is already an *unsettling* one: writers "write at a site of conflict rather than comfortably inside or outside the academy. . . . Learning a new discourse has an effect on the re-forming of individual consciousness . . . [which is] necessarily heterogeneous, contradictory, and in process" (488, 489). Given a recognition that the act of composing might be experienced more as a decomposing, we can call attention to this unsettling, rather than emphasizing coherence and unity. Further, foregrounding the conflict that arises as a result of trying to "insert" oneself into a preexisting form might allow the purposeful invention of new forms and a consideration of the limits of standard academic essay conventions. As Brodkey notes, revisioning our sense of the acceptable *form*s of composition entails reflection on the principles and priorities that inform our conventions:

> What is radical about the syllabus for Writing about Difference is not the topic but the view that rhetorical principles are historically and culturally contingent; hence our insistence that students cannot be taught to write independently of the con-

tent and context of writing. This principle, and the scholarship on which it rests, challenges the various instrumental approaches to instruction that have dominated writing pedagogy in this country from the outset. (1994, 252)

When Karen F. sought to write "Reflections," an essay in which she reflects on her initial awareness that she was inscribed, as a black female, in specific and motivated ways by the dominant culture, she also wanted to consider her recognition that no one, regardless of the position ascribed to them, is innocent of prejudice or capable of resisting the tendency to construct others in ways that place one's self *above*.[1] However, she experienced difficulty in attempting to link these ideas *in* written form. While the notions of simultaneously being inscribed *as other* and acting to *inscribe* others were intricately connected in her thinking, she had trouble conveying this connection clearly in writing. The process of writing the first draft, then, made this connection evident to her intellectually, but her felt pressure to shape these connections into a conventional, or as Karen described it "acceptable," form did not enable her to convey it rhetorically.

When we discussed this difficulty, Karen kept articulating her sense that she wasn't "really writing an essay." When I asked why, she claimed she could not fit her ideas into paragraphs that led from one to another, could not introduce everything together, because "no idea will even make sense without me first developing the idea before it." We discussed the possibility of writing in a form other than what she considered to be "the" acceptable version of an academic essay. We further discussed the political implications of prescribing a form that prevents a writer from articulating the complexity of her thoughts in favor of presenting a "composed" and linear text.[2] In the end, Karen opted for a form that allowed her to convey the complexity of her experience and reflection without simplifying them and also without losing the reader. Rather than construct a single introduction, with a unified body and a conclusion (her definition of the academic genre), Karen chose to divide her essay into three discrete sections, each of which opens with a single, italicized line that serves as both an organizing idea and a point of transition from one section to the next. Each of the three sections presents reflections on her various stages of "awakening" to the issue and practice of prejudice—first, her awareness of images intended to dehumanize members of particular groups; second, her first memory of experiencing prejudice in her own life, which leads her to consider how she has acted to perpetuate images of others and how she is struggling with her own prejudice; third, she considers the origins and sustaining conditions of prejudice in its various forms, concluding with her firm belief that "what goes around, comes around" (much like her essay). When her essay appeared in the publication, it was the clear favorite of the class—as much for its form as its content. One student asked Karen if she had been worried about not writing "the way you are supposed to," which led to a discussion about just what it is we are supposed to do when we write in school.[3]

Karen's struggle and success in creating a form were generated from her initial sense of a conflict between what she wanted to convey, what she'd realized through her writing of the first draft when she felt unencumbered by concerns of form, and how she felt compelled to say it, to contort those ideas into a certain shape. In the end, as she notes in the self-evaluation that accompanied her essay, wrestling with this conflict, rather than simply ignoring it or giving in to it, allowed for a more "difficult but provoking process:"

> *Excerpt from Karen Foster's Self-Assessment for Reflections:*
> This essay was a lot harder to write than the last one where I could just write and didn't have to think as much. This essay required more than just writing. There was a long, thought-provoking process before I could even jot down ideas and then again (!) after I had the ideas. Don't get me wrong, I liked it. It prompted me to a lot more thinking externally, about HOW to write. I'm not sure if my ideas are explained clearly yet, but I liked thinking AND writing controversially.

Conflict, either during the process of writing an essay or in discussions, peer critiques and general classroom dynamics is inevitable in any classroom. It is not always productive, but the aim of a critical classroom is to make space for generative conflict within individual processes and the larger group interactions. Distinguishing between destructive modes of argument (those that silence, dominate, violate) and productive modes is an ongoing negotiation but one that seeks to expose differences in order to enable students and teachers to consider their situatedness as writers and as thinkers. Brodkey usefully distinguishes between argument as *advocacy* and argument as *inquiry*, presenting the latter as a potential device for promoting a sense that *all* members of a classroom have a stake not only in their own position, but in at least recognizing and considering the positions of others.

> Argument as inquiry rather than advocacy makes it possible for teachers to institutionalize difference, or other politically sensitive issues, as a topic, since this view of argumentation values, and so sets out to teach students to value, informed opinions over personal opinions or even received opinions. . . . A rhetoric based on poststructural lines would . . . redefine the rights and responsibilities of students and teachers alike. Teachers would have the right to interrogate the contents of assertions students make about social reality, a right they derive from taking the responsibility for teaching students to distinguish between personal opinions and informed opinions. Students would then have a right to dissent from the realities posed in their classes, a right they would derive from taking responsibility for learning to distinguish between asserting a claim and laying out an argument in support of it. (1994, 241)

Generating productive conflict, moving toward argument as inquiry, is essential to a critical classroom. When Andalib (a former student) came to our class to interview us for a video project on racism and racial tension at our university, we invited anyone interested in and willing to discuss the topic to come to the table. Fifteen out of twenty students chose to participate; of the five who did not, four were white and one was Latino. Twenty percent of the white students and ninety percent of the students of color opted to participate. Before we began the discussion, I noted this disproportionate discrepancy and asked whether it signified anything. Charles, who had chosen to remain at his computer, said, "Yeah, it means you all think I'm a racist now." Fred said he did not assume that, but he found it noteworthy that the white students obviously perceived they *had* a choice about whether to be interested in or affected by race relations, whereas the students of color obviously did not. Another white student claimed he did not want to participate because he was "tired of being accused of creating problems just because I am white. White people aren't allowed to say anything about [racism]." "Aren't allowed according to whom?" I asked. Another non-participant claimed that every discussion of racism in his dorm and in his classes ended up as a lecture—not a discussion—whose purpose was to blame whites.

Clearly, the white students' bitterness results in part from an unwillingness to confront their own complicity in structures and relations of racism. However, their bitterness also results from a sense that this topic, in and of itself, is associated with experiences when they have been invited to participate only to be silenced and accused. While accusations may indeed be appropriate, how can we assign accountability in ways students might actually and reflectively consider and not simply recoil from, in ways that expect and rely not only on their listening (instead of recoiling) but on their actively participating?[4] I am not suggesting we should make discussions of racism comfortable or palatable. I am suggesting, though, that it seems to counter our purpose if we fail to find ways to engage white people in recognizing and contending with their complicity in racist relations, if we fail to find ways of moving beyond individual denials of racism to a consideration of the collective accountability of white people in relation to issues of racism and privilege. As Angela Davis insisted in an address she gave at the University of Massachusetts, rape won't stop until men stop raping. She went on to exhort her audience to find ways of engaging men in acknowledging their collective responsibility for ending rape. To do so successfully, we need to foster discussions that are not accusatory, hostile, or one-directional. Instead, we need to foster collective exchange that assumes that men and women are situated differently in relation to the act, the issue, and the myth of rape. If the goal is to act against racism and to foster antiracist, interracial relations, then we need to create the conditions that allow for critical interchanges while refusing to accept denial, silence, and detachment.

Pat, Fred, and I noted the tendency of white students to simply deny their individual responsibility for racism even if they were willing to acknowledge the existence of racism in our culture and classrooms. As Fred pointed out, he does not have a choice about whether to experience racist comments and discriminating actions; he can choose to remain silent, but he is nonetheless affected. Why, then, do white students get to simply deny their racism when he has no choice about whether to receive it? Jason explained that he struggles hard not to be racist and to "unlearn what I've learned." "So if someone calls me a racist, it's like I have to start all over and I haven't ever made any progress." I pointed out that we might need to perceive antiracist efforts as not finite or finish-able, but rather as an ongoing and lifelong struggle. Why are we so invested in not being *called* a racist and less concerned to do the work of intervening in racism? I asked whether they felt silenced by the accusations regardless of who made them; that is, if the accuser is white or black or Latino, does it make a difference in how they respond? As it turns out, the white students had only been accused by other white people, which we discussed as an indicator of the lack of dialogue going on among groups on campus.

I asked everyone present whether it was fair to say that no one person necessarily had the final word on what absolutely was or was not racist, regardless of the person's race. In other words, as a woman, I am not authorized to determine absolutely whether certain ideas or attitudes are always sexist *because* I am female. I do not represent womanhood, nor am I free of internalized sexist norms and myths. However, as a woman, I feel I have a right to claim that my experiential knowledge grants me authority that men do not have—not authority to be always "right," but my different situatedness grants me the right of a specific kind of relation to and authority on issues of misogyny and sexism. We discussed this for a while; and most of the students of color felt that if they *were* listened to by whites, they would be willing to acknowledge that this *might* be true. The white students had never thought about being able to *negotiate* such issues because they have never experienced what they considered to be a real discussion about them. Usually, the accusers were people (usually white people) in positions of power over them (dorm leaders or teachers or orientation counselors), and they did not feel they were really being invited to *respond,* but simply to *receive.* All the white students claimed to have learned more about racism by reading their peers' writing in this course because, as Jason said, "then you're alone and can think over what is being said. Also, reading their individual experiences blows away my preconceptions. Seeing it from their perspective changes mine." Fred asked if he thought this was because reading the essays, interacting with the writers in class "makes us human, gave us a face so we aren't objects to you anymore."

All the students commented on the use of small-group work in our class, which required them not simply to gather but also to accomplish thought-requiring tasks together. Several students reported dropping classes in which they were the only students of color because of their sense of alienation both socially and intellectually. Small-group work in classes, they noted, often puts students together without requiring that they *really* interact. As a result, those students who dropped courses felt even more alone in small groups. One of the white students commented that he had never considered what it must "feel like" to be in the minority. Dionne pointed out that he *was* a minority in our class. His response was that, on the first day, being in the minority excited rather than scared him, as he came to college expecting to learn more about other cultures, experiences, and perspectives. He was disappointed to discover that the campus was fairly segregated racially in his classes as well as in his dorm. Empowered as a white male outside of the classroom, he had no reason to feel threatened by his status as a minority in the classroom. Jason recalled his response upon reading the following passage from the conclusion of Fred's second essay:

> The way stereotypes affect me is that, when I walk by white people, I don't notice them anymore. They are like ghosts to me who are living in a different world. I try hard to change this attitude because I am a Christian but I get disappointed too many times, so I tend to give up. . . . I don't know if my kids will ever see a world where everybody is considered the same, but I'll keep praying for that. . . . To all you white people, I don't hate you or envy you. I just wish that you could see us people of color from a different point of view. Until then, I will never trust you. (Excerpt from Frederic March's untitled second essay)

Until then, Jason said, he had been angry that minority groups opposed being stereotyped and yet seemed to stereotype majority groups (his examples were feminists claiming "all men" were sexist or "bad" and African Americans naming "all" whites as racists and hateful). Upon reading Fred's essay, however—detailing what Fred said seemed like "harmless" incidents of prejudice (because they didn't entail physical violence or danger), but which angered, hurt, frustrated, and denied opportunities to him—Jason understood the reason for the mistrust. He was moved by Fred's effort to change his own attitude despite his perception that white people were unlikely to change theirs. To him, it "made sense" for Fred not to trust whites, whereas, as Fred's essay sought to demonstrate, it did not make sense for the white people whose behavior and attitudes he described to mistrust him.

The discussion went on for over an hour, and what emerged most clearly was the need for other such discussions and interactions to take place that allow for substantive and reflective conversations. As we all agreed, little progress will be made (unless revolutionary and armed struggle takes place) without interchanges *between* students of different races. Just as sexism, misogyny, and the exploitation of and violence against women will not end until men become involved in the struggle, racism will remain effectively entrenched without a cooperative and collaborative struggle that, while privileging the experience and voices of people of color, invites the participation and reflection of all people. Further, we concurred that white students need to be willing to acknowledge that they *are* privileged economically and socially by virtue of their whiteness, rather than to simply deny their individual accountability for racism. This discussion points to the importance of finding ways to articulate difference and engage in conflict that, without guaranteeing the legitimacy of every perspective, will allow for the *consideration* and evaluation of all perspectives.

When Andalib asked why such a discussion was able to happen among this group, all of the students pointed to peer critiques, regular class discussions, and the reading of one another's essays as enabling the discussion we had about racism. As Fred said, "Because of all the work and because the work forces us to help one another, we have the sense we are in it (the class) *to-*

gether." Fred's comment conveys his sense that collaboration needs to inform the classroom.

While conflict is inevitable (don't forget the students who chose not to join our discussion and the confrontation which resulted) and also potentially productive, a sense of negotiated community, with moments of laughter and informal communication, is also necessary. During the Interchange sessions, several students claimed the importance of balancing arguments, critique, and work with taking pleasure in their sense of a shared project as crucial to creating the conditions for collaboration and exchange. They connect these factors explicitly to their willingness to engage in critique, as well as their level of commitment to writing. As students became more invested in participating in the class relations, they also became more active as writers.

Karen S.: I remember feeling able to freely share my views in the class. A lot of times those views were attacked, but that is the point of learning. . . . Because we weren't judged on whether the instructor agreed with our views I never felt limited on a topic or afraid to say what I was really feeling. I also remember having a lot of fun in this class. We did a lot of work, but time in class always made me laugh. Learning comes easier in a relaxed environment. . . . Liveliness, the interaction our group had with one another. We did fight a lot during discussion, but we (most of us) always had fun in the class. When you gave us time to work on our writing, we spent a lot of time just talking and sharing ideas. We also spent a lot of time talking about what was going on in our lives, considering that most of us were freshman and were still a little confused by UMASS. Everything we talked about was relevant, whether to our lives, our writing techniques, etc.

Andalib: It's interesting, this connection or love for expressing my thoughts and feelings really increased after taking this class. Amy valued a continuous dialogue whether it was our circle time at the beginning of class or whenever we met [in small groups] to share something, and this infused me with a drive to write more and a greater interest in how people write and look at writing. And we discussed a lot the students' responsibility in the writing and learning process and . . . I realized how important knowing other students' views is to me. I needed live interaction [because] I think of myself as an anxious social writer—there was the purpose of expressing ideas and thoughts about life to others. What came about then was a balance between liking writing and a need to express an idea or message of importance to others. . . . It's true that there have been points when I have had to write and hated [doing] it. Those are the moments when I am not able to express what I really think and be honest in a paper.

Kafui: I know I value writing more because I now take pleasure in writing.

Karen F. : I value writing a lot. I always have. But [this class] has taught me that writing is not necessarily a task, it can be fun.

Josh: Another aspect of the class that I found very helpful and separated [it] from other classes is the ability to force students to work together in an environment that is friendly but yet critical. In other classes we may have to work in groups but we are never actually being critical, we just work together. In "our" [groups], I learned a great deal about myself and others. It was in these instances that I could learn to be critical of myself and others . . . to be critical *and* helpful.

Their emphasis on the importance of having a sense of groupness refutes the tendency to consider the critical classroom as a space limited to adversarial communication. At a job interview with a critically oriented composition program, I was asked how, as a critical educator, I kept "useless talk" out of the classroom. Confused, I asked what constituted "useless talk," and upon learning that the definition was "chitchat, non-critical conversation," I was at a loss. I explained I did not perceive such talk to be "useless" as it facilitates the development of networks within the class, if not among the larger group. Such networks seem important if we expect students to expose and critique substantive issues and representations of experiences, whether in their writings, peer critiques, or class discussions. The questioner claimed such a perspective put me in the "nurturing" camp and was inappropriate in a critical classroom. As a result, I questioned whether I was really more of a "nurturer" than I was willing to admit, or if I was too "soft" because I had not ever really considered the presence of such talk in my classroom. This example speaks to our (my) tendency to posit our choices as oppositional: *either* our classrooms are nurturing and therefore noncritical *or* they are critical and therefore not nurturing. Again, we need to recognize that a range of choices exists; and, while these choices might appear mutually exclusive in theory, as practices they serve the context of a class.

Shor and Freire (1987) repeatedly move to demonstrate that a critical classroom, particularly one organized around dialogue, is "rigorous." Presumably, they are responding to allegations that dialogic critical pedagogy is "soft," "easy." Rather than unproblematically assume rigor is an essential pedagogical quality, we should denaturalize the concept, work to define it *qualitatively* instead of proving our legitimacy by asserting *quantitative* rigor, as in claiming one's pedagogy is rigorous enough. The term is deployed as though it names a required condition for learning and teaching, and yet it is an unrooted signifier. What does it mean to be "rigorous"? Are we rigorous if we demand a lot of work—again a quantitative measure—and in relation to what standards? Is it proven by "tough" grading—and again, in relation to what or to whose standards? While I believe it is essential to expect active and reflective participation from all students (to set high standards for their development and work), it also seems important to help them achieve these expectations. Does that mean I am not rigorous enough if I not only aim for students to succeed but also help them do so? Rigor is an elusive criterion by which to "prove" or legitimize one's pedagogy. Like "nurturing" it is usually deployed as a fundamental basis for judging, either to reject or to sanction, a particular pedagogy. "Nurture" evokes images and practices associated with women's work as teachers, work that has traditionally been dismissed precisely because it is not perceived as the rigorous work of scholars and professors. "Rigor," then, became a quality that (de)legitimized particular teachers and practices a priori. The historical meanings of these terms are still operative. It would seem useful, therefore, to ground our discussions of such concepts in particular contexts of strategic deployment rather than to reject or embrace them as absolute markers or essential qualities.

Self-as-a-Kaleidoscope and Language as an Essential Piece

Much of the writing we do in class is, as Gramsci suggests, aimed at generating a self-inventory—choosing, considering, articulating, and reflecting on the moments that have led us to be shaped in a specific and contingent way and the role this shape plays in determining our understanding of the world. I hand out this paragraph from Gramsci on the first day of class and assign an interpretive response:

> Is it preferable to "think" without having critical awareness, in a disjointed and irregular way, in other words to "participate" in a conception of the world "imposed" mechanically, . . . that is, by one of the many social groups in which everyone is automatically involved from the time he enters the conscious world . . . or is it preferable to work out one's own conception of the world consciously and critically, and so out this work of one's own brain to choose one's own sphere of activity, to participate actively in making the history of the world, and not simply to accept passively and without care the imprint of one's own personality from the outside?
>
> For his own conception of the world a man always belongs to a certain grouping . . . He is a conformist to some conformity, he is always man-mass or man-collective. The question is this: of what historical type is the conformity, the man-mass, of which he is a part? . . . Criticising one's own conception of the world, means, therefore, to make it coherent and unified. . . . The beginning of the critical elaboration is the consciousness of what one really is, that is, a "know thyself" as the product of the historical process which has left you an infinity of traces gathered together without the advantage of an inventory. First of all it is necessary to compile such an inventory. (1987, 58–59)

Every semester, a few students return to class proclaiming they were *incapable* of understanding the text or that Gramsci's text was incapable of being understood. Other students react with active and passionate responses. By putting them together in small groups, assigning them the task of collaboratively generating some sense from the text and asking them to consider what might constitute the necessary categories of such an inventory, we begin to invent the outline of the course collectively.

To push the notion of collecting an inventory, each semester I introduce the image of the self as a jigsaw puzzle in which an individual piece is influenced by its relation to the whole, which, in turn, is determined in part by that individual piece. Several essays ask them to consider one of the pieces of that puzzle, how the piece was formed, and why it is an essential piece. The essays also require that the students put that individual piece into the context of the larger puzzle. That is, the main idea or focus of these essays (whether an experience or value or opinion or influential individual) needs to be related back to the whole, which entails considering which areas of the larger puzzle are influenced by and influencing of this piece and why. In this way, throughout the course, we can discuss the self as a fragmented whole, as a collection of pieces (moments and interactions) that can be understood more critically when they are contextualized, which take on significance only when considered vis-à-vis their place and function in the broader self as puzzle. Two years ago, a student suggested a kaleidoscope might be a better image than a puzzle as it allows for the shape of the self to shift at any given moment and depends on the perspective of the viewer. In passing a kaleidoscope to someone else, the image shifts; similarly, the interpretation of a text will necessarily shift when readers engage it. There is, then, no finite or ultimate "shape," but various pieces that will continuously reconfigure themselves depending on the perspective of the viewer. Indeed, her revisioning of my metaphor has offered me a new means of conceiving and explaining the notion of a self-in-process.

Ultimately, the goal of considering one's self-inventory is to introduce the concept and function of subjectivity. As Weedon suggests, the next step is analyzing how and why particular subject-positions exercise discursive, political, and ideological power *over* others:

> [S]ubjectivity is of key importance in the social processes and practices through which forms of class, race and gender power are exercised. We have to assume subjectivity in order to make sense of society and ourselves. The question is what modes of subjectivity are open to us and what they imply in political terms. Modes of subjectivity, like theories of society or versions of history, are temporary fixings in the on-going process in which any absolute meaning or truth is constantly deferred. The important point is to recognize the political implications of particular ways of fixing identity and meaning. (1987, 173)

The first two essays each semester (though they are never the same from one semester to the next as the specific assignment changes according to the composition of the class and the dynamics of the group) are devised and defined according to the components a given class decides is essential to a self-inventory, though the topics are fairly open-ended and broad. Each unit begins with readings, written responses, and discussions as a way of airing the various interpretations and positions that result from a common set of questions and readings. The first essay generally asks them to consider some aspect of their situatedness, while the second seeks to turn the lens outward, to reflect on their construction of others. During the weeks in which reading, responding, drafting, peer critique, and discussion are taking place, we begin reading articles about the role of language in shaping both the self an individual composes and the way an individual is constructed by others according to her language use. These first weeks, then, aim to initiate both a sense of identity as a composition undergoing continuous revision, and to offer moments for self-reflection on this process, as well as to introduce the idea of language as discourse, as a system that not only expresses a self-construction but constrains and enables the self that is expressed.

The first unit a few semesters ago sought to engage students in an examination of the self others composed for them and the influence this cultural inscription had on their self-construction. We began by reading two poems, "Untitled" by Nobuko Miyamoto and Chris Iijima, and "Child of the Americas" by Aurora Levins Morales. "Untitled" represents the Japanese American narrator's changing response to the question "what are you?" The poem thus reflects how self-construction is influenced not only by ethnicity but also by how one's ethnicity is "written" by the dominant culture at a given historical moment. As signified by the repetition of the phrase "*what* [not who] are you," the narrator presents his experience of being objectified as "other" in order to reinforce the political and ideological superiority of the hegemonic identity (Euro American, in this instance). "Child of the Americas" presents the voice of a subject who embraces her fragmented self as a means of being the author of her own experience. Rather than allow herself to be inscribed as "other," she pronounces her self to be a whole made of only *seemingly* incongruous parts. "I am new. History made me. My first language was spanglish. / I was born at the crossroads / and I am whole" (1986, 50).

These poems then offer two discursive and political representations ("Untitled" evokes historical events whereas "Child of the Americas" draws on images of food and body parts) of the self as a composite of pieces: one speaks with anger, frustration, pain; the other is celebratory, joyful. Reading them in juxtaposition allows for a discussion of various responses to the experience of attempting to write oneself while aware of the ways in which one is being culturally, politically, and discursively written by others. The first essay asks students to consider ways they have been "read" (and, therefore, written) by others and to consider how they resist, embrace, struggle with, negotiate, or strive for this inscription. I have sometimes assigned an essay that specifically requires them to consider their membership in a particular group. We begin by listing all the groups we can think of on the board: ethnic, racial, sexual, fraternity or sorority, religious, generational, scholastic, gender, athletic, and so on. I ask several prompting questions to generate reflection about the group, their membership and its impact on their present self-conception. A few of the questions as I have presented them in the written assignment include:

> How did you establish membership in this group? Did you **choose** to be a member? Were you born into this group? When did you realize you were born into this group and what constituted the other groups you weren't born into? Were you put into this group? By whom—peers, family, "society" (be more specific than this), the media, people of a certain race, class, professional position? If born or put into this group by others, did you at some point accept membership? Was there a formal ceremony to indicate or celebrate this acceptance of your groupness? Did you resist membership? Why? Did you abandon membership? What are some ways you attempted to demonstrate your membership (actions, attitudes, appearance) or to reject/resist it?

> When do you first recall knowing about this group? Did you aspire to membership or reject it? What did membership convey or deny? When do you recall recognizing the stereotypes associated with this group? Did you benefit from them? How

did you respond? What place in the larger culture does this group occupy? In the "society" of your high school? Here at UMass?

Is membership based on talent? Appearance? Behavior? Money? Traditions? Describe situations in which you are empowered by membership. And when you are disempowered by it. What privileges accompany this membership? Does a lack of privilege result? Who controls access to membership?

How has your status in the group changed over the years? Are you placed in (or seeking to place self in) same group here at UMass? If not, do you sense something is missing? Or is something gained? Or both? Recall specific experiences related to this membership—describe them in detail. How do they relate to the you who is now? If we see the kaleidoscope of you through this angle, what parts of your present "self" are most influenced? What if you'd never been in this group or fought being in it or sought to be in it? How would you-who-is-now be different?

The first unit, then, seeks to consider a piece of the composite self and its relation to an individual's shifting conception of "self" while also investigating the relation between individual and social constructions of identity. As Gramsci's inventory suggests, they begin interrogating one of the "traces" that has left them here in order to work toward a "consciousness of what one really is." The point, here, in the readings and writings, is not "self-expression," indeed some students choose to write about shared cultural experiences without ever using the first-person pronoun. Rather, the essays here function to prompt critical distance and reflective deliberation on the topic of identities, how they are inscribed socially and composed by individuals.

In the second unit this semester, the aim of our readings and discussion was to interrogate the ways in which stereotypes are sustained and how they function to disguise that which they sustain. For instance, in the discussion alluded to earlier, we focused on the claim that "all gay men are effeminate." While this statement clearly names what gay men are supposed to be, it also implies what straight men are supposed to be (*not* effeminate), while simultaneously upholding heterosexual men as embodying the "right" kind of manliness. So, the aim was to consider how the unsaid, the silences that cultural myths do not explicitly name, are as important as what they do say or name; without the former, the latter would be powerless. The aim of the essay was to consider how stereotypes are produced and sustained by individuals—considering in particular the role played by experiential knowledge (or the lack of it).

We began with three short readings: William Helmreich's "Stereotype Truth," a short student writing that resulted from an assignment to respond to the "Harper's Index" and his teacher's response to that writing. I handed those out with a series of directive questions for them to consider as they read:

> You'll be reading several different perspectives on the "truth" and "validity" of stereotypes and on the relationship between experience and the formation of stereotypes. As you read, consider the argument each writer is making and determine whether or not you believe there is anything legitimate in the writer's argument. As we discussed when reading the first publication last week, there may sometimes be a difference between having a foot planted firmly on each side of the fence and standing on top of the fence with no side at all. You needn't entirely agree *or* disagree—your position might be more complicated and allow for that, don't smooth it over to make it simple. How are these arguments constructed—what steps do the writers take to lead you in? Do they begin with specific experiences and arrive at general conclusions—is the transition made explicit or is it hidden and sneaky? Is it effective? Do they rely on some sort of "research"? What is construed as "fact"? Were you surprised at where they arrive in the end? Or did the beginning lead you to assume that end point?

The first reading, Helmreich's "Stereotype Truth," claims that stereotypes are not always the motivated result of ignorance or hate and seeks to ground particular stereotypes in the cultural and historical experience of the group being categorized.

> How have particular groups come to be identified with certain traits? Puerto Ricans are not thought of as grasping business but Jews are. Blacks are sometimes categorized as musically inclined but the Chinese are not. . . . Such stereotypes usually stem from the historical experiences of the group itself and the

experiences of those with whom the group has had contact. Although stereotypes are often highly inaccurate, a good many have quite a bit of truth to them. . . . Are Hispanics apt to be warmer and more emotional than members of other groups? There seems to be almost universal agreement on the validity of this stereotype among professionals and lay people who work with Hispanics. . . . Are blacks more musically gifted than others? Certainly music was a central feature of their African heritage. . . Music was integral to the black churches founded in this country. It was in them that African exiles were able to fully express themselves as they prayed, rocked, shouted, sang, and danced. When white society's fascination with blacks reached unprecedented heights during the Harlem renaissance in the 1920's, music became a way in which blacks could move up the socio-economic ladder. . . . Whatever the reasons, probably no other group in the United States has contributed as much to music, song, and dance. (Helmreich 362–63)

Helmreich's argument is slippery and requires, as the unit hopes to demonstrate, as much attention to what is unsaid as to what is said. For instance, his claim that stereotypes stem from "the experiences of those with whom the group has contact," ignores the influence or existence of assumptions and expectations about a group that exist even before contact with that group. He does not acknowledge that interaction or experience is itself influenced by preconceptions that are most likely already biased and not neutral and that the very terms with which he describes these groups are inscriptive, not simply descriptive. He further ignores the way in which the various stereotypes he seeks to ground in cultural and historical "truths" are not neutral or innocuous categories of description in the larger socioeconomic and discursive systems in which they operate.

This article is instructive, however, for the slippery way in which the argument is couched. Who, after all, can argue with *experience*? Further, while some students clearly agree or disagree with Helmreich's main idea, a significant number of students have more difficulty choosing one position. As Pericles, a Latino student noted, his experience demonstrates that members of his culture *do* tend to manifest their emotions more explicitly than white Americans. He was not sure that this was always interpreted by others as a *positive* tendency, even though he saw it as one. Within the context of a classroom, he suggested, his being perceived as "warmer and more emotional" is not necessarily to his advantage, as a teacher may be less likely to consider him as a serious and intellectual student. Albertina noted Helmreich's glossing over of the reality that music was not simply a "way in which blacks could move up the socio-economic ladder" but one of the *only* ways and that historically African Americans' professional success has been "acceptable" only when it is perceived by whites as "harmless," such as when entertaining whites. (We further considered the correlation between music in the 1920s and professional basketball today and the way these stereotypes not only prevent whites from perceiving African Americans as competition but also allow for a limited range of role models available in the dominant culture from within the black community.) Like Pericles, Lanh noted how even a seemingly positive stereotype might function to promote hostility and division by pointing to the assumption that Asian students are more motivated and competent academically. In classes, she had observed students who immediately perceived her as a threat, as the one "to beat."

Besides critiquing the unsaid, which informs Helmreich's argument, we considered the validity of what is said, as many of the students noted that they too had experienced the "truth" of certain assumptions either in their own cultural group or in their interaction with members of another group. Is there a way, we wondered, to name differences, to associate specific attitudes or behaviors with a particular culture without simultaneously devaluing those attitudes and behaviors? Anthony turned to Columbus as an example as we had read an excerpt from his journal describing his first contact with indigenous people. As Anthony pointed out, history itself would be different if Columbus had not immediately moved from observation to judgment, from description to evaluation. Upon seeing that "the natives" were dressed differently, Columbus assumes they are "heathens." Noting their generosity, he deems them to be naive and unlearned and "savage." Further, as we discussed, our cultural image of Columbus erases these inscriptions, offering instead an idealized image of Columbus as "civilization" conquering "the untamed savages" by force. What the journal makes clear is the role of discursive structures in forming Columbus's conception that he was superior and therefore granting him authority not only to judge, but to exploit the indigenous people. While his motive is to describe his vision of a "new" land and its occupants, he is simultaneously acting to inscribe and discursively take power *over* them. Anthony wondered what a journal entry written by someone seeing Columbus would sound like and whether it too would convey a sense of superiority and power over. But as Magdalana noted, the absence of accounts (or of our reading and valuing of them) of the "others" throughout history is the reason why the Columbus myth prevails.

After considering the possibility (and lack of historical examples) of describing differences without simultaneously ascribing hierarchical and comparative judgments about those differences, we discussed the second set of readings. In this exchange, a student in Karen Shoffner's class (who is a friend and former colleague in the Writing Program) details and legitimates the process by which his grandmother came to fear African American men. Karen's response documents some of her experiences as an object of prejudice, challenging the student to reflect on his position. Here are those writings in full:

> **Student's response entitled "Prejudice: Myth or Reality?" to an entry on the "Harper's Index":**
> Reading the Harper's Index brought to mind a little thought I've had now and then. . . . It goes something like this: Everyone agrees that prejudice is bad, but is there something more to it than just being mean? From my own experiences, I have begun to think that there is an important reason for everyone's prejudice. When something happens which can be largely attributed to a group, prejudice will surely follow. Can you blame a person for feeling this way? Case in point: my grandmother. She lived in Detroit for several years and was mugged and robbed several times. Since each time the offender was black, I can't say I blame her for being a bit apprehensive about being in the company of black people. Also, people say Poles are stupid. [According to Harper's Index,] 147,000 out of 175,000 business in Poland flow. Is there some link here? Probably not, but it is easy to find one if you want to believe it. See now, I feel that prejudice is bad, but I can see why people feel this way.

Karen Shoffner's response to "Prejudice: Myth or Reality?":
Prejudice is no myth, but let me tell you my side of the story. I have been called nigger more times than I care to remember. Rocks have been thrown at me in my own neighborhood. I've been loathed on sight simply because of the color of my skin. My father has been pulled over by police officers who've asked if he owned the car he was driving. A black man driving such a nice car could only have stolen it, so goes the rationale. Never mind that my father has a Ph.D. in chemistry and has a steady job. My younger brother was told by his drama teacher not to audition for lead roles in the school's plays; rather, he'd have a better chance of getting a servant role. And the list goes on.

I am not discounting your grandmother's experiences; they are horrific and shouldn't happen to anyone. If her attackers had been white, would she be uncomfortable around whites? Would she have been uncomfortable around you? The occurrences I detailed above, though not physically threatening like your grandmother's experiences, were wounding to our psyches. They were reminders that we aren't good enough and never will be to some people. I am distrustful of most people as a result. It is something I constantly fight because distrust is poisonous. I refuse to live my life in the shadow of discomfort and distrust; that would be only a half life. You say you don't blame your grandmother for her discomfort which, in my mind, is the seed of prejudice. I say you are condoning her attitude, an attitude that, if it remains unchecked, will grow into prejudice. No. Prejudice is no myth, but must we accept its reality so easily?

After reading the Helmreich article, the student's piece might be considered as a representation of the danger posed by Helmreich's sanctioning of stereotypes that "result" from experience. For, while the student claims that his grandmother's prejudice *followed* or was *caused* by her experiences, Karen's response points to the illusory and disingenuous "logic" of his argument by questioning whether the grandmother would be afraid of whites in general or, more pointedly, "of you." As this question demonstrates, the grandmother was acting on assumptions and images already available and dominant in our culture about African Americans in general and black men in particular. Lanh noted that chances are the grandmother already subscribed to these myths, given the unlikelihood that she had had much contact with people of other races as that interaction might have precluded her associating *all* black men with fear and danger.

This interchange between Karen and her student allows for a discussion about how racism cannot avoid drawing on preexisting assumptions, even when a writer claims to be using "raw" experience. The student's text demonstrates, that is, the way in which experiences are not simply or easily interpreted because our understanding of them is always informed not only by other experiences but also by assumptions, beliefs, and judgments that are not necessarily experientially based, but culturally produced. So his claim to be simply offering one example of how experience might validate racist attitudes reveals instead that our interpretations of experience are inevitably motivated and never simple. As Jason observed, the student himself claims it is easy to find a link "if you want to find one." He did not consider why one would be motivated to find such a link, nor did he acknowledge his *own* desire to find a link—not only between his grandmother's experience and her racism, but rather, in the essay itself, which ultimately posits prejudice as well-founded and acceptable. Similar to the description of his grandmother *within* the response, in composing the response itself the student draws on and contributes to our cultural condoning of racism as legitimate and necessary, without acknowledging his participation in the broader structures and relations that sustain such an acceptance. Instead, he posits his grandmother's and his own attitude as "natural," inevitable, understandable. Magdalana noted that the student's response reminded her of her own construction of homosexuals, which, until peer-editing an essay by Joseph, she had never questioned or considered as a *choice* rather than a *reality*. Here, she articulates the aim of these readings: to consider beliefs, assumptions, and attitudes as *constructions*, though their power relies on our conception that they are naturalized, normal, inevitable. Magdalana's remark also signifies the possibility for intervening in these processes once we realize they are choices.

Many students discussed the significance and appropriateness of Karen's "personal" response to the student; they question whether she had the right, as the teacher, to take his text "personally." Do teachers have a "right" to engage the substance of a student's argument and not simply its style or form? As with previous classes, the students did not see how Karen could have avoided confronting the message and felt it was important for him to be exposed to another position. They noted the thoughtfulness of her response, which, while powerful, is neither mean nor silencing. As one student noted, Karen also grounds her opposing analyses in experience and thus counters his assumptions that experience can be unproblematically interpreted. Fred noted that his implied audience seemed to indicate a lack of interaction with or consideration of the perspective of anyone different from himself. Noting the "let's be reasonable and honest here" tone, I observed that many students and teachers who occupy dominant subject-positions in the culture assume such a "voice" or posture easily and naturally as they have little experience recognizing that their opinions and attitudes are *not* universal or absolute truths. As at least one student has noted each semester, it seems important to consider why the student chose to write this response to this teacher. What were his motives or expectations in justifying and legitimizing racist assumptions as a white writer producing for an African American teacher? Some students read this as an intentional attack, while others believe it reflects his lack of awareness of any position other than his own, calling him "dense," "out of it." I interpret that to mean he is not self-reflexive because he is not "self" aware, but takes his reading and authority for granted; he assumes this is a "reasonable" argument that "rational" readers will sanction.

Having discussed the various ways in which stereotypes operate covertly and the ease with which we perpetuate them even while claiming to dispute them, we moved to a discussion of specific stereotypes. As discussed in Chapter 4, we considered the claim that "all gay men are effeminate" from discursive, political, economic, social, and historical perspectives. I made a column for each category on the board and we discussed the impact and function of this stereotype within them. This was more difficult to talk about as most students hadn't consciously considered the ways in which stereotypes determine social or political *realities*. That is, students were not familiar with discussing stereotypes beyond the idea *that* they exist, who benefits or suffers from them. Further, the discussion, as already noted, turned into a discussion about homophobia (with some challenging predomi-

nant attitudes toward homosexuals and others actively reproducing them). At the end of the discussion, I mentioned my surprise and frustration at the hypocrisy of those who, while critical
of Helmreich and the student in Karen's class, were now asserting the legitimacy of their homophobic behavior and assumptions on the basis of "experience," without acknowledging the
choices they made in interpreting that experience or acknowledging how limited that experience was. Here was a moment
when I felt it important to intervene in the discussion, where I
felt it appropriate and necessary to use my authority in order to
challenge them. I agree with R. Miller's advice that "taking of-
fense at the student's response . . . strikes me as being exactly the
wrong tactic here. It is of paramount importance, I believe, to
begin where the students are, rather than where one thinks they
should be" ("Fault Lines," 406). Still, it seemed appropriate not
to tell them they were *wrong* so much as to show them they were
acting in ways they themselves had already identified as problematic and unacceptable.

At this point, we moved on to the first draft of the essay, which
would emerge from these discussions and readings. Students were
able to choose any predominant cultural myth or stereotype, one
they experienced as object or perpetuated as agents or one they
did not feel they had any relationship to at all. The following are
the questions I handed out to them before they began the first
draft:

> We have spent time considering how and why stereotypes func-
> tion (largely because they are invisible or actively denied by
> those who act on them and by our culture—think of the stu-
> dent writing about his grandmother) and how and why they
> are perpetuated even when experience contradicts their valid-
> ity (recall Pat's description of how many of his friends who are
> white insist on believing he smokes pot and parties all the time
> *because* of their assumption about Haitians and black men even
> though they *know* he doesn't do these things). In class today, I
> want you to generate a list of possible topics and then you'll
> meet in small groups to consider some of the questions below
> in relation to your list. For the next class, a two-page single-
> spaced (yes, really!) draft is due and you'll be completing a
> self-assessment in class so that everyone can take home three
> essays and self-assessments to peer critique over the weekend.

Here are *some* questions to consider. And as you will surely note, there are *many* more which I didn't think of or we haven't explored yet in discussion. Use those too:

***Who is represented by this myth—is it a general myth assigned to all members of a group? Or does it name specific members of a larger group? How does this stereotype connote a negative image —think in terms of the language used? What is the implied norm you can deduce from this stereotype? Who is empowered by that definition of "normal" or "acceptable"?

*** Is there any historical, material (as in not purely imaginative) basis for this stereotype—whether it's in relationships between the objects and agents of the myth or in what Helmreich refers to as cultural and historical experience? Describe them. If so, do the circumstances that initially led to this assumption still exist? If not (as we discussed re Joseph's example and Ehren's), why is the stereotype still pervasive; what sustains it? When do you recall first becoming aware of this stereotype? How was it introduced to you? Was it a specific moment? Was it slowly through years of being immersed in cultural representations of people (in books, school, entertainment, politics)?

***Is this a stereotype you hold to be true? Where did you first learn this assumption? If so, do you have direct, personal experience that has led you to believe it? Describe these experiences. If not, then do you have other reasons to believe it? Have you seen it on television, in books, movies, music, and so on? Give some examples. Why do you believe it if you have no direct experience? Have you had any experiences which challenge this idea? What was your response?

***If you do not hold this stereotype to be true and yet it is pervasive in our culture, how have you been able to avoid buying into it? Why do others believe in it? Who do you imagine buys into it? Did you ever believe it? Was your belief in it challenged by some experience or some encounter? Describe. Do you try to counter this stereotype when you run into it? How? Do most of your friends believe it? Why or why not? Where did they learn it from?

***Who benefits from this stereotype? Who stands to gain from its remaining a mysterious "truth" even if it doesn't reflect reality? Describe the person whose reality it names (as we discussed re Lanh's example, this stereotype deflects blame for academic performance from the student who buys into it by allowing Asian students to be represented *as* the "problem"). Think carefully and in detail about how this stereotype is perpetuated and disseminated and discuss that. Can you think of a movie or a song or a show or a public figure who embodies this myth? Who does this myth separate from "the rest of us"? That is, if stereotypes serve to separate us into groups of acceptable and unacceptable "types" or behaviors, what do people not in the group you're examining supposedly have/possess/do that people in the group don't? What is the basis for making such a distinction (for claiming "no women possess the strength to be firefighters"). Or, to reverse this, what do people who are excluded from the stereotyped group *not* have/possess/do that distinguishes them from people inside of this group?

***Can you trace the history of this stereotype? When did it first become predominant? What purpose did it serve? Does it serve the same purpose now? Are there public figures who evoke this stereotype to assert and maintain power? To whom are they appealing? Why doesn't it hurt them to lose the support of the group they are stereotyping?

***Again, remember that even if you do not hold this stereotype to be true, others do. Why? What do they gain from buying into this? Are there any generative, constructive results? Why does it flourish???

Admittedly, there are too many questions here for any one essay to consider even most of them. Nonetheless, similar to the way in which I respond to essays by asking as many questions as I can, the questions themselves serve the purpose of at least complicating the issue and a writer's perspective on the issue. Rather than lecturing *at* students about the nature and function of stereotypes, I can pose questions that problematize or unsettle their understanding of stereotypes. Without offering or prescribing *the* answers to these questions, I can give them the responsibility and authority for reflecting on them and arriving at their answers. The essay, representing some of this thinking, then allows for a broad range of perspectives to be considered, for opposition to emerge, without my being the sole initiator of that opposition or directing the conversation toward specific and predetermined ends. Further, this unit aims not to *offer* them my vision of the ideal reality, but rather to generate reflection on how reality is an ongoing and shifting construction determined according to experience, assumptions, and our position in mutually determining discursive, political, and social relations of power and authority. If they conceive of reality in this way, they can consider the potential for revisioning.

Asking as many questions as I can think of represents my understanding of the role of the critical composition teacher. While I do aim to unsettle students' sense of themselves as agents and subjects, to engage them in a reflection of how they occupy both roles simultaneously in their writing and their lives, I do not aim to *give* them a new position or outlook. I primarily see my responsibility as accommodating the diverse range of interests in, attitudes toward, and conceptions about writing and the world by providing an array of tools for both writing and thinking more critically—that is, with an awareness *that* they write and think in specific ways and a consideration of how they might influence these processes. Rather than forcing *all* writers to use a specific tool, it seems more useful to present them with a choice of many tools and to require that they consider why a particular tool works best for them and when. With all students, I feel a responsibility to push them, to challenge them to develop as individual writers and thinkers who might also participate in a collaborative environment that recognizes, but does not devalue, differences.

Learning Language as Discourse

Many of the short assignments we complete in class attempt to move students to reflect on language itself as a social and political tool, which actively influences the process by which we identify a self and conceive of its position vis-à-vis the "world" we construct. Most students do not consider language as worthy of interrogation and critical examination as they have tended to perceive it as a neutral tool with which we simply and unproblematically express our preexisting ideas. Their writing has typically been judged according to criteria that attend to structure, style, grammar, organization, and thesis. Further, these formal elements are generally presented as unquestionable, "universally" agreed on, the standard and acceptable criteria that characterize academic writing. Two goals, then, emerge from these exercises. First, we attend to language itself as a signifying system that organizes, interprets, and shapes the reality or self we express. Second, we consider the implications of a standardized form for using language in the academy and the possibilities for variation and invention. As Giroux notes, in the dominant education discourses:

> Language is abstracted from its political and ideological usage. For instance, language is privileged as a medium for exchanging and presenting knowledge, and, as such, is abstracted from its constitutive roles in the struggles of various groups over different meanings, practices, and the readings of the world. . . . there is little sense of how language practice can be used to silence some students. (1986, 57)

The goal, then, is to expose the *workings* of language as well as to reflect on the function of imposing a standardized form of language practice (the five-paragraph essay, for example, which many of my students are still learning as *the* accepted "academic" form) regardless of the audience or purpose for which a writer writes. This goal informs our work all semester and is a large factor in how the course is structured.[5] Here, I want to consider two specific exercises that attempt to move writers toward a consideration of how definitions of "good" writing are fluid and context-bound as well as to recognize that the criteria by which we privilege certain forms of writing also imply the privileging of certain constructions of knowledge and authority.

The first exercise is a simple one in which students name all the "rules" of good writing they have learned in school over the years, and we list them on the board. A few rules have been mentioned in every one of the classes in which I have done this exercise and are, therefore, worth mentioning:

1. *Always* have a thesis statement in your introduction.
2. Do not use the first-person pronoun, "I."
3. Write essay in form of an inverted pyramid. (I am yet perplexed by this one.)

4. Do not directly address the reader.
5. Repeat your thesis statement in every paragraph.
6. Never use "slang" or "improper" English.
7. The conclusion should restate the introduction but in different words.
8. Be sure to have transition sentences between paragraphs.
9. Have 5 paragraphs (introduction, 3 bodies, conclusion).

These rules indicate the "formula" that both Josh and Paul allude to in the next chapter. Somehow, if students manage to erase themselves, ignore their readers *and* put all their ideas (although even *having* an idea has never once been listed as a "rule" for good writing), then they will be successful writers. After listing the rules, I begin posing questions. Do these rules make writing easier? Do the rules apply to all writing or are they determined by the context in which one writes? Why do we capitalize the "I"—signifying the importance of the first-person pronoun in the English language as other languages does not give it the same special status—and then require its erasure from academic writing? Is it difficult or easy to write without "I" or "you"? Who might be implied or imagined as audience? After asking them to describe their experiences following the particular rules they learned, we move to more reflective critical questions and discussion. Who benefits from these rules? What sort of thinking process is valued? What do you do when you do not have three ideas, but five or eleven, and so cannot contort your ideas into the five-paragraph format? Shouldn't an essay *lead* to a conclusion, argument, position, idea rather than begin with and end with the same one? Do you learn from reading this kind of writing? Do teachers seem to learn from reading it? Which rules give you difficulty and why?

Every semester, the discussion begins slowly as most students simply take these rules for granted as universal, objective criteria for academic writing. They have usually not considered the possibility that these rules were *invented* in order to serve a specific function and in order to convey a particular relationship between writer and writing, teacher and student, language and thinking. I have found that discussing their experience attempting to follow these rules is a good lead-in to considering their function and moving toward a recognition of the politics of form and criteria. In more recent semesters, after an initial discussion of these rules, I have handed out an excerpt from John Clifford's "The Subject in Discourse," as a means of engaging students in a consideration of the political implications of writing instruction within a broader socioeconomic context. Clifford, examining the subject position implied by such rules, concludes that rather than facilitate good writing they teach discipline and enact the same principles of inclusion and exclusion that operate in society:

> But form is also an attitude toward reality; it is rhetorical power, a way to shape experience, and as such it constructs subjects who assume that knowledge can be demonstrated merely by asserting a strong thesis and supporting it with three concrete points. . . . Writing subjects are allowed to feel that the rhetorical stance they are encouraged to take is the only credible one, really the only possible one. . . . Grammar was taught not because it was effective [as a method of writing instruction] but because it was good discipline. It was rigorous and arcane, and it privileged upper- and middle-class language conventions against those of the working class and poor. Teaching grammar, like teaching math or science, clearly installs the instructor as Subject who knows against those subjects who clearly cannot know, unless they apply themselves diligently and, of course, without wondering why. . . . Although traditional grammar instruction functions as an almost pure ritual of control and domination, it also serves as an effective sorting mechanism for race and class discrimination. . . (an excerpt from the excerpt of Clifford's piece, which I give to students, 43, 47–48)

While the excerpt requires some unpacking, it allows students to read and interpret an example of the "professional" discourse on writing pedagogy. Further, as Schwartz notes, there is "something to be said for making our own habits and assumptions . . . clear to students, not necessarily to politicize the classroom, but to reveal that it is and always has been a political space dedicated to political activities" (70). Given that many students are considering teaching and learning methods *as* issues, as choices, for the first time, Clifford's text provides a context beyond our local classroom and presents a "reading" of the pedagogy most of them have experienced but not questioned. Students, upon reading Clifford, most often note that they did not realize teachers teach in *specific* ways or that more than the *subject* itself is being imparted. The aim, then, is to demystify or denaturalize their experience as students so they might then investigate how their particular experience as learners, how their sense of themselves as writers, has shaped their attitude toward and success in writing and education.

After discussing the rules they have internalized over the years, we attempt to generate our own criteria. Asking them to think as readers, I call for a list of new rules, those *they* believe are necessary for successful writing. Here, students typically mention that a writer should be interested in her topic, should not jump around, should have a catchy opening that situates readers in the piece, should keep the reader's attention. Beginning to consider the idea that *having* something to say might determine *how* they say it, rather than vice versa, students generate criteria that corroborate Clifford's conclusion that "students want to become writers not because they have mastered syntax but because they are convinced they have something to say and somebody to say it to" (46).

I distribute this initial set of new, collaboratively invented "rules" and we refer back to, update, and revise it throughout the semester. The first publication assignment asks them to consider whether the essays they consider most successful have adhered to the rules we generated or whether they challenge those rules. So, for instance, an introduction remains an important standard requirement for a piece of writing, but we can consider the various shapes a beginning might take depending on the audience, purpose, and focus of a piece. One introduction might aim to grab the reader with vivid detail and unanswered questions; another equally successful introduction might immediately articulate the writer's position on a certain issue and establish the aim of the essay. As students reflect on their own and others' writings, they come to see that criteria are hard to define outside the context of the readers, aim, and reason for a particular essay. Recognizing the fluidity of evaluative categories and the role played by the agent of evaluation, students realize that a range of choices exist, and they can begin to consciously choose *how* to shape their ideas with a recognition that the form they choose will in turn shape *what* they say. While I do not assign specific forms, I encourage students to experiment with the variety of forms we identify when reading the publications. In this way, they experience the ways in which the conventions associated with a specific genre might actively constrain and enable the expression of their ideas.

Another exercise, which follows the discussion of rules, is aimed at generating reflection on how valuing a particular written product entails valuing a certain way of knowing and of constructing authority vis-à-vis that knowledge. Again, the exercise attempts to convey the link between privileging a certain form of discourse and the subject-position it implies. Seeking to contradict the predominant assumption that disembodied, universal standards of "good" writing exist—as well as to demonstrate that *all* criteria are subjective and simultaneously inclusive and exclusive—I developed this exercise to ask students to generate and account for their own criteria while then moving to consider the relationship these criteria posit between writer and text, words and worlds, authors and authority.

Responding to N.A.E.P. (due 2/9/95)

N.A.E.P. is the National Assessment of Educational Progress. Many of you probably recall taking tests every so often during your elementary and high school years. This is one such test that was administered in 1988, on a national level, in an effort to evaluate how well students were learning. In evaluating such tests (similar to evaluating the Writing Placement Exam you all took here at UMass), it is necessary for the evaluators to generate a specific set of criteria by which to judge the tests. The evaluators must decide what exactly makes for a "successful" or "good" essay and what exactly constitutes a "bad" essay. There are several ways of arriving at and defining the necessary ingredients. You could begin by deciding what a "good" essay *must* contain and then decide that essays that lack these things must be "bad." Or you could decide what makes for a "good" essay and what makes for a "bad" essay. You could decide to come up with the criteria as a committee, that is, before you've read any of the tests. Or you might decide to read some tests, get a sense of the range of writing going on in that age group, and then determine your criteria. But, at any rate, you need to decide what matters. A few things to consider whether or not you value: spelling, structure, style (as in??), voice, content, organization, development, topic sentence, imagery, vividness, tone/feeling. Don't forget, however, that if you choose to value one quality, you may be automatically deciding not to value another. For example, if you decide to value amount of information, are you then going to count that over clarity and vividness of the information that is presented? Or can you value both?

At any rate, I would like you to read the following examples and to define your criteria for the categories I will give below and then to put each essay into a category. You can do these three steps in whatever order you think will be most successful for evaluating the tests. You will be reading the work of fourth graders who were given from fifteen to twenty minutes to respond. I would like you to describe the order in which you complete the three steps and to explain why you chose to proceed in that order. The examples have been copied as written. Okay, here's the information you need.

QUESTION: *Informative Writing Task*

Identify a specific kind of animal and present relevant information about its qualities or characteristics.

Example #1 Bear's can Be mean But They won't Bother you if you don't Bother Them. Bear's are Defferent in many ways for instance Bear's sleep ontil spring and many other ways.

Example #2 Rabbits. Rabbits are very fuzzy soft animals (I love them). They eat carrots. Do make a mess. Some people do not like rabbits. Some people don't like animals but I don't know why! If I had a ribbit I would name it Fuzzy. That's a nice name, I think. Rabbits are different because they have tiny little noses and because their animals. They are speashal. Rabbits are very unuseual animals. It's funny but I hve a hard time eating a carrot. Rabbits are so small and they can ate carrots, they must have very strong teeth because carrots are hard for some people to bite. It's funny to think but how do rabbits get all that fur and what do they do all day??? If you have a ribbit your lucky.

Example #3 We went to the zoo and seen a tiger. It was orange with black dots. It was fun. We also seen a loine. It was ugly. We seen a ape. We also seen a zebra. It was brack white. It weit 2,0000 ponds.

Example #4 The Arctic Fox is a very tough animal. It thrives through long and cold winters. It reproduces more when there is more food. For instance, the average number of kits in one family is 10. Last year scientists studies came out 14 kits a family. The arctic Fox ranges from Northern America Eurasia and the northern islands. Sometimes the Arctic fox is white sometimes is a brown color. It really depends on the breed. Usually the Fox only has one breed but when one breed mates with another breed they sometimes have mixed breeds. The fox usually hunts small rodents like mice or sometimes what-ever it can find. Arctic fox's take care of there young and the father leaves the mother soon after mating, but the arctic fox mother teaches her kits to hunt.

CATEGORIES (in order from "worst" to "best"):

Unsatisfactory
Minimal
Adequate
Elaborated

Remember, these are the names designed by the evaluators. What difference would it make in your assessment if you'd been given *different* categories. For example: dull, okay, exciting or impersonal, active, personalized? In other words, you need to consider how the categories themselves reveal the particular bias and preference of the committee of evaluators— how these criteria themselves imply valuing some qualities over others and devaluing certain qualities.

Every semester, the fox and rabbit cause the most controversy. Typically, those who categorize the fox piece as elaborate, categorize the rabbit piece as adequate. On the other hand, a significant number of students reverse this, ranking the rabbit as elaborate and the fox as adequate. On questioning, the fox advocates generally point to the abundance of "facts," the evidence that the author is knowledgeable about her subject, the organized presentation of ideas, the "scientific voice," and their astonishment that a fourth-grader wrote this. As one student remarked "it sounds like a *Nova* special." Every semester, I ask whether or not it would alter their evaluation if they knew the writer was lying, had invented these "facts." The response has been a unanimous "no." What sort of "knowledge" are they valuing? Empirical, scientific, factual are typical responses. But the "zoo" and the rabbit writers also rely on empirical knowledge, I point out. The zoo writer has *been* to a zoo and has seen an ugly lion, while the rabbit writer seems to have had direct contact with at least one rabbit and has noted they are "fuzzy, soft, unseual" (*sic*). Aren't these also "facts?" Students dismiss the "zoo" writer because he did not follow the directions, which require that he choose one animal; whereas, the zoo writer simply lists animals. Further, they note that his piece reads more like a list of brief entries rather than an organized presentation of ideas. The rabbit writer, while presenting "facts," has a less structured piece than the fox writer and doesn't stick to "relevant" information. Relevant according to whom?

I ask them whether the different vocabularies affected their evaluation—while the fox writer uses more technical or denotative terms ("kits," "breeds," "rodents" and "thrives"), the rabbit writer relies more on poetic or connotative language ("speashal," "unuseual," "fuzzy," "like," and "lucky"). A rabbit advocate usually asks whether it is fair to judge the other pieces *in comparison to* the fox as this one is clearly advanced and doesn't seem a fair standard to set. This semester Fred was an avid supporter of all the pieces *except* the fox essay. He felt the others demonstrated an active and thoughtful writer, whereas the fox piece seemed to him simply a regurgitation of memorized facts. He could not see the point of valuing writing that, to him, didn't demonstrate an ability to process information, and he was visibly frustrated by and disappointed in the other students' admiration of the fox piece.

The rabbit writing is markedly different. It relies on a different mode of description. We see a difference also in terms of the relationship between the writer and her (an arbitrarily assigned gender-specific pronoun) subject and the way in which authority is constituted. As one rabbit fan noted, "she really makes you see and feel a rabbit, she gets to the essence of a rabbit." Unlike the fox writer's use of "scientific" data, the rabbit writer relies on personal experience to arrive at relevant information about rabbits. The writer is present in the essay, not only in her use of the first-person pronoun, but in terms of punctuation directives (exclamation points, question marks) and her positing of evaluative conclusions (that's a nice name, rabbits are special and unusual, it's funny, you're lucky). The fox writer, on the other hand, presents information but does not interact with it or arrive at conclusions and does not enter the essay directly, in a first-person voice.

The comparison of these two pieces in particular, the fox and the rabbit, point to the oppositions that generally inform definitions (either as presented to or perceived by students) of academic writing versus personal or, as Josh calls it, "journal" writing. The fox writer removes herself and eliminates traces of a situated author or "voice," whereas the rabbit writer actively interprets and judges the "facts" she presents. The fox writer evokes the authority of science, while the rabbit writer evokes the authority of experience. The fox piece demonstrates a writer who is detached from topic and conclusion, and the rabbit piece represents a writer who foregrounds her investment in them.

After discussing the evaluations as well as the criteria by which students arrive at them, we discuss what our different conclusions reveal about our situatedness, our values and definitions of "knowledge" and "authority," which inform our opinion about what constitutes "good" writing. Interestingly, when I ask students which writer they would most like to hang out with, *everyone* chooses either the zoo or the rabbit writer. But what about the fox writer? While most students articulate their awe at the "knowledge" and writing ability demonstrated by the fox writer, they do not perceive her as a very engaging or interesting individual. So, they value a type of writing but not the "persona" it conveys. But, as many of them point out, their own experience with school writing has shown them that form is inevitably privileged over ideas and they describe moments when they felt they'd written an important or thoughtful essay only to be dismissed for lacking the "proper" structure or for grammatical errors. It is worth noting, then, that they value the fox piece because (and in spite of) the fact that it exemplifies the very style of writing that they associate with their failures and frustrations as writers. The discussions also touch on the "naming" of criteria—the fact that, as evaluators, they felt constrained by the terms "elaborate" and "minimal" as though values were already being imposed on them.

Many students claim that their ranking would differ if they were able to identify their own categories of response.

The NAEP exercise raises issues about the legitimacy of standardized tests, points to the inevitability that a given text will be valued according to the subject-position of the reader. Further, the process of ascribing a ranking and having to account for it encourages students to consider their conception of the "successful" essay and the relationship it implies between writers, texts, and authority. That is, their sense that a text might be easily and unproblematically evaluated is unsettled as they have to defend not only *what* their set of criteria are but also *why* they chose that particular set. As Lu suggests, exposing the dominant codes of academic writing as constructed allows students (and teachers) to conceive of composing as a process of making choices, a process of "negotiation" rather than contortion or regurgitation:

> Although the product, their decision to reproduce the code, might remain the same with or without a process of negotiation, the activities leading to that decision, and thus its significance, are completely different. Without the negotiation, their choice would result from an attempt to passively absorb and automatically reproduce a predetermined form. . . . [I]f the student's choice to reproduce a code results from a process of negotiation, then she would have examined the conflict between the codes of [standard academic discourse] and other discourses. And she would have deliberated not only on the social power of these colliding discourses but also on who she was, is, and aspires to be when making this decision. (Lu, 1994, 455)

A final, and important, consequence of these assignments is that *my* criteria become repeatedly exposed and challenged as *my own* (they are not revealed as idiosyncratic but as situated and partial) rather than as *the* criteria. Students will ask "well, then, what is an 'A' essay to you?" I do not grade any of their writings (they grade themselves twice a semester, prior to our individual conferences, and we discuss their criteria for that grade and how or whether it differs from the grading criteria we generate as a class throughout the semester). I respond to the question by emphasizing the process of critical revision from one draft to another, the appearance of a writer being intellectually engaged in the writing process and in the class, and progress working through structural problems identified by peer readers and me on previous essays. While my aim is not to avoid the question, I also acknowledge that I cannot define *an* 'A' essay without reasserting a set of disembodied or transcendent criteria of the sort we have just deconstructed. While some students initially struggle with *not* having clear "rules," these exercises generate more reflection throughout the semester on the various conditions that inform the production and evaluation of "good" writing.

Grades are a central mechanism by which the institution inserts its rules and criteria, and imposes the gate-keeping function on our classrooms. While I cannot choose not to grade in my current university, I attempt to revision the purposes and function of grades within my class by constantly questioning the role they play in our experiences of and motivations for learning and writing. I do not simply "pretend" I do not grade or will not have to grade in the end. Such a strategy would do little to contest how grades work and would simply suspend their institutional effect until the semester's end. Nor do I assume students will simply feel liberated or more comfortable as writers because their work is not graded. Such an assumption would likely increase their anxiety over grades because they know grades are ultimately inevitable, and I would simply be delaying the act. This strategy would, in fact, most likely increase the power of grades and of my role and authority as the grader; to hide grades, to pretend they are not operative in or outside of the classroom, does not diffuse or challenge their effect. Rather, grades remain a central issue throughout the semester. I explain how I will evaluate their work with qualitative critique, which does not include quantitative assessment. I do not secretly grade their work and simply keep those marks from them. Nor do I suddenly announce my covert criteria at the end of the semester. But because we continually talk about the issue, practice, and effect of grading, we manage to work without using grades throughout the semester. This allows me to read their writing without thinking in terms of grades, which is as important as helping them write without their first concern being the grade.

At semester's end, we collectively generate the criteria by which all students will be graded. As the teacher, I tell them I reserve the right to contest any specific criterion (such as, say, attendance does not matter) they generate, but that I will provide a rationale and will make that decision immediately and publicly. During this discussion, students meet in small groups and decide what should be prioritized, on what basis their work during the course should be judged. We list all suggestions on the board and each group has to provide an explanation for any criteria they generate. In this way, we are not simply producing *different* manifestations of the same disembodied and purportedly "objective" standards by which grades are typically determined. We are acknowledging that we are not disinterested, cannot be impartial. Once we have generated our criteria, students have to determine how and on what basis we can judge whether or not they have been met. So, when they list "participation" as an essential component for evaluating every student's work, I ask them where we should look for evidence of this. For instance, is useful peer critique a form of participation? In every one of the ten semesters I have been using this system of grading, students generate qualitative criteria that one might assume they would not trust a teacher to measure. Commitment, responsibility, effort, consistency, "adding to the group," progress, and willingness to critique and revise are always mentioned as essential considerations in grading individual performance. As these categories indicate, an emphasis on contributing to the group always emerges as an essential component for a passing grade.

The standards by which they come to judge their work as writers, readers, and students, then, make explicit their understanding of the writing class as a collective process, one that depends not on individuals distinguishing themselves as the "authors" of exceptional products, but on writers and readers contributing to one another's critical processes. There is little attention given in their grading discussion to individual texts as products. Instead, their criteria value processes, participation in the collective process and evidence that individuals have actively developed a writing process, one they can articulate and reflect on to others. When they name attendance as important, their rationale is that students who miss class frequently cannot fulfill their responsibility to the development of the class as a group, and have not contributed responsibly to peer critique. In other words, they think beyond "well, attendance is mandatory" and can articulate why attendance is important. As criteria are elaborated, students can critique and contest either the category or the means of ensuring it. In this way, we generate a situated set of evaluative standards. Interestingly, the criteria are fairly consistent from one semester to the next, though the specific ways of naming them might vary. As a group, we determine what should be valued, and why specific practices are valuable and deserve recognition.

I would like to further note that grades are a useful way to intervene in the institution's normative practice. In their work outside of the classroom, as employees, parents, partners, community members, our students are not students, though they will remain—I hope—learners, and they will not receive any grades. Indeed, they might receive other forms of evaluation; their "work" in any capacity may be reviewed and judged. In light of this, perpetuating a letter grade as the standard signifier for commitment, ability, performance, success, and so on, seems misguided and not entirely useful. Teaching students to respond to other forms of evaluation is important and disrupts the grade code. Further, not grading or not using grades as the sole measure of classroom success allows us to evaluate other aspects of participation and critical engagement. It is difficult to "grade" accountability.

Writing about Writing: Publication Assignments and Peer Critiques

Publication Assignments[6]:
Excerpt from Publication Assignment #3:
Choose two writers from the publication whose work you admire here for the reason that you have watched it changing or improving or progressing or whatever word fits during the semester. Consider what makes this essay remarkable in their portfolio. Go back and read their essays in the Publications #1 and #2 and think about how this piece differs from those. What specific aspects have changed? Use the essays themselves to ground and support your criteria for evaluation. That is, as usual, you are expected to cite from the individual works to illustrate or support your interpretations and conclusions. You

might consider *any* aspects of the piece—such as those we have been discussing all semester, or you can use your sense of what aspects matter. Again, cite from all three essays and be specific.

Student Responses to the Publication #3 Assignment:

Albertina's changes are not at all the same as those I have discussed for Karell's work. Her essays have all been well-written and enjoyable and educational to read. What I note as a change is her writer's voice. Her voice in this third essay is much stronger and louder, more self-assured and I think this reflects a change in her behavior in class. . . . Her first essay, which was when we wrote about how we see ourselves versus how others see us, she didn't tell the reader much of anything except that she did not want people to know much about her. "I feel as though people can read me just by looking at me. . . . I try and create some type of distraction to steer them away from reading [me]. . . . My voyage to the silent world of thoughts has been a rewarding experience. I now know how to be a figment of someone's imagination." This essay was well-written but her voice wasn't clear. In the next weeks of school, Albertina started speaking more and letting her opinion be known. . . . Now she always participates and is outspoken. Her third essay reflects her change in behavior. With confidence, she talks directly about her economic experience, revealing more about herself to the reader—the way she is now and why. "I remember wondering how I would pay for things. I couldn't just hang around the school or go chill with my friends. . . . [but] a little hard work never killed anybody. I don't blame my parents for the hardships they encountered. Because of their determination despite everything, we at least have been given a chance to try and succeed for a better life for ourselves." (An excerpt from Pericles' response)

I've been watching Patrick's improvement from the first essay until the present. In "I Am Not Who They Think I America," he had no arguments whatsoever, and in that sense, the essay wasn't very convincing. To illustrate my point, here is a passage. "I was very mad when I first ran into this stereotype. For instance, her mother had no right to get mad just because I was in the room. Nobody has a right to assume anything about me based on the way I dress, or my color. . . ." This passage constituted an entire paragraph which for me had no clear purpose. He didn't explain his ideas or how he was illustrating them. . . . In his next essay, "Prejudice is a Real Thing" Patrick shows improvement, he is starting to argue his ideas more. For instance, he writes: "The police benefit from this stereotype because they use it to keep getting paid. When they see a black man in a nice car, they then have a reason to stop him and to be doing their jobs." Not perfect yet, but Patrick is going a step ahead. . . . In his third essay, "The Education System Needs a Little Change," Patrick shows he has learned a lot. He knows when he makes a point he has to convince the audience of it and therefore, he has to sit back down and think about how to do that. "Every year that we are in school, our teachers try to drill into us the type of person society wants us to be. By the time we are old enough to make our own decisions, we make them using the values they taught us." It's unfortunate that he doesn't illustrate this with an example to make it perfect (well, there is one but on the *next* page!). (Excerpt from Fred's response)

In a composition class that aims to generate reflection about the process and product of writing (which aims to present writing *as* a critical process in which students can intervene) it seems important to provide numerous occasions for reflecting on both the ways of composing and the end results. Peer critiques, along with publication assignments and self-assessments, offer a chance for writers-as-readers to consider composing and reading as processes that are neither mysterious nor spontaneous. Instead, each process entails a series of choices and, once writers can identify when and why they make certain choices, they can begin to assert control over those processes. As I often tell my students, knowing *why* a text does or does not work is as important as knowing *whether* it is effective; otherwise, you've no control over whether or not you replicate it (whether it is an attitude or an essay style). It is important to create opportunities for self-reflexivity on their changing practice and conception of these processes—chances to consider, critique, and push forward. These process-oriented techniques provide a way for them to write about writing—to reflect on *how* a text is written (with a new understanding that various legitimate forms exist). Without such moments, students may indeed develop a writing process in our composition classes, but they may not have more control over that process. It is important to engage them in the act of articulating their choices as well as considering the choices they did not make. In this way, we might seek to enact the link between engagement in the composition process and critical process.

Publications, then, play a central role in our composition class. They offer a vehicle for celebrating the fact that everyone got through another unit and for reflecting on individual and collective progress. In our Basic Writing course last semester, several students noted their confidence increased after reading the first class magazine, not because they considered their writing to be superior, but because they considered everyone's writing to be "decent." Given their sense that they had "failed" the writing placement exam, their estimation of themselves as writers had dropped; reading their peers' work helped them realize they were not in a class of "bad" writers. Having students read one another's work provides readers beyond the teacher; taking the publications *seriously* encourages them to write within a particular rhetorical context. Further, this allows us to rewrite the familiar, hierarchical distinction between "student" writing and "real" writing in which we study, learn from, and engage "real" writing and then ask students to practice. Reading students' final texts seriously and critically puts their writing into the pool of texts to be studied, thereby treating that work as *writing*, which need not be qualified by the signifier "student."

Publication assignments also allow for further consideration about criteria, for *ongoing* reflection about what constitutes a "good" essay and a recognition of the many forms such an essay might take. We can move, then, from generating and explaining evaluative criteria for fourth-grade writing responses to constructing and accounting for criteria appropriate to the writing within the specific context of our writing class. Discussing individual responses to specific essays demonstrates the fluidity of interpretation: one student's "favorite" essay is "confusing" to another reader; several students' choice of the "best" essay is considered by the writer to be incomplete. In attempting to account for diverse reactions to a single piece, both the writer and reader's situatedness in relation to a composition emerge as primary factors in their respective evaluations of the piece. Often, students claim an essay is their favorite because "I could relate to it." We might then talk about the difficulty a reader faces when trying to appeal to an audience he does not know and, sometimes, cannot relate to (whether a professor or a writing class). I often solicit advice from the writer whose piece we are considering, asking her to describe the process (drafts, peer critiques, discussions) by which she arrived at this product and to account for specific structural and substantive choices she made. Allowing writers to reflect on their process, these descriptions demonstrate the various ways of participating in the process of composing and deflects the pressure often put on (or taken on by) the teacher to *prescribe* both *the* ideal process and *the* product.

In my classes, I initially assign publication assignments which require that students consider various pieces of a particular product. Following are excerpts from the first and second publication assignments used in our Spring, 1995 College Writing course which preceded the third assignment which opened this section.

From Publication Assignment #1:
Choose two favorite introductions. Now, choose two not so favorite introductions. What do the successful examples do which the others don't? How do they do this? Similarly, what don't they do? That is, what makes them successful to you? Do they prepare you for the essay in particular ways? Make you want to read on somehow? Be sure to cite from the essays to demonstrate your point. Now, move from these specific evaluations to some general expectations you have about the function of an introduction and what strategies might successfully accomplish that function.

From Publication Assignment #2:
1) **Letter to a writer:** Here, you are to choose an essay that you found to be useful, successful, enlightening, well-written and to write the author a letter. I want you to concentrate on *why* you thought this was a successful essay. In other words, "Dear Lucy, your essay was really good. I learned a lot" is *not* useful, successful or enough to pass the assignment. I want at least a type-written page (as usual, single-spaced) where you *explain* why the essay was useful. This is not only for the writer's benefit but for your own. If you can figure out why you like the way a certain piece works, you can take some of the strategies into your own writing. Simply knowing that you like something is not as useful as knowing WHY. I will collect and evaluate these and then hand them out to the writers. When you write to them, you absolutely MUST cite from their work to

demonstrate your points. Do not vaguely refer to their piece, but rather use it to make your points.

2) An evaluation for me: Here, you are to think over the essays you have read and to reflect on what you consider to be the "good" (relevant, useful, complex, successful, clear, interesting, engaging are some things we've mentioned in class, define "good" however you want but be sure to justify your definition) results and what seem to be the "weak" (vague, confusing, wandering, no focus, 12 focuses, no support, undeveloped, however you define "weak") results. You can begin with microlevel aspects (introduction, focus, conclusion, purpose) or deal with overall essays. I want you to identify not only the results but what you think are the causes: what does or does not the piece do that has these consequences? How does it develop its points successfully? Or why doesn't it? I also want you to explain your evaluation, your criteria: account for your idea of what is "good" or "weak," and how an essay does or doesn't accommodate these criteria. *Why* do you think this works or doesn't work? Again, you must cite from the essays and not vaguely refer to them. Use the essays themselves to demonstrate your points. I will expect at least two typed pages for this assignment.

Many students have difficulty articulating *why* they prefer or resist a given text; for instance, at the start of the semester, many students will claim, "I don't know *why*, I just liked it. It was well-written." But, what makes it well-written seems to be an essential point if we hope for students to be able to demystify writing as something that does not *just* happen. Further, students often claim that a certain writer in the class "just is a good writer." This response ascribes some sort of authorial magic to one individual while denying it to others and represses considerations of composing as a process in which writers might make conscious choices and participate actively. The publication assignments, then, seek to engage readers in an investigation of the specific techniques that appeal to them or push them away; not only are criteria demystified but also the strategies by which a writer might accommodate or resist those criteria. By calling readers' attention to particular *pieces* of a product, the assignment moves them away from general, overall descriptive responses toward more critical evaluative feedback about the way in which a product is constructed.

Peer Reviews:
An excerpt from a peer review by Mariam:
Your essay is improving. You do a decent job showing some ways women face sexism and demonstrating that it is "all around us and mixed in with everyday life." I am glad you don't leave out that men are "victims" of sexism too. You back up your thoughts with incidences when and where sexism occurs. . . . Could you give more specific examples to illustrate the problem. You talk about commercials that show women as objects, well could you give specific commercials, discuss them in more depth. Show how they reflect sexism and how they portray men. . . . The paragraph "More recently, stereotypes . . ." doesn't really fit. It seems just thrown in so my advice is to develop it more and find a way to integrate it because you go from sexism to sexual harassment, two totally different topics unless you make them connect in here.

An excerpt from a peer review by Kafui:
I don't think you're a bad writer, maybe you were just not inspired by the topic, or maybe you're having trouble expressing yourself. But it seems to me, you didn't spend much time thinking about how to write this paper. It also appears that you're confused about what to say. First, you need an introduction where you guide the reader on what you intend to do, where you're taking him. In what seems to be the introduction here, you give a lot of information that you never argue for or even about later in your essay. You say in the introduction that stereotypes had an effect on how you view others. But you never explain how or why. You say you were exposed to *some* kind of stereotypes. Please explain, what kinds? You also often switch ideas before you have made your point. For instance you start saying how stereotypes were part of your everyday life and all of a sudden you tell us that they are bad, but some of them are true. Which, I think is contrary to your objective. You even admit later that a stereotype you held to be true is not in every instance. Doesn't that make this stereotype false? What does the incident with the kid have to do with what people think of you? . . . . You say the first part of the essay reflects your thinking prior to enrollment at UMass, but it sure isn't the impression I got. My understanding is that you still believe some stereotypes are true. And why have you dropped most stereotypes since coming to UMass? Why can't you judge a stereotype? (You did) You need to explain yourself.

An excerpt from a peer review by Fred:
I still think you need some work. From the introduction, I understand that you want to show us that when you were young up to today, you didn't understand that stereotypes influenced your judgments and you want to talk about that. Am I correct? When you say, "Stereotypes are not always bad . . ." you don't explain—why do you think some stereotypes are good? You go on saying, "people have tried to show how ignorant people are in judging a group"—why do you assume they are ignorant and not aware of their judgment? Do you consider yourself to be ignorant because you don't think all stereotypes are bad? But then you say "even I have been stereotyped in my life" is there some particular reason you think you were not supposed to be stereotyped? What do you mean when you call yourself a "typical white male"—is this stereotyping yourself or excusing? You say "But [I experienced] nothing like other races and cultures have." What sort have you experienced? Can you give an example to show the difference between stereotypes you went through and the ones that "other races" went through?

During my first two semesters teaching College Writing, the students consistently rated peer reviews and publication assignments as the least helpful or useful techniques presented in the course. I myself recall attempting to respond to a student's essay using the peer review questions I had assigned ("what's the focus?" "point to some places where you were engaged by the piece," "did you get lost? where?"). I felt thwarted, constrained, unable to write what I wanted to because the questions were in my way and did not solicit the comments I had in mind after reading the draft. Similar to students' frustration at feeling compelled to conform their ideas to a specific and imposed shape, I felt the "shape" of the peer review inhibited me from saying what seemed most important to say. I never imagined, much less thought, to encourage peer reviews that critically engaged the substance of an essay as do those cited above. My understanding of peer review was that it served to help a writer improve what was already written and not that it could challenge the writer to revision substantively or to consider the situated perspective that informed her piece.

Upon my initial discovery of the literature on critical pedagogy, my understanding of the function of these tools changed. According to my interpretation of the process-oriented training new teachers received, I introduced peer response as a vehicle for offering "sayback" or non-evaluative response. We practiced reading sample essays and responding to them without judging them. Conceiving of a ladder of possible responses, I envisioned critical feedback at the top and determined it would take at least four peer review sessions to arrive there. Primarily, I felt a need initially to protect the writers (from what? from whom?) from evaluative feedback because I did not distinguish between critical feedback and negative feedback. As the peer reviews excerpted here demonstrate, however, critical feedback might serve not simply to *criticize* a writer's product, but to present her with a perspective she might not otherwise have considered. Peer reading might engage a piece in order to generate a critique, offering readers a chance to *speak*, to represent their reactions to a piece.

How we name roles is important in establishing an initial attitude and relation to the activities at hand. To refer to writers, rather than authors, is to signify in the name itself the act and the product—writing. "Author" signifies authority over the text and is implicated in the historical understanding of authorship as a privileged position devoid of accountability or responsibility for texts or to readers. Similarly, referring to the text's recipients as an "audience" implies uniformity, homogeneity, a group that passively receives and celebrates the text. "Readers" allows for the differences among those who will engage the text and call attention to the act of reading—that is an active process and not a passive experience of absorbing or receiving the text. Thus, "peer review" is not an adequate name for the process of critical engagement, which we work to develop over the semester and "peer critique" is the term by which I now introduce this process. We talk extensively about the activities that are essential to critique because most students conflate critique with criticism, negative feedback. Critique is an action; it names the fact that readers act on texts by engaging them and attending not only to the "content" but also to the text's workings.

In order to engage in critique, we have workshops throughout the semester where we collectively and orally critique individual essays. Initially, students are typically hesitant to articulate what they consider to be negative feedback. They also move to discount their evaluations with phrases such as "it's just my opinion" or "maybe it's just me" or "I relate to this." Peer critique, then, becomes a process of learning how to contextualize one's response in relation to the piece, while also making explicit the evaluative criteria one brings to a given text as a situated reader. Learning how to perform critique is an ongoing project, not something I can tell them how to do—it takes practice, a sense of a shared group project, in order to be able not only to engage in generating but to engage received critiques.

> *An excerpt from Joseph's peer critique:*
> You make a good point when you say that "a person can hide their sexual preference, but a black man can never hide his skin color." But did you ever think that when a black person gets discriminated against, he/she can go back home and his/her family is also black so they will get support and comfort. When a gay person gets discriminated against, he/she can't always go home because his/her family is not all gay and the family itself might reject them. Also 1/3 of the teen suicide rate in this country is gay-related. That is a very sad statistic.

My original conception of peer reviewing would have effectively silenced Joseph. Further, while a noncritical peer review might have helped Eddie to revise his introduction or to fix some structural problems, it would not have challenged him to consider the impact of his piece on particular audience members (Joseph was not alone in pointing out that, in Eddie's description of a gay, black friend's depression and eventual suicide, he concentrated on racism as a determining factor to the exclusion of homophobia). He would not, that is, have received *critical* feedback, feedback that attends to the substance of a piece, to its construction of a position and not only its construction of an essay. Paul points to the absence of substantive peer critique concerning his "cowering, juvenile, justified essay on . . . my treatment of women:"

> **Paul:** I remember [the peer reader] reading the essay and totally avoiding the main issues. She told me I needed a stronger conclusion or to develop my outlook on certain points but she never got in my face and commented on the content which was, in

> retrospect, fairly rude and ignorant. She didn't respond to the
> content. She made the mistake of forgetting the paper and its
> message as a whole and just referring to the mechanics of it.
> She was probably disgusted with my view and unable to [deal]
> with my stupid justifications.

While Paul attributes the lack of critical feedback to the peer reader ("her mistake"), it was also built into the *form* of our peer review sheets, which primarily sought for the reader to help the writer improve what he had already written rather than to challenge or question or confirm the substance *and* style or structure of the essay. I was institutionalizing the silencing of readers by asking them to restrict their comments to issues of form. Even if Paul's peer reader had chosen to engage in the substance of his piece, he might at that time have dismissed her response as "angry" or "overly-personalized" because such responses were not built into our class. Had she opted for a critical response, she would have risked stepping outside the form imposed on her, a form that required that she ignore her subject position vis-à-vis the essay she was responding to. As a result of her having complied with the peer response norms in our class, he blames her for being passive, noncritical. Either way, the "blame" should rest not with this individual peer reader, but with my implementation of peer response.

For several reasons, I do not now introduce peer critique as "sayback" and progress toward critical, evaluative response. First, there is the potential for readers to feel victimized, violated or offended by an essay; asking them to refrain from voicing these responses seems a dangerous and futile exercise in silencing. Further, writers did not seem to experience peer critiquing as particularly useful when it was limited to either positive or neutral feedback (what is the focus of the essay? what is your favorite moment?). While certainly some positive reinforcement might encourage writers, it does not offer them suggestions for revising from one draft to another, nor does it necessarily indicate the reviewer's experience of reading the piece given that it precludes them from "freely" or honestly responding. Finally, there is a sense of increased engagement in the process of peer critique now, on the part of both readers and writers. When writers perceive their work as substantively engaged, not simply "reviewed," they are more committed to engaging their readers' ideas. I am not implying that writers then change their piece to accommodate the readers, but rather that they think more consciously and critically of their text, of the choices they made in composing that text.

Along with revisioning the function and format of peer critique, I now implement peer critiques differently in the course, again with the aim of enacting their centrality and of utilizing their potential to demonstrate the choices available to writers and readers. Some of the problems students in the past noted with peer critique sessions included their sense that they were always rushed, unable to complete them fully in the class period. Now, at the suggestion of a former student, peer critiques are usually homework assignments. Writers bring in three copies of a draft and their self-assessment and peer readers have more time to read, reflect on, and respond to the texts. Assigning peer critique as homework encourages students to take it seriously and to take their time. Additionally, some students preferred oral peer critique sessions—reading drafts aloud and discussing their responses—while others preferred performing and receiving written feedback on a draft they read to themselves. Similarly, many students prefer writing a letter or a self-generated response, whereas others prefer having some directive questions to consider and answer. In order to accommodate the various preferences and personalities, students, as writers and readers, choose the format they feel is most successful for them. While questions are always available, whether or not to read or consider them is up to the peer reader. Rather than mandate an oral, face-to-face peer critique session, I have writers and respondents meet at the beginning of a class when peer critiques are to be handed back to writers, in order to ask questions, clarify comments, explain a response, or seek more information.

I think one of the most important changes I have made is to stop collecting and writing responses to in-process drafts. Now, if an individual student wants my feedback, we have a one-on-one conference where one of us reads the draft aloud, and then we discuss it verbally. Otherwise, I don't see any drafts until the final is completed, at which point I read everything and comment on the overall revision process. In this way, my comments as the grader or authority figure don't supersede and speak over the peer critiques. Students who are concerned with revising their essays have to give serious and thoughtful attention to their peers' responses rather than simply revise according to their conception of my expectations. Another positive result is more one-on-one interaction with and among students that, along with their need to rely on one another, increases the "contact" among all members of the classroom and enhances the potential for developing a collaborative atmosphere based on shared responsibility and mutual commitment.

I intentionally use the word commitment because for most students, though not all students and not all of the time, it goes beyond getting the work done. They talk frequently in midterm and final one-on-one conferences and anonymous written evaluations about coming to "care" about the work in the class, about finding it to be important or meaningful, and about feeling a sense of responsibility to the class, to one another. This does not indicate that I am "superteacher," and in fact, they write and talk more about the class, about their classmates, than about the teacher in these evaluations. To me, this is a central component of a pedagogical site—in this instance a writing class—that works to negotiate a shared project and an earned and ongoing sense of community as readers and writers. I do not know many contexts in which twenty people come together and learn how to collectively function to the extent that, in the final analysis, they believe the group mattered to them as individuals. It is an example, I think, of seeing the self-in-relation, which I have emphasized throughout this text. This is not an idealized notion of a harmonious classroom where everyone gets along and we would come to class even if we didn't "have" to. There is conflict; there are always one or more students who never "enter" into the forming of the group and who, eventually, are no longer given access to it. We are not "free" from the institutional constraints and parameters, but neither are we operating according to their norms. It is a constant and shifting process of negotiations, mediation, reconfiguration.

It is important to discuss the progress students are making in performing peer critique, and the help writers are receiving from those peer critiques. After each session, I ask for examples of particularly useful responses, and the writers identify the reviewer and explain why their response was useful. This allows us to commend individuals and to keep reflecting on the various ways in which peer critiques might contribute toward a writer's revisioning. In a recent Basic Writing course, peer critiques were difficult and awkward for a majority of the students; many of them perceived themselves to be "bad" writers and did not believe they could contribute legitimate advice to another writer. In an effort to demystify the peer critique process and to re-present it as a readerly role, rather than a writerly one, I solicited examples of the most useful peer critiques writers had received and distributed them to the whole class. We talked about what distinguished these as useful. Dave then volunteered to have his draft peer critiqued by the entire class so that we could engage in a group discussion of a particular piece and discuss the various ways of representing its strengths and gaps to Dave.

The aim here was to consider the range of useful strategies for responding that are available to peer critiquers. The choice about how to respond will depend on a reader's relationship to the writer and topic. As shown in the excerpts above, some students choose to directly challenge the assumptions (the unsaid) or the gaps in an essay. Other times, peer critiquers choose to pose a series of questions for the writer to consider—either questions that arise because a piece is under-developed or unorganized, or because the writer did not consider his situatedness and the reader wants to offer some alternative perspectives. I perceive that my responsibility (for writers and readers) is to offer them a range of choices, a variety of tools and strategies, which might work for them. Their responsibility is to determine which tools work for them and to be able to articulate why. As the peer critique excerpts that opened this section demonstrate, enacting critical peer critiques engages readers more actively in responding to an essay. Each of the examples points to gaps in structure or contradictions between the writer's stated aim and the reader's experience of the essay; thus, students are not "ignoring" the formal or stylistic elements of a piece but are, rather, linking the form to the content. While their comments are critical, they are not thoughtless or negative and they indicate *active* engagement in tackling a text.

My aim is to move beyond peer critiques that present writers with the critical response of readers, a vehicle for readers to express and writers to consider the experiencing of a text that silences or objectifies or excludes particular subjects. I am now moving toward peer critiques that engage readers in a consideration of how their response is not arbitrary or inevitable, but is influenced by their subject-position vis-à-vis the text, by their sense of how it encodes or speaks for or over them. Peer critiques might, then, serve as a means for readers to consider how the process of reading and interpreting is simultaneously a process of writing and constructing the object of response.

During our Interchange sessions, the participants kept alluding to the importance of receiving critiques that engaged the substance of their essays. Their comments also point to the potential of peer critiques to serve a range of functions: establishing a sense of trust and collaboration among class members, in engaging them more fully in the composing process and in considering various perspectives (including their own). Peer critiques and publication assignments, when they play a central role in a course, might allow students to take one another and themselves seriously as writers, thinkers, and collaborators.

Patrick: Yes, I have a stronger connection between writing and thinking. I don't think other teachers spent a lot of time reading students' essays. Therefore, I didn't really have to think about anything, I just talked about anything just to beat the deadline. In this class I really have to think due to the fact that people will carefully read every single word. [This] makes me care more about my writing. In [a previous writing class], I didn't even look at my peer reviews because students just did it because they had to. They didn't think about it, they just wrote and the teacher didn't collect them. In here, it's a whole different thing. We have four peer reviews for every essay and the teacher collects them to make sure we're doing our job. So we really have to think about what we write.

I think it's ok for students to get mad when they peer critique an essay if they disagree with something that was said. Take me for an example, when I wrote my essay on stereotypes, everything I wrote was just MY opinion from experience. When [people] got mad about some of the things I said, they let me know and so I could learn from them.

Mariam: [This course] is different than any other writing course that I've participated in. The main difference is peer editing. . . .

In [other courses], the teacher would explain the topic and give a deadline. All I had to do was write the essay and hand it in on time. I didn't have to show I was making progress and if I was stuck, it was up to me to get help. To me this method was not effective. [This class] allows you to receive help and feedback, not only from one individual but from many. Some [peer critiques] enable you to write another essay. I think peer reading is very beneficial, but there's one problem. Sometimes the reviewer reads the essay and finds information they don't agree with . . . [but] they ignore it and say the essay is fine. I've learned it's better to speak your mind. Several times people have read my essays and said they are good and don't give me any ideas to improve. I think they are thinking that they don't want to offend the writer by giving negative comments or they think to themselves: who am I to tell this person how to write or what to change? I think I value writing more because before I would write just to complete the assignment but now I actually care what I have to say. The main reason is because I have an audience—before the only person who saw my paper was the teacher. Now your essay gets responded to in peer review and the publications. It's more rewarding. Being part of such a diverse class, I have learned a lot, more than any teacher could teach me.

Fred: I used to think writing an essay didn't require a lot of thinking. The reason is that no one had made me feel the need to do so. If I take the example of Kafui's peer critique of Dave's essay, this is the best way for me to explain what is in my mind at this instant. Kafui's conclusion to Dave was: "you need to sit down and rethink this entire essay." I entirely agree with that conclusion because I used to write just like Dave. I would put down a lot of ideas and leave them for somebody else to make sense out of it.

Karen F.: I like constructive criticism, Sometimes peer reviews can be repetitive. "I liked the subject." "Your essay was interesting." [Asking] why and how and because of what, for what reason, and are you sure????? When I see comments like those, I am provoked to think and analyze more. This results in a more thorough explanation of my ideas or theories.

Andalib: Definitely as [our] class developed and people trusted each other, the peer reviews became more content-oriented. I remember people asking me what I meant, what was I trying to say. And likewise I became interested in what other people were trying to say in their papers and wanted to see people develop stronger arguments.

Reflecting on the class, I realize I have learned a lot from the writing of others. Before the semester began, I had an expectation of students on a one-track goal of seeing college as a partying scene with a little school. Not many seemed concerned

> with the world or other issues around campus. In this class, I
> have read many observations and reflections that effected me.
> Essays where a few tackled writing on a deeper level and where
> the essays were thought-provoking and pertinent to the world
> around us. This class taught me a lot about people and that the
> youth ("us") today have a lot of important things to say and we
> can even say them *in writing*.

These remarks, some made two years after our class ended, are
important in demonstrating not only how writers can learn from
one another but also how these writers reflect on that process
and why it was important to them in terms of what they took
from the course. Underlying this book is a commitment to the
value of negotiating and sustaining a sense of community in the
writing class. This can have a great impact on the teaching and
learning of writing; further the experience of *creating* community—whether a group is successful or not in doing so—is an
important and radical departure from the normative classroom
relations and teaching practices of the university. As an institution, the university implies—via grading procedures, the physical configuration of the classroom, honors programs, remediation
programs, merit raise criteria, teaching awards "given" to or
"won" by individual "good teachers"—that competition and
individual performance are what count, what will be *measured*.
Students do not enter a classroom immediately identifying with
one another or assuming they can learn from and with one another. Grades serve to foster and promote the importance of individual performance and productivity, ensuring the teacher's
authority to judge and differentiate individuals, and inhibiting
students' sense that they are in a potentially collective space. How
many courses employ scale grading, where it is literally and a
priori impossible for all students to do well? Where, before one
student has even walked into the classroom, it has been determined that grades will be distributed according to some percentage system, so that a certain number can receive As, Bs, Cs, and
so on. Grades in such a system work similarly to "wealth" in
capitalism; an A is meaningful only so long as everyone cannot
get one, and only so long as we firmly believe that grades are
objectively "earned," not subjectively determined, whether according to the criteria of the institution or the teacher. We need

to believe grades are *earned* in order to believe they are meaningful signifiers, and so we are forced to arrive at criteria for grading that are disembodied and detached from the pedagogical situation.

Notes

1. "Reflections" is cited at length and discussed in terms other than style and form in Chapter 7.

2. A more detailed discussion of the political implications will follow in the section "Learning Language as Discourse."

3. Again, a more detailed discussion of this issue follows in "Learning Language as Discourse."

4. Further, we need to devise ways of participatory conversations that allow for a full range of positions to be expressed without simply *reproducing* the same silencing strategies used to construct and sustain the ideas, attitudes, and relations we seek to challenge and change.

5. We read, for instance, several essays that assert that language is a political tool, one that constructs its users and inscribes a certain version of social reality. Gloria Naylor's article in the "Hers" column of *The New York Times* was discussed in Chapter 2 as demonstrating how a word's meaning changes according to the context in which it is used. Amy Tan's "Mother Tongue" extends this idea to include the fact that not only a word's meaning but our perception and evaluation of a speaker or writer depends on the language she herself chooses to speak in. June Jordan in "Nothing Mean More to Me Than You and the Future Life of Willie Jordan" and James Baldwin's "If Black English Isn't a Language, Then Tell Me, What Is?" reflect on the political implications of devaluing one form of English in order to posit an other form as *the standard* English. Given their argument that Black English grew out of and gives voice to historical experiences and specific subject-positions, the connection is made explicit between the privileging of a language form and the privileging of those who most closely resemble the subject-position implied by that form. Devaluing another language form as "slang" or "inappropriate" entails a silencing of the experience represented by and the subjects who choose to speak in that form. All of these articles serve to provoke reflection on the way in which language itself shapes us— the identity we construct for ourselves and others and make explicit the

connection between political, social, and discursive structures and relations of power and domination.

6. Again, publications are the bound collections that include each student's essays at the end of a given unit. They are handed out to everyone in the class in the form of a journal—cover, table of contents, and so on.

CHAPTER SEVEN

Revisioning Communities in the Contact Zone

Turning our *teaching*, our enactments or attempts to engage (in) pedagogy, into texts is challenging; we lack forms of representation that do not flatten these texts out, reduce their textures. Classrooms, at any given moment, are complex and multidimensional. How do written narratives represent and reflect on this? As Joseph Harris acknowledges, writing critically about our teaching presents the "extraordinary difficulty of representing the work of teaching in ways that allow anything more than the most tightly filtered insights into our courses" (1993, 786). The absence of re-presentations of specific classroom moments reflects not only our failure to substantively engage the dialectic between pedagogical theory and practice, but a lack of models to emulate, critique, and consider. Deciding in this manuscript *how* to incorporate our classroom without deforming it— by simplifying or idealizing or appropriating—has been as difficult as deciding *what* to include. I have chosen from the data those moments that illustrate both the potential and problems of teaching writing as a critical process. I would like to present them in order to invite further reflection and critique, recognizing that the narrative I construct around these moments, the meaning I invest in these texts, is not only enabled, but also limited, by my having been a participant.

An Extended Rap about Our Rap on Rap

During one class, Karen F. and I had an in-class conference to discuss her essay, which attempts to consider accusations that rap music is contributing to, if not directly responsible for, violence, particularly among her own generation. Karen was skeptical about those who say the reason they support the censorship of rap is because they want to decrease violence; to her mind, attacks on *real*—not represented or imagined—conditions would be more effective. Why not deploy the time/money/energy/collective action against real violence by working for change in our material culture? Why do they think that censoring music will really impact violence? As she wonders in her self-assessment, "Who possibly *really* believes that our kids will be okay if we monitor their music? How will silencing Tupac decrease despair or injustice?" I suggested she consider what is really at stake for those in favor of censorship: Whom do they represent? Who are they? Why rap music and not Metallica? What are they really seeking to silence if their efforts would so obviously have little substantive impact on violence? She got stuck on these questions because she was so focused on the ineffectiveness of censorship as a means of promoting peace (which, as she pointed out, is the implied aim of censorship proponents given that decreasing violence implies increasing peace).

We decided to ask anyone interested to gather at the table (I taught in a computer classroom) in order to seek various perspectives on the issue. We were joined by five students: Jason, a white American from Long Island; Magdalana, an African American from Chelsea, Mass.; Joseph, a Latino from Boston; Albertina, a Cape Verdean American from Dorchester, Mass.; Patrick, a Haitian American from Boston. Karen is an African American from "never in, but always near 'the projects.'" The lines were drawn immediately. Jason was the sole supporter of the position that rap has *nothing* to do with violence and in his belief that if, by some fluke, kids who listened to "gangsta rap" were propelled to enact its narratives, the fault rested with the parents rather than the music. Magdalana, Albertina, Joseph, and Patrick did not advocate the censorship of rap, but insisted that it did indeed appeal to African American kids in the city by offering them role models from within their own environment. As Albertina pointed out, *political* rap encourages people in despair to fight back, to make a change, struggle for equalities. "*Gangsta*" rap, however, presents protagonists who operate within the system, not to change the system, but to exploit it and emerge, as she describes, "on the top of the bottom that is the ghetto."

Repeatedly, Jason denied the correlation between rap and violence, claiming he had listened to rap since adolescence and had "never once thought to kill someone because of it." Magdalana asked whether or not he'd ever seen anyone killed outside of television or the movies. He had not. Magdalana and Albertina argued that it is easier to distinguish certain behavior as wrong if you never *witness* it, if it is unfamiliar, absent from your environment. But for kids who experience what the songs discuss, the distinction between "entertainment" and "reality" is more blurred. As evidence, Joseph talked about his thirteen-year-old brother who, heavy into rap, had started wearing the clothes, talking the talk. Joseph himself was concerned about his brother's potential to over-identify with the rap stars who were not only advocating certain actions, but were experiencing violence and trouble in their lives outside of the music. Jason's response was that Joseph was denying his little brother's ability to distinguish between the lyrics and life. "He isn't a lump of mushy clay—he's young but he has a brain and he *should* know right from wrong. My parents taught me that."

During the discussion, Jason worked to shift the blame from music to parents, claiming the answer wasn't to be found in censoring music, but rather in instilling a "moral structure." Albertina asked whether or not it was easier to have certain morals when you were privileged (which she defined as economically secure, living in a house with a yard in the suburbs, having at least one parent around most of the time, and white). She also claimed it was easier to differentiate between the music and reality if you lived a reality that didn't reflect the music. Jason continued denying the connection between how one interprets and responds to a stimulant and the context in which one receives that stimulant. But, to do so, he had to deny the arguments based on experience offered by the other students. Further, he had to deny his own experience as a determining factor in his own argument. He simultaneously became louder and began interrupting other speakers, visibly defensive and verbally hostile. The others became increasingly frustrated and disturbed by his unwillingness to even listen to them, much less to acknowledge the legitimacy of their perspective.

I was yet hoping to address Karen's initial question to the group, which was: what are the *real* motives of those who advo-

COMPOSING CRITICAL PEDAGOGIES

cate censorship? I asked them why, if eliminating negative role models was their aim, the would-be censors did not seek to silence Nirvana with their message of despair, alienation, hopelessness, of being acted upon by an unfair, meaningless society. Jason claimed this was precisely the reason he related more to rap than to "alternative" music: rap offered more powerful voices and a message of individuals being able to *act*. I asked whether there might be a correlation between the need to "censor" for public safety and the fact that the censor's targets were representing, *giving voice to*, black, male (in the case of gangsta rap), urban, economically powerless experiences. Is it not only the message itself (Nirvana's despair or NWA's advocacy of resisting and retaliating against police) but the messengers they seek to silence? And from whose perspectives, or according to whose interests, is *gangsta* rap constructed as the most threatening, the *most* dangerous music? The group was not interested in these questions as they were more focused on whether rap might *sometimes* or *never* contribute to an individual's decision to act in a certain way. They did not seem interested in pursuing this train of thought and, rather than put parameters on the discussion, I let it unfold where it may. Jason did, however, draw a correlation between the historical response to Elvis, the Beatles, and Ozzy Osbourne and the present response to rap. He wanted to move the discussion away from whether rap contributes to violence to whether it should be censored *even* if it does contribute. But the others did not participate in the discussion about censorship beyond agreeing with him that adults always look for the wrong ways to contain and control the outlets of young people.

At this point, it was interesting to note that their single point of agreement, their shared belief that censorship is neither *the* or *an* answer, went unacknowledged. The only moment of alignment went quickly by as Magdalana, Albertina, Patrick, and Joseph sought to convince Jason that rap can have a direct impact sometimes, and Jason continued to counter their point. At this point, Karen F. and Jason became more clearly aligned as Karen took Jason's side that it was ultimately up to parents to control their children. Albertina asked Karen where she had grown up and whether she had had two parents. Karen had grown up "on the edge of comfort," she said, and with two working parents. A physical rearrangement of the group was apparent at this point as Karen moved back from the table and Albertina and Magdalana moved closer together, away from Jason and Karen. The "other" side now clearly included Karen. I started to wonder whether, just as Jason was denying the role experience played in the formation of his perspective, Albertina and Magdalana were not only foregrounding, but prioritizing, experience as the *only* legitimate place from which to stake a claim. Not only was the substance of each side's position in question but also the basis for determining that substance.

During the discussion, Jason interrupted me as well as the other students; when he did, I asked him to wait to speak until I was through. Several times he continued to speak over me, and I shot him an effectively silencing glance to show him that it was my turn to speak. The other students spoke louder when he interrupted, or faster, and made visible their frustration with his silencing tactics. But not one of them asked him to be quiet or made explicit reference to his confrontational strategies. Instead, they kept attending to the content, not the form, of his argument. The next day, Magdalana called me to say she was upset and hurt. She felt Jason didn't respect me as a teacher (because I am so "nice," he takes advantage of me). Further, she was annoyed by his unwillingness to listen and by my unwillingness to *order* him to be quiet. She believed that, as the teacher, I should use my power to force him to play by the rules. Talking to Albertina and Patrick after class, she came to the conclusion that I had "let him win." They wondered why three of the five white males in the class don't treat me with "enough" respect and why they seem to consistently disrupt the goings on of the classroom by challenging me in "unnecessary and unproductive" ways.

Such is an interaction in what Mary Louise Pratt terms "the contact zone:" a "classroom which [functions] not like a homogeneous community or a horizontal alliance." A classroom where texts/issues stand in "specific historical relationships to the students in the class, but the range and variety of historical relationships at play [are] enormous." And a class where "everybody [has] a stake in nearly everything we read [and discussed], but the range and kind of stakes varied widely" (454). This interaction also raises many of the issues I have been attempting to ad-

dress and consider concerning the enactment of a critical classroom. Enabling and facilitating conversations is a primary function of the role I construct for myself as a critical composition
teacher. In this instance, I perceived my choices as a dichotomy:
either I silence Jason by imposing our collective "right" answer
on him, or I attempt to demonstrate (but without calling attention to this demonstration) how to engage in a *conversation*, an
interchange, rather than a contest to simply be the loudest voice.
I now recognize that the choices available to me were more complex and I will return to this issue in the section "But What about
the Teacher?" Here also is an instance when a student refuses to
acknowledge subjectivity (the existence of his own or the legitimacy of others' experiential knowledge), and thus a *conversation* was impeded.

Considerations and Constructions
of Students as Agents and Subjects

Given that my classes have been so heterogeneous[1], I was made
aware early on of the impossibility of simply establishing divisions or constructing my students according to singular categories such as race, class, gender. Because of the aims I articulated
in the previous chapter—engaging students in a consideration of
their "selves" and their texts as constructions, foregrounding how
they can, to some degree, author these constructions, and a recognition of discourse's role in "shaping" these constructions—
the dominant lens through which I view students is determined
according to whether or not they seemed to feel "entitled" or
"devalued" (silenced) as speakers and writers, according to the
ways in which they assume, reject, or struggle with discursive
authority.[2] I aim, then, for individual students to enable them to
locate themselves somewhere in between the two extreme positions of agent and subject, in terms of their words and their worlds.
While they need to recognize that they cannot entirely "master"
and thus control discourse, they might also begin to conceive of
choices in the process and product of composing (in terms of
criteria, product, ideas, etc.); they might, that is, exercise discursive agency. Similarly, the class aims for students to be able to

turn their critical lens inward *as well as* outward—to generate reflections on the "self" and the texts they compose and also their construction of "others" and, ideally, the relation between the two.

At the start of this book, I evoked Taylor, the student whose declared helplessness was a motivating factor in my decision to investigate and practice a critical pedagogy. Taylor's inability to recognize herself as an agent, as one who interprets and therefore imposes meaning on texts, the world or her own life was manifest in her struggle to insert herself into her writing. She often could not think of topics worth writing about, declaring repeatedly that she had "nothing to say" about anything important or interesting. For Taylor, writing was an exercise in erasing herself, what we might recognize as "automaton" writing where the writer takes no control over her text by claiming she "just" writes. Paul, on the other hand, had what might be called a heightened sense of himself as a discursive and social agent. Immediately upon entering the class, he made it clear he considered himself a successful writer and a self-actualizing individual. His first essay, traced the realization of his "glorious vision":

> Three years ago . . . I was only five feet, two inches and weighed a measly one hundred and two pounds. This was a very frustrating point in my life. For one thing, I commanded no respect from my peers. . . . I was always one of the last kids picked in gym class. Then, one clear September day, I had a glorious vision: I, Paul, would become a true athlete. That was when I began weight training. . . . So here I am today, five feet, eight inches, one hundred and sixty-three pounds. Quite a change if I do brag so myself (and I do). . . . [W]hat I'm trying to say is that I feel somehow a bit wiser from having altered my destiny . . . and I can view stereotypes from both sides of the coin.

Paul's purpose in the essay was to reflect on the internal changes that accompany the transition from being categorized negatively (as "geek" or "nerd") to being stereotyped positively ("jock" or "popular"), while simultaneously considering the broader issue of how stereotypes function not only to exclude or disable but also to include and enable. As the section above represents, both stylistically (the strong, determined "voice") and in its content, his absolute belief in self-determination, and the lack of a broader social context according to which he might consider his desire to be a "jock," or the construction of "real" men versus "wimps" in our society, ultimately override his attempt at social analyses. Instead, he locates power to determine stereotypes as residing with the stereotyped, rather than in sociolinguistic structures and material relations. His assertion of the ultimate ability of all individuals to act as agents, to "alter their destiny," signifies a lack of awareness of the ways in which even his "nerdy" self was inscribed with privilege, and that some inscriptions might be more malleable than others. In other words, there is no sense of his subject-position as determined beyond the local level of personal experience.

Paul, then, represents the other end of the spectrum on which I have already located Taylor. Rather than an erasure of agency, he erases his subjectivity, unable to recognize that he is positioned in a particular way in the world and that this location is influenced by and, in turn, influences his understanding of self, others, and world. Both Paul's inflated sense of the individual as a free-agent and Taylor's sense of herself as subject *to* the world around her and to the "rules" of writing as imposed and determined by someone else result in a lack of critical self-reflexivity in their writing and reading. Paul might not recognize the role experiential and structural determinants play in his inscription of a text (or the world) and may therefore assume he's found *the* meaning revealed by the text. Taylor, believing she is not authorized to determine meaning will wait for meaning to emerge, without recognizing the role she plays in ascribing meaning to a text or an experience. As Schwartz observes:

> The apparently sensible nature of the world not only keeps students quiet; it leads to a potentially dangerous understanding of the individual's relation to this world. Reading or understanding comes to seem a passive or uncomplicated *reception* of the truth, facts, or reality that some authoritative figure has discovered; writing or explaining is merely the straightforward reproduction of the preexisting truth that has been uncomplicatedly received. (1989, 61–62)

While Taylor tended to describe past experiences vividly, she struggled with analyzing them, with considering the ways in which they influenced and shaped her present self. Given her tendency to erase herself and to see life as simply and arbitrarily unfolding, it is not surprising that she had difficulty entering into the text, even of her own life, and imposing meaning. Paul, while he analyzed past events in the context of his present identity, was more likely to arrive at a universal interpretation, such as he does when identifying stereotypes as *always* surmountable. As Schwartz suggests the absence of "self"-awareness (resulting either from the "entitled" agent or the "silenced" subject) leads to a sense that we come to see the world/meaning as natural and inevitable, rather than as a result of our location vis-à-vis and interaction with it. Schwartz offers the metaphor of "conversation" as a means by which to encourage critical self-reflexivity from both "types" of students.

> What I "give up" in conversation is rather a particular kind of closure or certainty: no exchange occurs without some risk, however minimal, to my ideas and opinions. And the substitute I receive in exchange for the old certainty is a new role, one constituted by responsibility to another. . . . I take on the responsibility for my own views, for thinking reflectively about what they are and why I hold them. . . . I must recognize, that is, that I have a world view and that not everyone shares it; that I am like others, in short, not because we necessarily all think alike but because my view, like any other, makes "good sense" only within a limited context. (1989, 63–64)

A goal, then, for a critical composition classroom is to develop a sense of writing as a means by which we not only represent but also arrive at our sense of the world, a tool with which we can not only describe but also interrogate our conceptions of self, other, world, and the relationships we impose between them. Before students can revise these conceptions, however, they have to recognize them *as constructs*, as a choice rather than an inevitability.

> [T]he goal of reading closely is not to establish coherence but to turn attention to language as a system of power and to the reader as a constituent in that system. . . . to make interpretation less mysterious by making the processes of reading [and composing] explicit, and helping students to be more aware,

more reflexive about their own readings. The idea is not to waken the ideologically complacent, but to teach ways in which discursive authority functions. It must be added that teaching does not "free" students, but demonstrates how components of ideological systems come to appear as "choices" and "freedoms." (Donahue and Quandahl 1989, 3)

Writing itself might then be presented as a "conversation": a conversation between the individual writer and the experiential, social, political, and discursive factors that have shaped her; between writers occupying a particular subject-position and imposing meaning and readers who are positioned and also act to inscribe, and not simply discover, meaning. Paul describes his increasing sense of the relationship between writing, thinking, and "self"-awareness when he reflects on his history as a "successful" writer. Feeling legitimate as an author, having been "authorized" by others, he was convinced there was not much left for him to learn. Now, he attributes that early success to a conception of authority as deriving from *form*, to his acquisition of "the correct formula":

> **Paul:** The relationship between writing and thinking is such a complex and individual process, but most teachers I had been exposed to ignored this concept entirely. I was always taught to simply write in a format: introduction, body, conclusion. When I graduated from high school, I had so exhausted the options of that format, I thought I knew everything about writing which actually made me a worse writer. I had such a program in me, I couldn't use writing to think and I had no idea how to formulate a paragraph anymore when asked to write in a different manner. Only when a teacher took the time to individualize the process of writing, to display a clear, yet variable framework . . . was I able to make progress in my writing and thinking. I would say the most important thing I carried out of this class is the ability to analyze and filter through memories, experiences to try and determine the "catalyst" moments. What I mean is the specific things, instances, which have led me here, caused me to think and react in the ways I do. This has helped me write better and made me expand the way I think and react to others' thoughts more, well, thoughtfully.

Here, Paul makes clear the connection between questioning his subjectivity and improving his writing skills: looking for the "causes" has helped him to become a better writer. Rather than deriving his authority solely from having the right "form," he now grounds his ability to "write better" in his self-reflexive engagement with the way he is situated in the world and the text.

Though Taylor was unavailable for this study, I selected other students who, like her, began the class feeling absent from their writing and with a sense that "academic" discourse demanded the erasing of oneself as authority from the text. Again, the presentation of writing as a *way of* thinking, and not simply a product of "finished" and appropriately dressed or formulated thoughts, allowed them to insert themselves more into the composing process and to gain a sense of themselves as discursive agents. The following Interchange comments reflect students' experience of the course as a process of coming to envision themselves more as discursive and critical agents and therefore demonstrate the change that might result for individual student writers in a critical composition classroom.

Karen F.: There definitely needs to be a connection between writing and thinking. If you think about that game where someone says blue, and then you say the first thing that comes to your mind, sooner or later, there is a relation between the words. If you do the same for an essay topic, jotting down and really *considering* your ideas, you'll begin to find connections and then you have a reason to write. Getting a sense of writing as a thought-provoking process has allowed me to consider the differences between good writing and bad writing and to become more involved in my writing. Using this in writing essays for other classes, I can see how my ideas, not just the writing, are more organized, linked, and clear.

Beth Anne: I want to ask everyone a question. We are all talking about how important the connection is between thinking and writing. I believe they are almost the same thing. One is expressing yourself to yourself and the other is expressing yourself to others. If this is true, shouldn't everyone who can think themselves through high school be able to write effectively? I always felt like my connection between writing and thinking was messed up somehow during my early education. Does anyone else feel that way?

Andalib: Before Basic Writing, writing was really a struggle for me. I had always felt like a slacker which stemmed from a lack of purpose in writing and in my education. Of course, I knew they were important, but *how* they were important confused me. Here, writing was geared to thinking about the world around me, about my place in it. I saw that I was the key factor in my learning process. My teacher and fellow students were very important, but most important was my ability to learn, to reflect, to change and to become firmer in some old ideas too. Basically, learning to take learning in my own hands. In each essay, we were challenged—if not in the actual content, in the quality of the content and in thinking through and developing it and ourselves.

Josh: In the average class, one is asked to write a paper, but not to think. I mean, we are asked to jot down information, learned or read. In here, I knew I was being graded for my thought processes, for demonstrating thinking, and for attempted revisions, not for content and grammar. By doing this I had to think through the constant revisions. Now, a paper is not complete without revision. I have to get out ideas . . . first, but then I read and really look at what I am saying, what's important and *who* would see it as important, where to expand and push. Writing now gives me a chance to really think *and* to say what I am thinking.

Kafui: If I compare the teaching style between the class I am now taking with Amy and other writing classes I've been in, I would say that [this] course has been the most useful. Why? Well, the writing class I've taken in the past, teachers would pay more attention to technical aspects of writing as opposed to the construction of ideas. . . . Those [grammatical] exercises never incited us to think or learn how to think. Whenever we had to write an essay, . . . there wasn't sufficient time. Added to that, there is the fact that you have to write about a subject you may never have thought of. As a result, I've always thought of myself as a bad writer because I never had any ideas for *those* topics. Thinking and writing are two complementary things. You can't do one without the other and expect a good result. . . . I now value writing more because I now take pleasure in it. It was my ambition when I was younger to go to law school but I wasn't any good at [writing] or at least that is what I was led to believe until I took [College Writing].

So writing as revisioning, writing as a conversation between a writer and her ideas, between a writer and her readers, might offer occupants of both extremes of the agent-subject spectrum a chance to become invested in and responsible for the texts they produce. Making explicit the link between writing and thinking gives both "types" of students an investment in the process. While students may not initially accept or exercise their authority, we need to keep offering them tools for doing so rather than immediately assuming they are unwilling or unable. As Ron Scapps notes:

Many students are already convinced that they cannot respond to appeals to be engaged in the classroom, because they've already been trained to view themselves as not the ones in authority, not the ones with legitimacy. To acknowledge student responsibility for the learning process is to place it where it's least legitimate in their eyes. (In hooks 1994, 144)

Josh, a student who, like Paul, tended to question everything we did as a class, to challenge the usefulness of each assignment, began the class feeling that, while he did have something to say, the product was not valued by those in a position to judge or evaluate his work. Like Taylor, then, he came to believe that successful academic writing entailed the erasing of one's "self," the regurgitation of the teacher's ideas, the following of rules for the sake of adhering to rules. On several occasions, during the course of our interchanges, he attributes his increased investment in the process and product of writing to a growing sense that he could be "present" in his writing and could write about ideas, experiences, and issues that mattered to him without being deauthorized.

Josh: Here I was a little freshman inducted into the brave new world of the English department. I wasn't too happy with taking [Basic Writing]. I was a little disturbed by the idea of flunking my first exam in higher learning, that would be the writing placement exam. . . . In the beginning, I just kind of slacked. It really wasn't intentional, but I had never had to write revisions. In the first essay about myself, I thought I had written the best damn essay of my life and AMY wanted me to change it . How annoying—so like every college student I protested. I finally started to get the hang of these revisions a year or two later, but I know where I started to learn the skill and I [always] use revision today. In other classes, a paper was usually based from research or lecture notes, basically I just had to find the information and spit it back out. In this class, we actually had to come up with a topic and explain why it mattered. In the process of drafts, I had different types of thought processes. In the first draft, I just wanted to have ideas, the second is where I was more critical . . . . I spend the third draft smoothing things out, trying to find a logical sequence for my paragraphs to fall under. In the idea of a *thought* process, I mean coming to terms with and being able to analyze one's own paper.

Excerpt from Josh's end evaluation of "Life," his first essay in College Writing:
In my essay "Life," I chose the two most joyful experiences I could recall and examined them from a theological and philo-

sophical point of view. I have been struggling with who I am and writing this piece helped because I was figuring out how certain people have helped to create "me." This essay felt like a breakthrough for me, not necessarily in my writing, but as a good start to my life as a *college* writer.

Josh: One aspect of the class I found frustrating in the beginning was the whole psychology idea. Who am I? Why am I? I felt at some points as though I was writing in my journal which is fine, but I didn't understand how this was *college* writing. But, then, some of the topics I felt really proud to write about and actually enjoyed. . . . My point is that the psychological idea helped and made me learn not only about English and goals but about revising and figuring out my true thoughts. . . . When I have written a paper now, it's easier to get the idea out but after re-reading, . . . what is important is that I start to really look at what I'm saying and whether or not I need to rephrase or expand, it really gives me a chance to *think*. [My emphasis]

Josh: In high school, I kind of acted like a flake with the will to learn hidden somewhere. . . . My learning disabilities have always been a problem, but I was impressed by your style of teaching because I never felt that grammar or something was the important part of my piece. When I wrote in high school and someone checked my paper, I felt like I had to change the whole thing to fit into society's little shape and that just became a really frustrating aspect of writing to me. So here, in [Basic Writing] I felt like I could concentrate on my thoughts more than my grammar and by doing so I felt I was able to write ideas that really had meaning to me.

Josh: For me, the problem with society's norm tended to be in high school, where I would write a paper and no matter how good my ideas were or weren't (who cared about my ideas, I wasn't supposed to really have any) in the paper, if it didn't have the five-paragraph ideal, it was blown to bits and my parents were called because I had a "writing problem." "You have to catch them while they're young," they would say. . . . I think the number one thing, so to speak, I brought with me from this class has to do with believing in peer reviews. Before this class, I would let one or two people read over my paper basically just for grammatical errors, but never for actual input or variation to the paper. I always felt like it was my paper and other people just never understood what I was trying to say. Since the class, I feel more comfortable with putting new ideas in a paper and [peer review] not only helped me become a better writer, but to deal with people in a different manner. The reviews only felt forced in the beginning, but [later] I found myself turning even to kids in my hall for an opinion and not just on grammar. I was really looking for missing links.

* * * * * * * * * * * * * *

> Of the many methods used to make students occupy submissive subject positions, perhaps the most familiar . . . is the way teachers seem overly concerned with error, misspelling, syntactic lapses, and usage distinctions of the most subtle dimensions. If we include rhetorical shortcomings in structure, development, focus, and logic, the stage is set for an elaborate drama in which the Subject cannot be challenged and in which subjects must be wanting. . . . The good student who can negotiate this minefield intuitively knows that little depends on the ideas in the essay. . . . As a result, the "I" that "writes" the essay is so decentered, so alienated from actual experience that many students have as much emotional identification with their school writing as they do with geometry. (Clifford 1991, 48)

Josh alludes repeatedly to his sense that "college" writing had some concrete and immutable form—a form with which, based on past experience, he would feel neither comfortable nor competent. Seemingly, not only teachers but peer readers as well were acquainted with this form, though Josh was not, which left him feeling alienated not only from the writing process but also from control over how his product was evaluated. In a course where students were encouraged to use writing to consider how they have come to be positioned in the world, and to grapple with that position (and in a course where readers were encouraged to respond to the substance of a piece, not merely its form) Josh began to experience a new sense of authority which, in turn, provides for a revised understanding of himself as a writer and of the function of writing.

While I cannot "give" Andalib or Josh agency, any more than I can "liberate" them from a sense of impotence as social or discursive actors, I can provide processes that encourage them to recognize the ways in which they determine the world, even as they perceive it to be acting on them. As Josh and Andalib indicated above, students' passivity often stems from their sense of not really being certain what purpose their writing is serving. Helping them to take responsibility for *finding* a purpose, rather than imposing a purpose on them, might be a means of engaging them more fully in the composing and learning processes.

For Joshua, writing can become a vehicle for action, a process by which the agency he exercises might be exposed. For Paul, writing can become a means of *reflection*, a chance to recognize that he is positioned not atomistically, but along a continuum of available subjectivities, and to consider why he has arrived at this particular position. While I cannot force him to abandon his ideal of free agency, I can challenge him to consider the factors that enable him to believe this is true *for him* as well as to recognize the constraints that might prevent this ideal from being possible for everyone.

Revisioning the Rap on Rap

The tensions that emerged during the discussion on rap might be understood by considering the role Jason occupied in the subject-agent array, as well as by considering the role I chose versus the expectations my students had of me. All the students were relying on personal experience as the foundation for their argument; Jason's experience, however, stood in sharp contrast to the experience of the majority. Further, he was unwilling or unable (probably somewhere in between the two) to recognize the determining influence of his own background and subject-position. Struggling to defend his "right" to interpret rap music *absolutely*, Jason was forced to discount and deny the experience of everyone else at the table. On the other hand, Magdalana, Albertina, Joseph, and Patrick sought not to contradict Jason's interpretation but rather to *localize* it, to convince him to acknowledge competing, but equally legitimate, interpretations and to recognize that his was simply one of many possible positions. The students, seeking to ground their contradictory positions in personal history, became increasingly specific in their articulation of influencing factors, moving from the more general categories of "white" versus "black," city versus suburb, to the specific experience of growing up white and male on Long Island in an economically privileged nuclear family. They drew on their own histories, not as a means of forcing Jason to give up his own interpretation, but as a means of forcing him to acknowledge the ways in which his subject-position was influenced and specific, rather than universal.

> Identity politics emerges out of the struggles of the oppressed or exploited groups to have a standpoint on which to critique dominant structures, a position that gives purpose and meaning to struggle. Critical pedagogies of liberation respond to these concerns and necessarily embrace experience, confession, and testimony as relevant ways of knowing, as important, vital dimensions of any learning process. (hooks 1994, 88)

But Jason's insistence on denying his own subject-position—his denial of the influence of geographic place, race, class, gender, and family structure on his interpretation and response to rap—entailed his devaluing of the other students' experience. To acknowledge personal testimony as a legitimate basis for their interpretation would have required that he attend to his own judgment as constructed and partial. Instead, he insisted on arguing in absolutes and universals, for one "right" answer, one "truth."

Magdalana and Albertina's visibly distancing themselves from Karen and Jason represented the fact that their argument is grounded not only on experience but also on a recognition that their shared experience places them together, apart from others. They had not only to voice their knowledge to Jason (and later Karen) but also to assert the legitimacy of experiential knowledge as a "relevant way of knowing." But, the potential of identity politics to preclude a recognition of even shared intellectual and political ground was also evident in the discussion: Magdalana and Albertina glossed quickly over the point at which they aligned with Jason and Karen—their common assumption that censorship is not the solution, regardless of how we define or where we locate the sources of the "problem" in question.

Conceiving of values, opinions, and interpretations as *either* right *or* wrong, as "out there" somewhere waiting to be discovered, Jason lacks an awareness of how the seemingly *"ordinary* experiences of life . . . not only fill time but they also shape language, behavior, and imagination" (Shor 93, my emphasis). Nonetheless, his impatience with the discussion, his apparent perception that he was not really being heard (despite the fact that his was the loudest voice), reflects the dissonance experienced when one's secure sense of self and of the place that self occupies in the world is disrupted, called into question, identified as not simply "natural."

> Like our presence in the world, our consciousness transforms our knowledge, acting on and thinking about what enables us to reach the stage of reflection. This is precisely why we must take our presence in the world as the focus of our critical analyses. By returning to our previous experiences, we grasp the knowledge of those experiences. The more we can uncover reasons to explain why we are as we are, the more we can also grasp the reason behind our reality and thus overcome our naive understanding. (Freire 1985, 100–101)

In the case of this discussion, there was a lot at stake for Jason as he was being forced to confront the existence of a particular and partial (incomplete) subject-position that determines his opinion and prevents him from speaking *for* others. The other students were prompting him to acknowledge that there are reasons why he thinks as he does, socioeconomic factors that determined his experience and his interpretations. As a white, heterosexual, economically privileged male, however, the identity constructed for him by the dominant culture is both positive and powerful, preventing him from having to contend with (or recognize) socially, discursively produced representations of himself. In other words, his very ability to "erase" his subjectivity makes possible his belief in absolute agency (that parents, if not individual children, can control and determine the influence of rap). Having seen himself positively in books, in school, on television, having been "written" in appealing ways all over the culture, it is with ease that he now ignores himself. Unless an individual experiences dissonance or friction between his own self-image and the image produced by the dominant culture, he might believe he has a "choice" about *whether* to construct his own identity. Without having been made to choose, he might not be forced to recognize identity *as* a construct, as something produced outside of oneself, by experiences, environment, language, images, and the socioeconomic structures that are informed by and inform them.

Having experienced his composite self as seamless, not having had to confront his situatedness (race, gender, economic status, sexuality), Jason is unable to negotiate a space between what he sees as the irreconcilable positions of agent and subject. His response is familiar: (predominantly) male students frequently deny the existence of sexism, or white students deny that racism "really" still exists. *Acknowledging* the existence of racist or sexist social and discursive structures and relations would entail confronting the privilege granted to them by those structures and relations, if not an admission of their complicity in perpetuating (passively or actively) them. Karen F., however, having *recognized* herself represented as an object, is aware that others have constructed a role, an identity *for* and *over* her. She cannot, then, simply ignore the idea of subjectivity, as she has to *contend* with the identity, the subject-position, offered to her.

An excerpt from "Reflections" by Karen Foster:
When I was younger, a lot of words did not exist in my vocabulary. "Stereotype" was one of them. . . . When I was in kindergarten, I always had friends who were white. At that age, I did not know the difference. . . . I only started noticing the differences that were supposed to be there when I saw how black and white friendships were portrayed on television. These children's parents did not get along with each other. I found this kind of strange; my best friends' parents got along well with mine. I wondered what the anger was about. Looking back, I can say television was the first outlet to teach me about more than just stereotypes—prejudice, racism, and hate. You know what I'm talking about. When was the first time you noticed that all black people are able to dance? Or that we all excell in basketball? Or on picnics, we only bring watermelon, and fried chicken? I was still young at the time, so I found most of these images to be humorous. Why not? To me they were true. I love fried chicken and watermelon. I could dance. But wait a minute . . . even if Dr. J. tried to teach me, I couldn't play basketball, even if my life depended on it.
. . . .I continued to watch T.V. But I was getting older and I started to notice: why were blacks always living in the ghettos of inner cities ("Good Times")? Why were they always only criminals ("Hunter")? Why were they always trying to steal something (any show you watched)? . . . . I remember asking my mother "Why!" She couldn't give me a straight answer. All

she said was that these portrayals were stereotypes and they were used to make one group seem better than another.

Karen's awareness of these representations propels her to consider not only the ways in which she is imagined by others but also, in turn, the ways in which she herself imagines "others." Having already turned the lens outward, she is propelled later in the essay to turn it inward:

> *An excerpt from "Reflections" by Karen Foster:*
> But come to think of it, we've all held and said a stereotype one time or another. Admit it. "What do a blonde and a balloon have in common?" "What do you call a black, Jewish and gay person?" "Don't try to act black." "Why are you talking like a white person?" Tell me, what *does* a white person talk like? When someone laughs at these jokes you feel better, not even because you made the person laugh, but maybe because that person thinks the same way you do about "other" people. . . . I've realized someone could be talking about me in the same way. It hurts and I'll admit it. I still talk mess with someone I don't like, but I don't attack their ethnicity, complexion, height . . . things they can't change. And why should they? Who am I to decide? Why should my standards mean everything? . . . There are standards as to what the perfect human being is: an Anglo-Saxon male with upper-middle class status. If you measure up to this standard, you might feel you have the right to criticize or put down anyone who does not. As for the rest of society, there is a feeling of resentment. In order to fill these insecurities [we] turn to putting down someone else who does not measure up.

It is important to note that Karen not only *experienced* the process of being constructed and constructing but also articulates and reflects on the experience. As Freire suggests, it is by returning to her previous experiences that she "grasps the knowledge of [those] experiences." This knowledge, this *reflection* on why "we are the way we are" propels her to *action*, signified by her turn to self-reflexive critique. As bell hooks says, "Coming to voice is not just the act of telling one's experience. It is using that telling strategically—to come to voice so that you can also speak freely about other subjects (*Teaching*, 148).

But What about the Teacher

Magdalana's critique of the role I chose as the teacher stems from at least two related issues. First, I believe she confused Jason's combative, defensive posture with his victory—doesn't the *loudest* one always *seem* to win? I pointed out that I had not let him interrupt me but that I decided (had made a conscious choice) not to speak *for* her and the others. Not only would I not be there to do that in most situations, but to do so seemed simply another way of denying them their voices. We also discussed Jason's argumentative strategies as a reflection (and result) of the fact that he *was* listening but didn't like what he was hearing. Unable to substantively challenge their argument, he relied on bullying tactics, consistently redirecting the conversation and recasting the debate. So, perhaps we should not look at the discussion simply as a "loss" for her side, but as a moment when Jason's conceptions of himself and of "others" and of his right to speak *for* and *over* everyone had been unsettled; hence, his turn from offensive to defensive strategies. Second, she wanted me to be a more outspoken advocate for her and those she perceived as her allies. Because she invests me with the loudest voice, she feels strongly that my voice should be used to impose not only order but to ensure that "truth" prevails. Silenced and interrupted, she and the others felt verbally beaten. Despite the dissatisfying results of this engaged discussion, exposing and confronting the ways in which different participants assume and exercise authority is, as Jay suggests, necessary if our aim is to enact, and not only to espouse, a participatory pedagogy.

> In the classroom, the authority of one person's experience quickly runs up against that of someone else, so that the limits of such authority may be usefully marked and analyzed. Clashes of cultural identities do not always yield to happy multiculturalism, however, or cheerful tolerance. On the contrary, the differences between cultural groups are often fundamental, sometimes deadly, and are better brought into the open than repressed (at least in the classroom). Multicultural pedagogy inevitably confronts the problem of how a social structure can successfully accommodate persons who find the beliefs or truths of others to be unacceptable and intolerable. (1994, 620–21)

A few years ago, I most certainly would have silenced Jason in order to allow the other students to speak and also to convey a message to him that he did not ultimately have the power to determine what or who was heard. In this instance, however, given my determination to *enact* a participatory classroom, I hesitated because Jason was alone in representing his particular position, and he was a minority in the group as a male and a white person. Could I really force him to listen to the other students, or would I be simply forcing him to heed my authority? hooks posits that a fundamental task of the critical teacher is to facilitate dialogue that implies not only prompting students to talk but also to listen:

> This doesn't mean that we listen uncritically or that classrooms can be so open that anything someone says is taken as true, but it means really taking seriously what someone says. . . . I see it as a fundamental responsibility of the teacher to show by example the ability to listen to others seriously. (*Teaching*, 150)

Evoking my authority as facilitator when debates become mean and threatening, or fall into a dualistic and repetitive cross-debate, is a strategy I am comfortable with; here, however, I felt imposing my voice as teacher would be counter-productive. I felt that by intervening, Jason would perceive he had been forced to abdicate rather than realize he had been substantively challenged and unable to meet the challenge. Further, I am aware of my tendency to listen more "seriously" to those students with whom I agree or am sympathetic. In this instance, I felt neither aligned with nor compassionate about Jason's position, given both his insistence on denying the validity or influence of experience and his combative argumentative tactics.

> Reimagining the classroom as a contact zone is a potentially powerful pedagogical intervention only so long as it involves resisting the temptation to either silence or celebrate the voices that seek to expose, critique and/or parody the work of constructing knowledge in the classroom. (R. Miller 47)

In the past, the most consistent criticism I have received on course evaluations is that I am *too much* of an advocate. The only group specifically named as the object of my advocacy is women and/or feminists. In this instance, also, I find it interesting that Magdalana and the students she spoke to would have felt I *could* advocate for their position. They know my economic background, that I am ten years older, from a white, Midwestern suburb and that I do not listen to rap (except for the group Salt-n-Pepa which, the students noted, occupied a distinct genre from the groups in question). Given that their argument was rooted in the belief that personal experiential knowledge is primary, it is ironic that I—whose experience was the most markedly different (even simply generationally) from everyone else in the group—might be perceived as the most forceful and powerful spokesperson for their position. Obviously, these students assumed I *would* act as their advocate and invested me, as teacher, with the final word, the ability to impose right-ness, truth. While I was allied with the rest of the students, my alliance was a reaction to Jason's rhetorical strategies, more than a reaction to the content of his argument. I was sympathetic with his efforts to complicate the issue and to keep trying to get back to the issue of censorship as a misdirected and motivated attempt to control young people, rather than a genuine attempt to make strides against violence.

And yet, Magdalana's criticism unsettled me. Should I have enforced more structure onto the conversation? Should I have imposed an interpretation as *the* "truth" at the end of the discussion? The problem is, that at the time the discussion took place, I was conflating these two positions. Rather than considering an array of choices or of roles, I only envisioned two: *either* I could impose order and therefore impose a "truth" *or* I could choose not to intervene directly and hope my own refusal to be interrupted was teaching him something. However, I could have imposed structure, evoked my authority as teacher-facilitator, without simultaneously silencing the debate. I could have advocated reciprocity in speaking and listening to one another, without advocating a particular "right" answer. As Magdalana pointed out, I had failed them, not because I did not speak up for her side, but because I didn't require that *everyone* present participate as active listeners while she and the others were speaking.

Part of my decision not to evoke my authority as the teacher-facilitator resulted from questions that arose for me after an earlier class when we had a heated discussion about sexism and advertising. Again, a few students were louder and spoke more frequently, claiming that neither they as individuals nor the system of advertising is complicit in or benefiting from sexism. At the end of the discussion, I was disgusted with the general denial that either the system of advertising or the individuals who passively or actively participate in that system are sexist. Therefore, I took two minutes and offered my understanding of the "truth:" to me, denial accompanied by an unwillingness to really engage in the opposition's arguments signifies complicity, absolutely. Further, I noted, given that we have been raised and conditioned in a society and economy which are not only informed but *sustained* by the subjugation of women and the privileging of men, how could any one of us claim to be innocent or "free" of sexism? Wouldn't this be an ongoing, never-ending process, one of many small and infinite steps rather than one that we might simply and finally complete? Later, I questioned my need to impose order and judgment onto the chaos of a discussion that, though tense and at moments unruly, was productive in engaging all the participants to account for their positions. Why did I need to ensure that my ("right") side was heard last and loudest? Why is it so difficult to leave a discussion that is not "finished" or "definitive," but is messy and complicated and open-ended?

Several students approached me after class, from competing sides in the discussion, to express their relief that—for once—I had provided a clear endpoint, had intervened in order to allow them to leave with something clear and tangible, rather than unsettling and unresolved. Nonetheless, I remained skeptical about imposing *my* perspective, and drawing consciously on my institutional authority in claiming the last two minutes because I could not face going home again and trying to sort through where our discussion had taken us. I chose to exercise my power for my own peace of mind—that I might know I had *imparted* something—as much as to advocate for the underrepresented position. Hadn't I chose a critical end over a critical process?[3]

Looking at my different response to the discussions on rap and sexism, I realize that I feel more comfortable serving as a spokesperson when a particular side is under-represented and that, in such an instance, I have no difficulty evoking my institutional

authority. Perhaps this accounts for part of my hesitance in intervening during the discussion on rap: despite Jason's combative
strategies, he was clearly the underdog in terms of the *substance*
of the debate. But my mistake was in conflating the *process* of
enacting a critical conversation and espousing a specific, authoritative *end* of the conversation. Further, despite Jason's being alone
on his side of the issues, he was *not* simply or unproblematically
underrepresented given the discursive and social authority invested
in the subject-position of whiteness, maleness, and class privilege. I need, then, to be more attentive to how conversations take
place and to consider the array of options available to me at a
given moment rather than constructing my choices as oppositional and mutually exclusive.

So, the "role" we choose to occupy is open to negotiation
and is likely to shift according to the situation at hand. Nonetheless, this fluidity is not often reflected in the scholarship as prescriptions about how to exercise *or* share *or* deny authority tend
to advocate one choice at the exclusion of the others. In "Risks,
Resistance, and Rewards," for example, Cecilia Rodríguez
Milanés notes her discomfort at having "yelled" at her students
for their passivity and detachment and for not complying with
the contract they had collaboratively devised and by which their
performance was to be evaluated. As Rodríguez Milanés describes,

> I shocked myself. I took out a copy of the contract, waved it at
> them, and reread out loud some of the requirements, remind-
> ing them that they had authored this contract. . . . I was angry
> . . . . Guilt began to pulse at my temples. There was silence. I
> like to think that some of them hung their heads in shame, for
> that was exactly what I was doing. (1991, 123)

This is a troubling response, because it implies a classroom
can operate without explicitly directive moments from the teacher,
whether they manifest themselves in anger, frustration, or disappointment. Like my own construction of choices during the discussion on rap, Rodríguez Milanés envisions no options between
doing nothing and evoking a traditional posture of teacherly authority. In this instance, however, as in the discussion on rap,
such an evocation is not only appropriate but necessary. One of
the most challenging and critical tasks of *any* teacher, regardless

of her pedagogical orientation, is to engage and motivate students. Nonetheless, we have all had the experience of being *unable* to move twenty or more disinterested students. If we have been self-critical and considered alternative means to encourage them to be active and interested, if we have considered our complicity in creating the situation and still have no success, I see no reason not to express frustration.

Rodríguez Milanés seems to have internalized the myth of the super-teacher—an image that informs implicitly or explicitly various models of pedagogy—the teacher who never loses her cool or expresses any emotions which are not clearly supportive, encouraging and positive, or non-authoritative. The idea of a critical classroom, however, is that it depends on the active participation of at least a majority of the members. Having negotiated the expectations of the course in collaboration with her students, why should she feel "guilty" for holding them to their end of the bargain? Surely her students would have a right to express anger and disappointment if she failed to respond to their writing or to show up for class? Weren't her students exercising their power in choosing *not* to fulfill the requirements they had helped to devise?

Here, Rodríguez Milanés seems to interpret critical pedagogy as implying that a teacher cannot *ever* use her power or exercise the authority granted to her by her position within the institutional structure. Whether or not we exercise this authority, it *always exists*; we cannot ever completely or equitably distribute power. So, the issue might be *how* we exercise our institutional authority, rather than *whether* we do. Moreover, as Gore observes, "As Foucault (1977) and others (e.g., Walkerdine 1985, 1986; Walkerdine & Lucey 1989) have argued about disciplinary power, practices which decrease overt regulation can increase surveillance and regulation through covert and more dangerous means" (68). A better strategy than denying or repressing power, then, might be to expose it consciously and directively, as a means of strategizing how to disperse it. In the moment Rodríguez Milanés describes, it seems to me she was using her authority in order to engage students in a recognition of their own authority—to name their passivity and lack of engagement *as choices* with consequences for the whole class and not simply as natural or inevitable student roles.

In considering our roles as teachers, it is important that we not assign absolute, transcendent parameters. Rather than assuming we *can* "empower" or "share" power, we need to consider how power is exercised by students and teachers in specific, micro-level operations in the sites of specific classrooms. If we adhere to Foucault's conception of power as "exercised," and existing "only in action," (1980, 89), then we cannot prescribe how power is to be used or rejected. We cannot declare all exercising of power in a particular manner to be repressive, without considering the local and actual context in which it is exercised. As Gore notes, "the perpetuation of a dichotomy between empowerment and oppression also stems from a shift in conceptions of power as repression to power as productive, such that empowerment is linked with a productive conception of power and oppression is linked with a repressive conception" (1992, 59). Gore suggests we move from the notion of "empowering" (implying a one-way transference of power) to considerations of how we might "exercise power toward the fulfillment of our espoused aims, ways that include humility, skepticism, and self-criticism" (68). We might, that is, exercise power, as I interpret Rodríguez Milanés to do—in order to help students exercise their power inside and outside of the classroom, by pointing out their responsibility and accountability for determining the class and holding them to the criteria they collaboratively generated.

While metaphors of the teacher as "nurturer," "coach," "emancipatory authority" abound, the role a teacher takes on should vary according to the context in which she acts. Further, no *one* of these personae or strategies is likely to succeed with all students, for all teachers, or in every classroom. Conceptualizing a broad range of possible roles and interrogating how contexts (including our construction of students and self) determine the role we choose seems a more useful and fluid exercise in determining the functions teachers fulfill in critical classrooms. Further, the critical classroom relies on "conversations" *between* students and teachers, on their mutual responsibility for the process and product of learning. The de facto exclusion of particular roles or voices (anger, frustration, disappointment) because they are defined *in the abstract* as noncritical or nonnurturing, denies the opportunity for everyone in the classroom to participate in determining the dynamics and relationships. While, as Rodríguez Milanés suggests, anger is not an *essentially* appropriate response, surely there are situations in which it is necessary and appropriate. Similarly, students should be able to express anger about failed expectations, concern for how they are being "read" by teachers or the roles constructed for them.

To avoid immediately conflating anger with destructive or uncritical authority, the class must engage in continuous reflections and discussions about the class. Students and teachers together can discuss their goals and expectations, thus establishing a collaborative (if not absolutely consensual as not all participants will agree) framework for the course that then provides a basis for a range of responses. Magdalana, then, can express her disappointment that I did not deploy my institutional authority to make Jason listen. I, in turn, can articulate the choices I perceived as available to me and reflect on how I might choose differently given that I now recognize the existence of other choices. In the situation that arose during our discussion on rap, I chose not to assert my institutional authority because of apprehension about how Jason would respond. It seemed to me that Joseph, Maggie, Albertina, Karen, and Patrick were holding their own. And yet, clearly, my "gaze" here was directed primarily at Jason; perhaps I should have been more attuned to the impact he was having on the rest of the students. As Magdalana pointed out, on more than one occasion, a few students have appeared to disrupt and destructively determine the agenda and dynamics.

One such occasion, which Magdalana mentioned in particular and which several students referred to on their mid-term course evaluations, arose when Charles wrote an essay defending the idea that white people can dance. The essay begins by noting famous white dancers (Barishnikov, Astaire) and goes on to locate various dance forms as emerging from the needs and traditions of specific cultures. Not until the end does he introduce his own love for, and training in, break-dancing, hip-hop, and other forms he identifies as "African-American dancing." Clearly, Charles has a particular relationship to his topic—he wants to defend not only his right but his ability to dance any dance. In my comment to him, however, I noted that the way in which he assumed authority seemed duplicitous as he attempts to first construct an "objective" or "absolute" argument. Soon, though, the ground shifts as he moves to localize, and by the end, when his personal stake in the topic emerges, I felt duped and suspicious. First, he declares Barishnikov and Astaire are "beyond any doubt, regardless of your criteria, two of the most successful and amazing dancers in the history of dance," while paying no attention to the form of or audience for their dance. His second move is to establish that our appreciation for one dance form over another is determined in part by our association of that form with a particular ethnic group. In the same essay in which he is calling attention to the nature of categorization as a construction, one biased and determined by both our subject-position and the social construction of the form in question, he is also attempting to pose absolute judgments. Further, by denying his investment in the topic until the end, he is attempting to use a disinterested, detached voice as a means of establishing credibility and authority. I suggested he consider opening the piece by detailing his own history with various forms of dance and then explain his frustration at being categorically denied "access" to particular forms because of his whiteness.

An excerpt from my response to Charles's essay:
While you seem to have taken the approach that denying personal involvement results in increased credibility, as one reader I disagree. As Glenna and Robin [peer readers] point out, it's a bit confusing to suddenly leap into your personal history with the topic as this section actually would better illuminate the preceding section by introducing it. In the section on how we wrongly continue what was once an appropriate association between cultures and dances and dancers, there is more unsaid which informs this section than said. See Glenna's questions on peer review and mine in margin. Further, you are arguing against absolutes rather loudly and yet in the previous paragraph, you spent several lines *telling us* that Astaire and Barishnikov are among the best *period*. There, it seemed you were searching to prove white men could dance. But, these men dance a very particular sort of dance, each of which is typically associated with specific audiences (in terms of class and race).

So, how do they serve as a counter-example rather than a reinforcement of what you argue against later? I think all these
pieces do somehow fit together, but you need to work through
the connections more clearly and to at least address/explore
the contradictions in here if you can't, finally, resolve them.
Again, I suggest you consider opening the piece by situating
yourself vis-à-vis the topic. I felt skeptical to find how relevant
this was to you personally *only* at the end and to now have you
consider how this relevance determined your argument.

When I handed this essay back in class, Charles read the comment and immediately refuted my interpretation. He believed that
foregrounding his investment would diminish his authority and
did not believe the experience was necessarily relevant to or informing the argument. He could, he claimed, eliminate that section of the essay without substantively changing the claims. But
could he eliminate that part of his personal history, the experience itself, without substantively revising the claims in the essay,
I asked. He believed he could. Class that day was supposed to
revolve around a discussion of their research projects, but Charles,
even as the group was gathering, moving from terminals to the
table at the front of the room, was still challenging my response.
Other students voiced opinions about how authority is most usefully and effectively constructed by writers, about where personal
reflections most appropriately enter an essay. Charles had tended
to dispute my readings all semester, to withdraw during group
work, and to continually express his surprise at having not tested
out of the College Writing requirement. At our mid-semester conference, he mentioned that he had expected the course to be a
"joke," and so didn't plan to take it too seriously. He did not like
revising, drafting, or peer editing (which he excels at in terms of
substantive, reflective, and challenging comments). We had engaged in a battle of will all semester and this was not the first
time a conflict became a part of the larger class discussion.
   While the class voted to postpone discussion of the research
project in favor of reading and responding to Charles's essay and
the broader issues of how authority is constituted and functions
in an essay, several students were frustrated by this decision. They
felt Charles was often able to re-direct the agenda of the class
because he actively challenged me. As one (white female) student

noted on her mid-semester evaluation, "a few kids (who happen to be white and male) are always disrupting the discussions. I don't think we should react the way we do because it gets in the way. Plus I think it's funny that in such a diverse class when we're always talking about power they are still deciding more than the rest of us. Because they are louder."

I had never been in a class where white males were such a significant minority and I had been especially attuned to Charles who seemed to feel constantly uncomfortable. I tried to ensure his sense that his contributions to discussions and agendas counted, as I am conscious of doing with any students who seem to feel themselves on the margins of the class. In this instance, however, those in the minority within the classroom were inscribed with majority status everywhere except the classroom, a status conferring power and authority which obviously carried over into our writing class. While my hope was to challenge Charles's easy means of taking on authority without simultaneously taking on accountability for that authority, I allowed him to determine the class agenda that day. In the hopes of unsettling his sense of himself as objective, removed, detached from his own opinions and values, to demonstrate that he does have a determining and situated subject-position, I gave over group control of the discussion. By so doing, I handed over control to him, thus reinforcing the very authority I sought to challenge. Some of the other students clearly (and rightly) feel Charles's privilege to determine events is reinforced by this strategy rather than questioned. So while the *end* of the discussion, its impact, was that the group convinced Charles to consider other ways of claiming and using discursive authority, the *means* to that end, the discussion itself, reinscribed his authority. Of course, we did vote, and a majority chose to discuss Charles's essay. While it was not a case of the tyranny of the minority (white males or me), it was an instance where a member of the dominant's ease in challenging the authority of the teacher and the classroom became the propelling factor of our discussion that day.

The roles we occupy as teacher rely on our construction of students; in turn, the roles students (to some extent) choose to occupy depend, in part, on their construction of the teacher. Despite my having ensured Charles the opportunity to participate actively in the course, he clearly did not see me as an advocate. And yet Magdalana did perceive me as an advocate despite her sense that I did not fulfill the role adequately. We cannot, once and for all, determine *the* positions to be occupied by teachers or students, not even in such general terms as I used to categorize mine above as agents versus subjects. As Josh demonstrates in his comments, for him the course was a means of making a transition. Gradually, he revisioned his sense of himself from a writer subjected to rules and structures imposed on him by those with societal authority to a writer who could intervene actively in his compositions. He thereby found more meaning in the process and produced texts that he and others considered to be valuable. Paul, on the other hand, shifted from a sense that any text he authored was successful by virtue of his having followed the right formula, to a sense of accountability for the substance of his writing. With each of these students, my role shifted along with their revisioning of themselves as writers. As Paul became more conscious of and responsible for the ways in which his writing constructed himself and others, I became more of an ally and my comments included more praise. As Josh became increasingly confident that he did have something to say to others and not only for himself, I challenged him to consider how readers might respond and why. Not only, then, does my role shift within a given class, but it undergoes a transition vis-à-vis individual students.

Closing Reflections on Teaching Writing as a Critical Process

The only absolute condition underlying the roles we construct for one another is that teachers are situated in positions of institutional power, elevated in the institution's hierarchy, and students are not. This institutional authority, the way it is accommodated and resisted by students and teachers, needs to be more often acknowledged and confronted in our discussion. Because neither we nor our students can simply ignore, reject, or deny it, we need to consider both those moments when we attempt to evoke authority critically—that is, in an attempt to en-

courage students to recognize or exercise their own authority —
and the moments when we use our authority (to grade, to com-
mand attention, to direct discussions) to silence, to have power
over, rather than power *for*. Further, recalling Freire's claim that,
students "are so *ideologized* into rejecting their own freedom"
(Shor and Freire 1987, 21), we should not assume that a simple
giving up or sharing or transferring of power is possible. We
should not, that is, assume we *can empower*. But it seems to me
we should grant students more agency than we typically do when
we assume that *any* expression of a personal belief or political
opinion, any advocacy at all, will effectively silence them *because*
we are in positions of institutional authority. And, we might also
consider whether silencing *can* be effective, can be one useful
choice in the array of options rather than always the negative or
noncritical choice. As Magdalana suggests, sometimes the silencing of one student is perceived as the authorizing of other students' right to speak. How do we make such decisions? Seemingly,
critical teachers have to strategize ways of representing the complex, and sometimes contradictory, roles we play in the classroom without fear that this inevitable complexity, the impossibility
of ever fulfilling a decontextualized and disembodied set of criteria (as articulated by the scholarship on critical pedagogy), automatically results in our failure to enact a critical agenda.

The positing of our teacherly roles as mutually exclusive
choices reflects the broader tendency to construct our pedagogical choices as oppositional, either/or. Rather than continuing to
argue for one specific pedagogy *over* another, we might begin, as
this text has attempted to do, to consider the conversations that
take place between and among pedagogies. While process pedagogy presents writing as a process in which students can intervene, critical pedagogy presents meaning itself as open to
negotiation and contingent on the authority one constructs and
which is constructed for one. Both pedagogies aim to enable students to take an active role in their learning processes and to
encourage the teacher to consider the role she assumes. Seemingly, then, there is some common ground where we can work to
synthesize these theories in practice as a means of utilizing their
respective strengths and trying to be aware of and responsive to
their potential limitations for individual students and situations.

But continuing the combative, mine-versus-yours mode of debate leaves us not with a choice, or with a pedagogical process in which *we* might intervene, but with prescriptive, descriptive arguments. It is time to try to enact an interchange rather than a cross-fire.

Leaving the Contact Zone, Returning to Communities

As a teacher, I envision my responsibility as not only to individual writers but to the community of writers and readers which we seek to develop during the course of the semester. "Community," of course, is a highly contested term in various frameworks. One must question whose voices are silenced, which identities are glossed in efforts to *enforce* or *impose* community. Historically the concept of community signifies both inclusion and exclusion—membership is gained at the cost of repressing aspects of one's social identity, and inclusion is only meaningful if exclusion is a possibility, for one's self or others. I have already engaged Pratt's suggestion that we think in terms of "contact zones," a signifier without the historical implications of community; others suggest working towards collectivities. These are useful alternatives for conceiving of the relations, dynamics, and possible configurations of our classrooms. Even as I deploy those concepts strategically in and about my teaching, I cannot forego the possibility of communities. For groups marginalized from mainstream political and economic decision-making and resources, the notion and practice of community often remains important internally, central to sustaining the struggle for equality and in composing group identities that contest dehumanizing normative images. Arguments for "community," for instance, are central to theorists of race, gender, and sexuality, who insist not only on the need for continued community but also on the criticism of communities imposed from without. If a central goal of critical pedagogy is the conceiving of one's self in specific, immediate social and material relations to others, is teaching for *social* transformation, how then can we abandon the possibility of communities?

Obviously, one cannot simply assume a community exists in a given classroom by virtue of people having been assigned the same room at the same time. Students do not share enough in their identities *as students* to foster an immediate sense of group-ness or collectivity. Immediately on entering the classroom, they begin to form groupings on the basis of physical, linguistic, in-scribed and assumed signifiers. Nonetheless, isn't it possible to work on, to engage in practices of negotiating and enacting com-munities? A writing class might be a useful context in which to experiment with fostering a sense of responsibility beyond one's individual performance as teacher or student, a sense of account-ability for one's product. Writing, after all, is predominantly en-visioned (like voting, like owning) as a solitary act. Authority is largely understood to be within the power of the individual writer. Texts are invented, created, and therefore "owned" by their au-thors. How texts imagine, impact on, represent others, and how texts are "written" by readers, is ignored or glossed over in this romanticized vision of writing. A writing class which wants to emphasize the process of negotiating a community of writers and readers must confront these myths, consider how they function, why and to whose advantage they are sustained. We must criti-cally reconsider what we "know" about writing and reading, about authors and student writers, in order to construct different possibilities as a group.

At the end of each semester, I meet with each student from my writing course for final conferences. Each student brings his or her portfolio, including a new collection of writings on their development over the course of the semester as a writer, as a member of the class, as a reader. Using the various texts they have produced (including their responses to other students' texts), they are expected to reflect on how they have understood and engaged in the process and product of writing over the course of the semester. We discuss their portfolios, the course, their sugges-tions, and so on. In this most recent round of conferences, I was surprised to note that when asked what was the most important aspect of the class—what had most significantly challenged and impacted them as writers, fourteen out of seventeen students re-sponded that it was the other students—their interactions with classmates, the whole class, or the group itself. When I asked them to elaborate, they did not all tell only happy stories about learning from one another. Some of them told stories of being frustrated, of feeling they or their texts were misread. Others talked about having to work to overcome their feelings of inadequacy as writers for half the semester before they felt they could really contribute to the group. Most of them mentioned their exasperation with one student in particular who did not believe he needed to revise, who made them feel like they were wasting their time when they responded to his texts, who seemed to them unwilling to learn from the group since he was already, in his mind, a "real" writer.

One woman discussed her frustration at being pegged early on as the "angry black woman" as a result of her classmates' response to an early piece of writing she published. But she insisted on finding a point of entrance into the group, not at the sacrifice of her values or the silencing of her voice, but because she believed she had something to teach many of her classmates and because she wanted to communicate with them. Her commitment to participating in the negotiation of the community stemmed from what she felt she could contribute. They did not, then, simply detail experiences of cooperation, harmonious collaboration, and productivity. They did, however, detail experiences in which the composition of the group, the differences and specific situatedness brought by each member, mattered and was significant to them as a group, and as individual writers and readers. They did not simply or "naturally" or always value one another. Thirteen of the fourteen students said they believed one of the most important aspects of the course was that each student had responsibilities towards others students and that, over the semester, they had learned to take these seriously. Several said they had initially "blown off" the response assignments, telling the writer, "this is good; I like this" but without seriously engaging the piece. We discussed peer critique often, it was a central part of the course and their grades were largely dependent on it. But the institutional authority I used to emphasize these particular assignments was only one influence. They also attributed their increased investment in peer response to seeing their own pieces taken seriously, engaged with obvious time and attention by their classmates. It was not so much the content or tone of the responses that stuck with them, but the fact that someone had taken their work seriously, not just treated it as an assignment to be completed. This led them to invest more time and commitment to their responses, to feel a sense of responsibility. It also, according to most of the students, led them to feel more committed to all aspects of our work as a class, discussions, projects, and so on.

What these writers seemed to take from the course, then, can be called a sense of community, a belief that their contributions mattered to the group, not only to their own performance or standing, and a belief that others' contributions mattered to their work. It was not an imposed community, one they were coerced into joining and conforming to, but a community they worked out among and for themselves as members. Membership was earned by a commitment to the group, by fulfilling one's responsibilities to the group. This experience changed their understanding of writing as well. Many students talked about learning that they had a lot to learn from other students' writing, when they initially believed only I could teach them anything. Several students mentioned that being exposed and expected to respond to such a wide range of writing styles and topics led them to question what they had previously thought constituted "good writing."

As I mentioned earlier, there was one student who felt his authority as a writer was inherent; he was a *born* writer, gifted by genetics or God. Writing, he used to say, was his destiny. He had, then, nothing to learn from the class and nothing to contribute since his gifts were natural and could not be explained, improved on, or taught to others. At the start of the semester, he had been granted by most students the position and identity of "*the* writer." During final conferences, however, many students talked about being frustrated by his behavior towards the class, not interested in reading his texts or having theirs read by him. He had not, it seemed, become a part of the community and, at a certain point, he was no longer welcome. Communities function to exclude as much as to include; but it is important to recognize that inclusion/exclusion in and of themselves are not inherently good or bad, and we might suggest they are inevitable processes. The point is to make explicit and to account for the conditions that determine inclusion and exclusion. Like Burke's concept of identification (we identify the shepherd only with nurturing and tending to the sheep and not with raising them for slaughter), we tend to identify community as *either* inherently enabling *or* repressive. Expressivist pedagogy idealizes community as a utopian possibility in our classes. Others, suspicious of "community's" utopian, humanist identifications, resist and reject it altogether.

But community as an abstraction, as a *concept* means little, or at least its effect remains elusive; what is "community" when it is considered only outside of its material, embodied enactments? Like writing, it is a process and a product. We can reflect on specific enactments or experiences of community, but how do we make the decision to idealize or reject it as a concept, an idea, completely detached from lived relations? At SUNY Albany, where I was in a teaching community, all of the teachers in our writing studies major met every other week to reflect on our classes, and to extend our understandings of what we are doing in our curriculum and as writing teachers. From the start, it was evident that some teachers entered the discussion with a negative sense of "community." Some teachers had experienced such groups to be repressive and constraining, enforcing conformity and imposing constraints on our teaching. Others were skeptical of the possibility that we *could* negotiate a community together, suspicious that we were being asked to enter into an existing community, with prescriptive norms and expectations. It took two years, and a lot of mediating and starting over, but we *achieved* community—not by stifling opposition, but by engaging it and not always satisfactorily. Our sense of a shared project, however, provided a motivation for us to keep finding ways to work together. In addition, many of us came to recognize how this community energized our teaching, and enabled us to reflect on our pedagogies and to understand our classrooms within a larger, collective context. I came to understand how this group demanded increased accountability; I needed to be able to articulate why, not only what, my students and I are doing. I found this accountability, because it was not imposed but generated through shared inquiry and critical exchanges, to be generative. So, like my students, I have come to see that a sense of one's work in relation to the work of others, and a recognition that one is working within specific and shared contexts, can be a transformative experience.

I would like to suggest, then, that such a collective process of coming to negotiate, identify, and value a sense of community is an *enactment* of social transformation. A university does not necessarily foster a sense of collectivity amongst its various populations. Students, whether in a writing class or a dorm, are not necessarily united, do not inevitably share positions or identities, even when we impose homogeneous identities (as "students" or as "student writers" or "basic writers" and so on) on them. I am not suggesting that this experience of group-ness will immediately translate into these people working towards radical democracy in contexts outside of our class. But given the institutional roadblocks (grading, awarding the achievements of individual teachers and students and so on) such moments are important realizations of the possibility of collectivity. For a student to feel a sense of responsibility for helping her classmates learn, for students to believe they can teach and learn from one another, for the bottom line not to be the individual performance, the individual textual product, the individual's grade—well this is a radical departure from, and disruption of, the normative relations that generally inform and are affirmed by our classrooms. As Jay suggests, it requires a pedagogy of interruption to contest and interfere in the standard operating procedures and assumptions which direct the classroom behavior, goals, and attitudes of teachers and students.

While we look outside of the classroom for "proof" that our critical pedagogies are successful, I would like to suggest we can look in the classroom. Our students, as I have suggested and attempted to support throughout this book, are not only students. The patronizing and patriarchal tone with which we often refer to them in our pedagogical discourses denies them not only agency but existence outside of the classroom. For twenty or more individuals thrown together semi-randomly into one room at one time, for students and teachers who are functioning within a competitive environment which situates them and conditions their interactions before they have ever even met one another, to be able to negotiate collective praxes, to enact community (not to impose, enforce, or declare it) is radical praxis. Such a process requires action and reflection, specific strategic instructional acts, and ongoing reflection on the social visions that inform and are informed by those acts.

I have reflected on some of the concerns and problems I have encountered in how all members of the classroom participate in constructing one another, and of the tensions which arise in a critical composition classroom. I would like to end with students' reflections on how their experience—as writers, readers, co-inquirers—is affected when they perceive authority to be, if even only temporarily, more equitably distributed. I have been doing a lot of talking in these pages about the ways I perceived students and writers to be positioning and representing themselves and one another. Here, then, are those students and writers—talking about the teacher, providing their perspective on how I was positioned and positioning, and their experience of classroom relations. They do not portray me as Super-teacher, nor do they attribute the valuable experiences they had in class to my "personal" gifts or idiosyncratic talents or quirks. That they are critical readers of our classroom is demonstrated by how they call attention to the processes and conditions that allowed for our work together, rather than commending individuals or thanking fate. Their remarks make clear their awareness that what they identify as the *products* of our classroom work were made possible because of specific *processes* that we engaged in collectively. Finally, their reflections indicate that, however irresolvable the tensions and questions concerning power and "appropriate" roles are in the abstract, we should continue the struggle to *enact* and not simply *theorize* a participatory classroom that invites and acknowledges the various and sometimes conflicting roles individual participants will play in creating that classroom.

> **Karen F. :** I do not think anyone in our class has more "power" than the next person among the students. And, between Amy and the class, the power is divided. There is always that sense of authority that a teacher has over their students. A better learning atmosphere is when a teacher does not use this authority to "make" a student just do assigned work by the rules. By this, I mean that there is usually a way of learning or teaching that a student or teacher believes they have to conform to. Personally, I learn and feel more comfortable in an atmosphere where I am able to interact freely with both students and teachers. . . . I learn more by indirect teaching than by direct. I feel power is equally distributed in our class. The open workshops and peer-review sessions help to accomplish that sense of equalness . . . and also allow me to feel free to ask for help from the students *or* the teacher.

Karen S. : I thought there was a balance of power in our class. Amy sometimes liked to dominate, especially on political issues, but she always stopped herself and let us talk. And I don't think she wanted to be "right" but that she got frustrated with people who weren't willing to expand their minds. They came to class with their own views and ideals and weren't even willing to examine others. I think she pushed them to do so, to think and not just to write. I think she cared more about the fact that we actually THOUGHT than what we thought. A thought comes to your mind. Any thought about anything. You can let it pass, or you can delve deeper into it. What does it mean? Why does it mean? How does it mean? That's critical thinking—not just accepting something at face value, but challenging it as far as you can. . . . As a junior now at this university, I have encountered very few professors who will budge on anything. . . . I don't feel I have a voice in many of my classes. We have to write what the teacher wants us to write and say what the teachers wants us to say.

Paul: I define critical thinking as any thoughts that lead me on to a new and unexplored train of mind. We all know how boring our own heads are if we don't challenge ideas and reach some new enlightenment, or even a fresh perspective on an old idea. I guess that would mean I take critical thinking to be one, well, the most important thing a writer/human can do for itself. . . . You tend to reach some conclusions that you hold onto for a while. To stop the process would mean either your life is perfect or you're a Neanderthal.

Andalib: I felt like our voices as students were valued. This was balanced by the fact that we had to respect Amy's requests. I remember the only time Amy got really mad was cause nobody had done their homework. The thing is, because there was a sense of respect in the class, I think we realized the wrong and we all tried to be punctual. In her use of a strong voice, she somehow made us realize that the class and what we got out of it was mostly dependent on our effort and contributions. Not guilt, but awareness.

Josh: Karen, you have a really interesting point, I really thought our class had a type of respect factor not found in most classes especially at a large university. Amy had her ideas and goals that would not be altered. She drew the line at certain specifics that would benefit her style of teaching. I remember we were never able to talk her out of those discussion sessions. But, by the end of the semester, we were deciding whether to do two or three drafts and how many peer reviews we felt [necessary]. This came about because Amy respected our *education*. We didn't just talk our way out of assignments; we had to have legitimate reasons as did she.

Karen F. : Most of my classes so far at the University have been very formal. . . .even in some of the classes I am taking now which are smaller (25–30 people), there is still no interaction among students. Every action, comment, or thought is addressed to a teacher, and not another student. In our [writing] class, sometimes our discussions seem to exclude Amy and involve everyone else in the class. If you think back to . . . [when] we had a discussion about the quote Amy put on the board. I can't remember the exact quote, it had to do with people being able to succeed only if they pull themselves up by their own bootstraps. That discussion took on its own agenda. You started by having to explain the comment and then the class took over, talking about all the meanings, the ridiculousness of that statement applied to welfare and social security reform.

Paul: I would say—again—that the single most important concept in getting someone to actually enjoy/attempt writing is an individual, conscious effort to question the students, but let the students ask the questions to themselves. That is, [the course] . . . invigorated me to question myself and my process. . . . It was a self-learning process through questions and prodding by the teacher. In this way, I could take credit for myself which would increase my excitability when I wrote, which would "spur" me to write more. This whole master plan not only helped me to write well, but to know when I wrote well.

Andalib: Critical writing. It means to look at things in a new light and to relate what one may think or feel to other things in life. To be able to observe *and* think *and* write *and* to relate those processes to oneself. The discussions enabled that for they made people rethink and have different opinions on their papers. . . . Those verbal interchanges inspired me and helped me get to ideas, to write more. . . I feel inspired to write and write better after I have discussed and learned from others, so there are feelings *and* ideas involved.

A Final Word

Four years ago, I "defended" the original version, or first draft of this book, because it served as my dissertation. Present at my defense were my committee members, some family and friends, and also Andalib, one of the undergraduates whose thinking and writing figures into this book in a central way. Andalib had read chunks of the dissertation and asked me if he could be present for the defense. Because it was summer, I had not thought to invite the students who had participated; but he was willing to drive a few hours for the event, and I was more than delighted to have him there.

At one point during the question-posing section of the defense, a member of my committee asked how, or finally whether, such teaching or thinking about teaching ***really*** had any political or material effect on students, their lives, our culture. He noted that while all of this was intellectually useful, perhaps it remained, finally, esoteric, abstract, an intellectual exercise. He wanted, he said, some kind of "evidence" that specific and substantive changes did indeed take place. This is the most commonly asked question, I think, of radical pedagogies and of political movements and philosophies. "Does it work? Give me some proof. How do we ever really know if we're being *effective?*" On the one hand, it is an incredibly important question. To not pose this question is to assume we are meeting our goals simply because we declare ourselves to be doing so. This question prompts important self-reflexive thinking and invites students to work as active participants in evaluating and retooling our pedagogies. An important question indeed. On the other hand, I wonder whether this question does not keep us from pursuing options and possibilities because we are unwilling to invest in the kind of revisionary work and teaching necessary to exploring the possibilities without some kind of tangible proof, or a guaranteed outcome. That is, to desire and look for evidence is important; but to need it before proceeding is problematic in that it forestalls change, forestalls even the possibilities this kind of work aims to promote and pursue.

After the question was posed, I moved to respond to it. But it was the question that also troubled me. "Who do I think I am? Do I really think this matters, can I prove this has an effect?" I had done a lot of thinking and writing that sought to articulate and explore the contradictions I had experienced and theorized in the discourse of critical pedagogy. And while I believed my critique was legitimate and necessary, I had not yet learned to reject the terms of assessment promoted by the very discourse I sought to revise. Therefore, I struggled with this question, struggled to answer it both honestly and forcefully, to acknowledge my uncertainty without allowing that to be "evidence" that, finally, the whole project needed to be abandoned. After all, the *lack of uncertainty* in the work of Giroux and McLaren is precisely what I found to be most troubling and suspect in the first place. The decisive declarations that characterize work in American critical pedagogy scholarship made me skeptical. I wanted to expose and pursue the fissures and holes covered up by the rhetoric but made visible in my efforts to take up that rhetoric in my classrooms. I stumbled my way through this question for a while, finding it difficult to be complex and clear at the same time, to speak into an existing assumption (we need "proof"), which I found both vital and problematic.

When I finished, Andalib spoke up, "Can I say something?" I was, as were my colleagues, committee members and friends, taken aback (in a good way) at his sense that he could and should participate in my dissertation defense. Such an institutional moment is not a collective enterprise, but rather the penultimate culminating moment in which the individual thinker/writer/scholar/researcher proves her stuff, gains credentialing and authority to enter into the academy as a full and contributing member. I was delighted by Andalib's sense that he too had something at stake in answering this question. He had been involved in every meeting with my student focus group, he and I had kept in regular contact since he had been in my course a few years ago, he was always interested in and supportive of this project. It delighted me, then, that he felt he could and should join my voice in responding to a question that was not only about my text, but about someone else's interpretation of his experience in our class and discussions. My chair, Anne Herrington, smiled. I remember her smiling. She said that, as long as it was okay by me, it was okay by her. I smiled too and urged him to go on. He turned to the questioner and leaned forward in his chair. I did not take notes, so I have only my memory to go on. He talked about how he knew this class had resulted in long-reaching effects for him and for at least some of the other students because they talked about those effects. He said he did not go about writing or thinking in the same way anymore. He talked about how, as a writer deemed "basic" by the university, he knew he had important ideas to contribute but worried they would not be heard. Taking this class convinced him he could be heard, not only because he believed he *should* be heard, but because it taught him to figure out how to write in different situations, how to think about the way people would hear and respond to his writing, how to make himself heard. And he said that maybe everyone in the class did not go out and join political causes or protest specific events, but they did work together in the class. This alone, he said, made the experience different from most classes, where the teacher does all the teaching. In his other classes, he said, students tended to cluster together in groups formed around obvious affiliations early in the semester, or they were put into a competitive relationship, each vying for the approval of the teacher, or for the grades. He talked about conversations he'd had with other students in the focus group, at times when I was not formally convening the group, and their sense of what it meant to be in a classroom where people were working together, challenging, and supporting one another. He talked about how he had been struck simply by how much each student remembered of his or her experience in the writing class, that they could recall particular moments and what they meant, remembered the names of their classmates, remembered not only the essays they wrote, but the various stages of the drafting and revision process.

What strikes me in this memory, though, is not so much what Andalib said, but the fact that he felt entitled to speak at all. No other person present, beyond myself and the committee members, felt authorized to participate in the conversation. But for Andalib, we were not simply talking about my dissertation, we were not simply questioning a theoretical framework for understanding the work of teaching writing, we were talking about his experience in our writing course and his sense of the experiences of other students as they had been represented to him. Andalib was not "defending" me or my text; rather, he wanted a voice in this discussion, he wanted to be heard because, in his perception, the students' reflections on those courses were as important as my own. And in this moment, he was our teacher, intervening in the discussion in order to pose important questions, prompting us to deliberate over our assumptions. If the aim of radical pedagogies is to question "how and in whose interests knowledge is produced and reproduced" (Gore 5), then it seems Andalib, at least, understands what it means to *enact* radical pedagogy.

Notes

1. Of the nine composition courses I have taught (six sections of College Writing and three sections of Basic Writing), the percentage of white students has ranged from 30 to 75 percent. Given that African Americans, Latinos, and Asian Americans make up only approximately 11 percent of the student population at the University of Massachusetts, and given the number of colleagues who have had *all* white classroom populations, my classrooms have been fairly atypical. In five sections, at least one gay, lesbian, or bisexual student has been out to the class, while in two other sections a student has been out to me and a few students, though not to the class at large. Further, this semester, for example, eleven out of twenty students are working at least part-time and receiving financial aid, and describe themselves as "working" or "lower" class.

2. Of course, I am establishing a dichotomy here, while recognizing that it ultimately collapses given that many students (and teachers) occupy both extremes at once, while others constantly shift. So, rather than a position being determined once and for all, I see it more as a construction which requires ongoing revision and allows for mobility and fluidity. The point, however, is for us to be able to work towards achieving a balance between the poles, the recognition that occupying one does not entail denying, ignoring, or rejecting one's place simultaneously on the other.

3. In further discussion about the experience of that class, the students decided to write reflective short writings on how generative debate might best be facilitated in a classroom and to consider, in particular, what role the teacher should play. Most students found the messiness of the discussion to be positive, claiming it forced them to better consider and articulate their position. A few students commented that they felt silenced by the discussion, because they couldn't find an entry point. One student said it gave her a headache because it depressed her whenever her peers discussed issues of exploitation and discrimination because she saw it primarily as a futile exercise in denial. All of the students except three felt the teacher should provide some sort of wrap-up, not necessarily one that offers "the" definitive perspective, but one that contextualizes and comments on the various perspectives represented.

WORKS CITED

Althusser, Louis. 1971. "Ideology and Ideological State Apparatuses (Notes towards an Investigation)." In *Essays on Ideology*, 1–60. London: Verso.

Anzaldúa, Gloria. 1987. *Borderlands/La Frontera: The New Mestiza*. San Francisco: Spinsters/Aunt Lute.

Baldwin, James. 1994. "If Black English Isn't a Language, Then Tell Me, What Is?" In *The Composition of Our "selves."* Ed. Marcia Curtis et al. Dubuque: Kendall/Hunt, 101–3. (Originally published in *The New York Times*, July 28, 1979.)

Bauer, Dale M. 1990. "The Other 'F' Word: The Feminist in the Classroom." *College English* 52 (April): 385–96.

Berlin, James. 1988. "Rhetoric and Ideology in the Writing Class." *College English* 50 (September): 477–93.

———. 1991. "Composition and Cultural Studies." In *Composition and Resistance*. Ed. C. Mark Hurlbert and Michael Blitz, 47–55. Portsmouth, NH: Boynton/Cook.

Bigelow, William. 1990. "Inside the Classroom: Social Vision and Critical Pedagogy." *Teacher's College Record* 91 (Spring): 437–48.

Brannon, Lil. 1990. "Is a Critical Pedagogy Possible?" *Journal of Education* 172.1:16–18.

Brodkey, Linda. 1992. "Articulating Poststructural Theory in Research on Literacy." *Perspectives on Literacy Research*. Ed. Richard Beach and J. L. Green, 293–318. Urbana, IL: NCTE-NCRE.

———. 1994. "Making a Federal Case out of Difference: The Politics of Pedagogy, Publicity, and Postponement." In *Writing Theory and Critical Theory*. Ed. John Clifford and John Schilb, 236–62. New York: Modern Language Association.

———. 1987. "Modernism and the Scene(s) of Writing." *College English* 49 (April): 396–418.

————. 1989. "On the Subjects of Class and Gender in 'The Literacy Letters'." *College English* 51 (February): 125–41.

————. 1989. "Transvaluing Difference." *College English* 56 (October): 597–601.

Bullock, Richard, and John Trimbur, eds. 1991. *The Politics of Writing Instruction: Postsecondary.* Portsmouth, NH: Boyton/Cook.

Carby, Hazel. 1987. *Reconstructing Womanhood: The Emergence of the Afro-American Woman Novelist.* New York: Oxford University Press.

Carrie, Frederic. "Untitled." Unpublished essay, excerpted with permission of the author.

Christensen, Linda. 1989. "Writing the Word and the World." *English Journal* (February): 14–18.

Christian, Barbara. 1987. "The Race for Theory." *Cultural Critique* 6 (Spring): 51–63.

Clifford, John. 1990. "Enacting Critical Literacy." In *The Right to Literacy.* Ed. Andrea Lunsford, Helene Moglen, and James Slevin. New York: Modern Language Association.

————. 1991. "The Subject in Discourse." In *Contending with Words.* Ed. Patricia Harkin and John Schilb, 38–51. New York: Modern Language Association.

Clifford, John, and John Schilb, eds. 1994. *Writing Theory and Critical Theory.* New York: Modern Language Association.

Culley, Margo, and Catherine Portuges, eds. 1985. *Gendered Subjects: The Dynamics of Feminist Teaching.* Boston: Routledge & Kegan Paul.

Curtis, Marcia, et al., eds. 1994. *The Composition of Our "selves."* Dubuque: Kendall/ Hunt.

Daudi, Philippe. 1983. "The Discourse of Power or the Power of Discourse." *Alternatives* 9:275–83.

Delpit, Lisa. 1986. "Skills and Other Dilemmas of a Progressive Black Educator." *Harvard Educational Review* 56 (November): 379–85.

————. 1988. "The Silenced Dialogue: Power and Pedagogy in Educating Other People's Children." *Harvard Educational Review* 58 (August): 280–98.

Distasi, Paul. "Untitled." Unpublished essay, excerpted with permission of the author.

Donahue, Patricia, and Ellen Quandahl, eds. 1989. *Reclaiming Pedagogy: The Rhetoric of the Classroom*. Carbondale: Southern Illinois University Press.

Elbow, Peter. 1983. "Embracing Contraries." *College English* 45 (April): 327–39.

———. 1986. "The Pedagogy of the Bamboozled." In *Embracing Contraries: Explorations in Learning and Teaching*. New York: Oxford University Press.

———. 1993. "The Uses of Binary Thinking." *Journal of Advanced Composition* 13 (Winter): 51–78.

———. 1981. *Writing with Power: Techniques for Mastering the Writing Process*. New York: Oxford University Press.

———. 1973. *Writing without Teachers*. New York: Oxford University Press.

Ellsworth, Elizabeth. 1989. "Why Doesn't This Feel Empowering? Working through the Repressive Myths of Critical Pedagogy." *Harvard Educational Review* 59 (August): 297–324.

Faigley, Lester. 1986. "Competing Theories of Process." *College English* 48 (October): 527–42.

———. 1992. *Fragments of Rationality: Postmodernity and the Subject of Composition*. Pittsburgh: University of Pittsburgh Press.

———. 1994. "Street Fights over the Impossibility of Theory: A Report of a Seminar." *Writing Theory and Critical Theory*. Ed. John Clifford and John Schilb, 212–35. New York: Modern Language Association.

Fitts, Karen, and Alan W. France, eds. 1995. *Left Margins: Cultural Studies and Composition Pedagogy*. Albany: SUNY Press.

Flannery, Kathryn Thomas. 1990. "In Praise of the Local and Transitory." *The Right to Literacy*. Ed. Andrea A. Lunsford, Helene Moglen, and James Slevin, 208–14. New York: Modern Language Association.

Foster, Karen. "Reflections." Unpublished essay, excerpted with permission of the author.

Foucault, Michel. 1972. *The Archaeology of Knowledge; and the Discourse on Language*. New York: Pantheon.

———. 1984. *The Foucault Reader*. Ed. Paul Rabinow. New York: Pantheon.

———. 1990. *The History of Sexuality, Volume I: An Introduction*. New York: Vintage.

———. 1977. "History of Systems of Thought." In *Language, Counter-Memory, Practice: Selected Essays*. Ed. Donald F. Bouchard. Ithaca, NY: Cornell University Press.

———. 1981. "The Order of Discourse." *Untying the Text: A Post-structuralist Reader*. Ed. Robert Young, 48–77. Boston: Routledge & Kegan Paul.

———. 1980. *Power/Knowledge: Selected Interviews and Other Writings, 1972–1977*. Ed. Colin Gordon. New York: Pantheon.

———. 1977. "Preface To Transgression." In *Language, Counter-Memory, Practice: Selected Essays*. Ed. Donald F. Bouchard, 29–42. Ithaca, NY: Cornell University Press.

———. 1983. "The Subject and Power." *Michel Foucault; Beyond Structuralism and Hermeneutics*. Ed. Hubert L. Dreyfus and Paul Rabinow, 208–26. Chicago: University of Chicago Press.

France, Alan W. 1993. "Assigning Places: The Function of Introductory Composition as a Cultural Discourse." *College English* 55 (October): 593–609.

Freire, Paulo and Donaldo Macedo. 1987. *Literacy: Reading the Word and the World*. South Hadley, MA: Bergin & Garvey.

Freire, Paulo. 1970. *Pedagogy of the Oppressed*. Trans. Myra Bergman Ramose. New York: Seabury.

———. 1985. *The Politics of Education: Culture, Power, and Liberation*. South Hadley: Bergin & Garvey.

Fuss, Diana. 1989. *Essentially Speaking: Feminism, Nature, & Difference*. New York: Routledge.

Gallagher, Chris. 1998. "Composing Inquiry: Rethinking Progressive Pedagogy and Literacy." Ph.D. diss. SUNY–Albany.

Gilbert, Pam. 1988. "Student Text as Pedagogical Text." *Language, Authority, and Criticism: Readings on the School Textbook*. Ed. S. De Castell, A. Luke, and C. Luke, 195–202. London: Falmer.

Giroux, Henry. 1992. *Border Crossings: Cultural Workers and the Politics of Education*. New York: Routledge.

———. 1988. "Border Pedagogy in the Age of Postmodernism." *Journal of Education* 170:162–81.

———. 1988. "Literacy and the Pedagogy of Voice and Political Empowerment." *Educational Theory* 38 (Winter): 61–75.

———. 1986. "Radical Pedagogy and the Politics of Student Voice." *Interchange* 17 (Spring): 48–69.

———. 1983. *Theory and Resistance in Education: A Pedagogy for the Opposition*. South Hadley, MA: Bergin & Garvey.

———. 1995. "Who Writes in a Cultural Studies Class? Or, Where is the Pedagogy?" In *Left Margins: Cultural Studies and Composition Pedagogy*. Ed. Karen Fitts, and Alan W. France, 3–16. Albany: SUNY Press.

Giroux, Henry, and Peter McLaren, eds. 1994. *Between Borders: Pedagogy and the Politics of Cultural Studies*. New York: Routledge.

———. 1989. *Critical Pedagogy, the State, and Cultural Struggle*. Albany: SUNY Press.

Gore, Jennifer. 1993. *The Struggle for Pedagogies: Critical and Feminist Discourses as Regimes of Truth*. New York: Routledge.

———. 1992. "What We Can Do for You! What *Can* We Do for 'You'? Struggling over Empowerment in Critical and Feminist Pedagogy." *Feminisms and Critical Pedagogy*. Ed. Carmen Luke and Jennifer Gore, 54–73. New York: Routledge.

Gramsci, Antonio. 1988. *An Antonio Gramsci Reader: Selected Writings, 1916–1935*. Trans. Q. Hoare, Giroux Nowell-Smith, J. Matthews, and W. Boelhower. Ed. David Forgacs. New York: Schocken.

———. 1987. *The Modern Prince and Other Writings*. New York: International Publishers.

Hairston, Maxine. 1992. "Diversity, Ideology, and Teaching Writing." *College Composition and Communication* 43 (May): 179–93.

Harkin, Patricia and John Schilb, eds. 1991. *Contending with Words: Composition and Rhetoric in a Postmodern Age*. New York: Modern Language Association.

Harris, Joseph. 1993. "The Course as Text/The Teacher as Critic." *College English* 55 (November): 785–93.

———. 1997. *A Teaching Subject: Composition since 1966.* Upper Saddle River, NJ: Prentice Hall.

Helmreich, William B. 1981. "Stereotype Truth." *The New York Times*, 15 October. Sec. A, p. 27, column 1.

Herzberg, Bruce. 1994. "Community Service and Critical Teaching." *College Composition and Communication* 45 (October): 307–19.

———. 1991. "Composition and the Politics of the Curriculum." In *The Politics of Writing Instruction*. Ed. Richard Bullock and John Trimbur, 97–118. Portsmouth, NH: Boynton/Cook.

———. 1991. "Michel Foucault's Rhetorical Theory." In *Contending with Words: Composition and Rhetoric in a Postmodern Age*. Ed. Patricia Harkin and John Schilb, 69–81. New York: Modern Language Association.

hooks, bell. 1981. *Ain't I a Woman: Black Women and Feminism.* Boston: South End.

———. 1984. *Feminist Theory from Margin to Center.* Boston: South End.

———. 1989. *Talking Back: Thinking Feminist, Thinking Black.* Boston: South End.

———. 1994. *Teaching to Transgress: Education as the Practice of Freedom.* New York: Routledge.

Hurlbert, C. Mark, and Michael Blitz, eds. 1991. *Composition & Resistance.* Portsmouth, NH: Boynton/Cook.

Hutcheon, Linda. 1989. *The Politics of Postmodernism.* London/New York: Routledge.

Jarratt, Susan. 1991. "Feminism and Composition: The Case for Conflict." In *Contending with Words: Composition and Rhetoric in a Postmodern Age*. Ed. Patricia Harkin and John Schilb, 105–23. New York: Modern Language Association.

Jay, Gregory. 1994. "Taking Multiculturalism Personally: Ethos and Ethnos in the Classroom." *American Literary History* 6.4 (Winter): 613–32.

Jordan, June. 1994. "Nobody Mean More to Me Than You and the Future Life of Willie Jordan." From *On Call: Political Essays.* Boston: South End Press, 1985. Collected in *The Composition of Our "selves"*. Ed. Marcia Curtis et al. 104–17. Dubuque: Kendall/Hunt.

Kecht, Maria-Regina, ed. 1992. *Pedagogy is Politics: Literary Theory and Critical Teaching*. Urbana: University of Illinois Press.

Knoblauch, C.H. 1991. "Critical Teaching and Dominant Culture." In *Composition and Resistance*. Ed. C. Mark Hurlbert and Michael Blitz, 12–21. Portsmouth, NH: Boynton/Cook.

Kozol, Jonathan. 1981. *On Being a Teacher*. NY: Continuum.

Lather, Patti. 1991. *Getting Smart: Feminist Research and Pedagogy with/in the Postmodern*. New York: Routledge.

———. 1992. "Post-Critical Pedagogies: A Feminist Reading." *Feminisms and Critical Pedagogy*. Ed. Carmen Luke and Jennifer Gore, 120–37. New York: Routledge.

Lazere, Donald. 1995. "Teaching the Conflicts of Wealth and Poverty." In *Left Margins: Cultural Studies and Composition Pedagogy*. Ed. Karen Fitts, and Alan W. France, 189–208. Albany: SUNY Press.

Lindemann, Erika, and Gary Tate, eds. 1991. *An Introduction to Composition Studies*. New York: Oxford University Press.

Liston, Daniel P., and Kenneth M. Zeichner. 1987. "Critical Pedagogy and Teacher Education." *Journal of Education* 169:117–37.

Lu, Min-Zhan. 1992. "Conflict and Struggle: The Enemies or Pre-Conditions of Basic Writing?" *College English* 4 (December): 887–913.

———. 1992. "A Pedagogy of Struggle: The Use of Cultural Dissonance." *Journal of Teaching Writing* 11.1 (Spring/Summer): 1–18.

———.1994. "Professing Multiculturalism." *College Composition and Communication* 45 (December): 442–58.

———. 1991. "Redefining the Legacy of Mina Shaughnessy: A Critique of the Politics of Linguistic Innocence." *Journal of Basic Writing* 10.1:26–40.

———. 1990. "Writing as Repositioning." *Journal of Education* 172.1:15–28.

Luke, Carmen, and Jennifer Gore, eds. 1992. *Feminisms and Critical Pedagogy*. New York: Routledge.

Luke, Carmen. 1992. "Feminist Politics in Radical Pedagogy." In *Feminisms and Critical Pedagogy*. Ed. Carmen Luke and Jennifer Gore, 25–53. New York: Routledge.

Malinowitz, Harriet. 1993. "Lesbian and Gay Reality in the Writing Class." Ph.D. diss. New York University.

Manchester, Beth Anne. 1993. "Shame." In *The Freshman Writing Program Anthology*. Ed. Anne Herrington and Patricia Zukowski, 18–20. University of Massachusetts at Amherst.

Marshall, Brenda K. 1991. *Teaching the Postmodern: Fiction and Theory*. New York: Routledge.

McDowell, Deborah E. 1980. "New Directions for a Black Feminist Criticism." *Black American Literature Forum* 14 (Winter): 153–58.

———. 1988. "Language, Social Structure, and the Production of Subjectivity." *Critical Pedagogy Networker* 1.1 and 1.2:1-10.

McLaren, Peter. 1988. "On Ideology and Education: Critical Pedagogy and the Politics of Empowerment." *Social Text* 19:153–85.

———. 1988 . "Schooling the Postmodern Body: Critical Pedagogy and the Politics of Enfleshment." *Journal of Education* 170.3:53–83.

Miller, J. Hillis. 1983. "Composition and Decomposition." In *Composition and Literature: Bridging the Gap*. Ed. Winifred Bryan Horner, 38–56. Chicago: University of Chicago Press.

Miller, Richard E. 1994. "Composing English Studies: Towards a Social History of the Discipline." *College Composition and Communication* 45 (May): 164–79.

———. 1994. "Fault Lines in the Contact Zone." *College English* 56 (April): 389–408.

Minh-ha, Trinh T. 1989. *Woman, Native, Other: Writing Postcoloniality and Feminism*. Bloomington: Indiana University Press.

———. 1991. *When the Moon Waxes Red: Representation, Gender, and Cultural Politics*. New York: Routledge.

Miyamoto, Nobuko, and Chris Iijima. 1971. "Untitled." In *Roots: An Asian American Reader*. Ed. Amy Tachiki, et al., 98–99. Los Angeles: Continental Graphics.

Moi, Toril. 1988. "Feminism, Postmodernism, and Style: Recent Feminist Criticism in the United States." *Cultural Critique* 9:3–22.

Morales, Aurora Levins, and Rosario Morales. 1986. *Getting Home Alive*. Ithaca, New York: Firebrand Books.

Mouffe, Chantal. 1988. "Radical Democracy: Modern or Postmodern?" In *Universal Abandon: The Politics of Postmodernism*. Ed. Andrew Ross, 31–45. Minneapolis: University of Minnesota Press.

Myers, Greg. 1986. "Reality, Consensus, and Reform in the Rhetoric of Composition Teaching." *College English* 48 (February): 154–73.

Naylor, Gloria. 1986. "Hers." *The New York Times*. 20 February: Sec. C2.

Needle, Michael. 1999. "'My Character Just Happens to Be Homophobic. . .': Coding and De-coding Homophobia in the Writing Classroom." Unpublished Seminar Paper, April.

North, Stephen M. 1991. "Rhetoric, Responsibility, and the 'Language of the Left.'" In *Composition and Resistance*. Ed. C. Mark Hurlbert and Michael Blitz. Portsmouth, NH: Boynton/Cook.

Nowlan, Robert Andrew. 1995. "Teaching against Racism in the Radical College Composition Classroom: A Reply to a Student." *Left Margins: Cultural Studies and Composition Pedagogy*. Ed. Karen Fitts and Alan W. France, 245–54. Albany: SUNY Press.

Phelan, Shane. 1994. *Getting Specific: Postmodern Lesbian Politics*. Minneapolis: University of Minnesota Press.

Pratt, Mary Louise. 1991. "Arts of the Contact Zone." *Profession 91*, 33-40.

Ohmann, Richard. 1995. "Afterword." In *Left Margins: Cultural Studies and Composition Pedagogy*. Ed. Karen Fitts and Alan W. France, 325–32. Albany: SUNY Press.

Orner, Mimi. 1992. "Interrupting the Calls for Student Voice in 'Liberatory' Education: A Feminist Poststructuralist Perspective." In *Feminisms and Critical Pedagogy*. Ed. Carmen Luke and Jennifer Gore, 74–89. New York: Routledge.

Orner, Mimi, Janet L. Miller, and Elizabeth Ellsworth. 1996. "Excessive Moments and the Educational Discourses That Try to Contain Them." *Educational Theory* 46.1 (Winter): 71–91.

Radhakrishnan, R. 1990. "The Changing Subject and the Politics of Theory." *Differences* 2.2:126–53.

Recchio, Thomas E. 1994. "On the Critical Necessity of 'Essaying.'" In *Taking Stock: The Writing Process Movement in the '90s*. Ed. Lad Tobin and Thomas Newkirk, 219-235. Portsmouth, NH: Boynton/ Cook.

Rich, Adrienne. 1979. "Disloyal to Civilization: Feminism, Racism, Gynephobia." In *On Lies, Secrets, and Silence: Selected Prose, 1966– 1978*, 275–310. New York: W.W. Norton.

Rodríguez, Milanés Cecilia. 1991. "Risks, Resistance and Rewards: One Teacher's Story." *Composition and Resistance*. Ed. C. Mark Hurlbert and Michael Blitz, 115–24. Portsmouth, NH: Boynton/Cook.

Schilb, John. 1991. "Cultural Studies, Postmodernism, and Composition." In *Contending with Words: Composition and Rhetoric in a Postmodern Age*. Ed. Patricia Harkin and John Schilb, 115–24. New York: Modern Language Association.

———. 1985. "Pedagogy of the Oppressors?" In *Gendered Subjects: The Dynamics of Feminist Teaching*. Ed. Margo Culley and Catherine Portuges, 253–64. Boston: Routledge & Kegan Paul.

———. 1992. "Poststructuralism, Politics, and the Subject of Pedagogy." In *Pedagogy and Politics*. Ed. Maria-Regina Kecht, 48–69. Urbana: University of Illinois Press.

Schwartz, Nina. 1989. "Conversations with the Social Text." In *Reclaiming Pedagogy*. Ed. Patricia Donahue and Ellen Quandahl, 60– 71. Carbondale: Southern Illinois University Press.

Sedgwick, Eve Kosofsky. 1990. *The Epistemology of the Closet*. Berkeley: University of California Press.

Shor, Ira. 1980. *Critical Teaching and Everyday Life*. Boston: South End.

Shor, Ira, and Paulo Freire. 1987. *A Pedagogy for Liberation: Dialogues on Transforming Education*. South Hadley, MA: Bergin & Garvey.

———. 1987. "What is the 'Dialogical Method' of Teaching?" *Journal of Education* 169:11–31.

Simon, Roger I. 1994. "Forms of Insurgency in the Production of Popular Memories: The Columbus Quincentenary and the Pedagogy of Countercommemoration." In *Between Borders: Pedagogy and the Politics of Cultural Studies*. Ed. Henry A. Giroux and Peter McLaren, 127–44. New York: Routledge.

Smith, Barbara. 1985. "Toward a Black Feminist Criticism." In *The New Feminist Criticism: Essays on Women, Literature, and Theory.* Ed. Elaine Showalter, 164–81. New York: Pantheon.

Spelman, Elizabeth V. 1988. *Inessential Woman: Problems of Exclusion in Feminist Thought.* Boston: Beacon.

Spellmeyer, Kurt. 1989. "Foucault and the Freshman Writer: Considering the Self in Discourse." *College English* 51 (November): 715–29.

———. 1991. "Knowledge about 'Knowledge': Freshman English, Public Discourse, and the Social Imagination." In *Composition and Resistance.* Ed. C. Mark Hurlbert and Michael Blitz, 70–80. Portsmouth, NH: Boynton/Cook.

———. 1994. "On Conventions and Collaboration: The Open Road and the Iron Cage." In *Writing Theory and Critical Theory.* Ed. John Clifford and John Schilb, 73–95. New York: Modern Language Association.

Tan, Amy. 1994. "Mother Tongue." In *The Composition of Our "selves".* Ed. Marcia Curtis et al., 137–41. Dubuque: Kendall/Hunt. (Originally published in *Threepenny Review.*)

Trimbur, John. 1980. "Cultural Studies and Teaching Writing." *Focuses* 1:5–18.

Tuman, Myron C. 1988. "Class, Codes, and Composition: Basil Bernstein and the Critique of Pedagogy." *College Composition and Communication* 39 (February): 42–51.

Villanueva, Victor. 1991. "Considerations for American Freireistas." In *The Politics of Writing Instruction: Postsecondary.* Ed. Richard Bullock and John Trimbur, 247–63. Portsmouth, NH: Boynton/Cook.

Weiler, Kathleen. 1988. *Women Teaching for Change: Gender Class & Power.* South Hadley, MA: Bergin & Garvey.

Weedon, Chris. 1987. *Feminist Practice & Poststructuralist Theory.* Oxford, UK: Blackwell.

Welch, Nancy. *Getting Restless: Rethinking Revision in Writing Instruction.* Portsmouth, NH: Boynton/Cook, 1997.

Yagelski, Robert. 1994. "Who's Afraid of Subjectivity? The Composing Process and Postmodernism or a Student of Donald Murray Enters the Age of Postmodernism." In *Taking Stock: The Writing Process Movement in the '90s.* Ed. Lad Tobin and Thomas Newkirk, 203–18. Portsmouth: Boynton/Cook Heinmann.

INDEX

Eddie (college student), 231
education, purposes of, 33–34
Elbow, Peter
  on classroom relations, 95n3,
    103, 166
  and outside action, 149
  process pedagogy of, 48n2, 50
Ellsworth, Elizabeth
  on classroom relations, 109
  critical pedagogy critiqued by,
    104, 124–29, 136
  poststructuralism of, 178n3
  on situated pedagogy, 151,
    173
empowerment. *See also* agency;
  authority
  in critical pedagogy, 101–4,
    125
  of students, 27–33, 165, 267,
    273
ethics, in writing, 172, 176
evaluative criteria, for writing,
  210–22, 225–27, 238–39. *See
  also* reading: critical
expressivist pedagogy, 37–38,
  49–53. *See also* composition
  pedagogy; process pedagogy
  community in, 278
  critique of, 158, 161–62
  definition of, 6–7
  subjectivity in, 83

Faigley, Lester, 18, 48n3
feminist pedagogy, 58, 89. *See
  also* progressive pedagogy
Fitts, Karen, 11–12
Flannery, Kathryn Thomas,
  156–57
form (of writing)
  authority of, 250–51
  conventions of, 183–85, 255
  politics of, 210–14
Foster, Karen, 22, 25
  on classroom relations, 280,
    282

essays by, 141, 184–85,
  241–45, 259–60
on peer review, 237
on rap music, 257, 268
subjectivity of, 259–60
on writing, 192, 251
Foucault, Michel, 9, 39–40
on discourse, 74, 101–2, 150,
  159, 160–61, 168, 169
poststructuralism of, 156–57,
  178n3
on power, 74, 165–66, 267
and revision of pedagogy, 130
on social construction, 72,
  137n2
France, Alan W., 11–12, 70
Fred (college student). *See* Carrie,
  Frederic (Fred); March,
  Frederic (Fred)
Freire, Paulo
on action and reflection, 54,
  144, 149–50
on classroom practice, 138n6
on experience, 258, 260
and Ira Shor, 103
on power of students, 273
on rigor of critical pedagogy,
  193
on social construction, 65–66,
  177

Gallagher, Chris, 3, 4–5
gender, 110, 137n3
Gilbert, Pam, 48n2, 48n3, 77
Giroux, Henry, 48n3
authority of, 103–4
Border Crossings, 104
critique of, 105–8, 109,
  122–28, 284
on discourse, 13, 41
on diversity, 76
and pedagogical practice, 56,
  101, 105–8, 130, 136
on production of knowledge,
  51, 88

NCTE Annual Convention
(1998), 103
normative binary, 11, 99
North, Stephen, 73–74, 149
"Nothing Mean More to Me
Than You and the Future Life
of Willie Jordan" (Jordan),
239n5
Nowlan, Robert, 119–21

Ohmann, Richard, 62, 87, 153–54
oppositional pedagogy. *See*
progressive pedagogy
Orner, Mimi
critical pedagogy critiqued by,
104, 136
"Interrupting the Calls for
Student Voice in 'Liberatory'
Education," 178n1
poststructuralism of, 178n3
on situated pedagogy, 151

Pat (college student), 187–88
Patrick (college student). *See* Bien
Aimé, Patrick
Paul (college student). *See*
Distasi, Paul
pedagogy
of argument, 53–54, 122–29
context of, 53–56
definition of, 3–7
and politics, 33–41, 38, 47,
75–78, 87
process of, 133–37
and reflection, 7–13
revision of, 7–13, 87–94
synthesis of, 273–74
"Pedagogy of the Bamboozled"
(Elbow), 95n3
"Pedagogy of the Oppressors?"
(Schilb), 30, 116
peer review, 66–72, 81–82, 86–87,
222–39. *See also* publication,
in classroom

and authority, 148
and community, 190, 276–77
form of, 229, 232
in process pedagogy, 52
students' concerns about, 170,
173–75
Penn State Conference on
Rhetoric and Composition,
103
Pericles (college student),
200–201, 223
personal narrative, 52, 57–65,
79–84, 85–94
vs. cultural critique, 85
Phelan, Shane, 9, 129
Plato, 166–67
political action
as pedagogical goal, 141,
144–45
vs. reflection, 149–53
politics
of form, 210–14
of language, 41–45, 162–67,
209–22, 239–40n5
and neutrality, 62, 76
and pedagogy, 33–41, 47,
75–78, 87
in poststructuralism, 157–58
postcolonial pedagogy. *See*
progressive pedagogy
postmodern pedagogy. *See*
progressive pedagogy
poststructuralism, 156–67, 177,
178n3
power
in classroom, 267, 273,
280–82
and discourse, 165–66,
167–68, 170, 173, 177
and language, 41–45, 66,
239–40n5
practice
of critical pedagogy, 8, 72–78,
98–101, 179–82
vs. theory, 5, 15–17, 19–21,
54, 99, 122–29, 130–33

Sheila (college student), 144–45
Shoffner, Karen, 202–5
Shor, Ira, 103, 193
social construction, 141–43,
    162–67, 196–98. *See also*
    subjectivity
    and language, 30–33, 41–45
    students' recognition of,
        80–84, 152, 249, 258–60
social imagination, 141
social relationships, 108–10
social transformation, 279
Sophists, 166–67
Spellmeyer, Kurt, 141, 181
Spelman, Elizabeth V., 137n3
Stenberg, Shari, 96–99, 133–36,
    137n1, 138n7
stereotype
    analysis of, 110–16, 123,
        137n4, 198–209, 247–48
    in student writing, 171,
        259–60
"Stereotype Truth" (student
    essay), 199–201, 203
student
    agency of, 246–56
    assumptions about, 117–19,
        148–49
    empowerment of, 27–33, 165,
        267, 273
    as object of pedagogy, 99,
        106–8
    role of, 7, 12, 125, 166,
        280–82
    situation of, 118–19, 168, 170
    subjectivity of, 246–56
student writing
    context of, 62–65, 77, 80–84,
        181
    writing courses' focus on,
        96–98
"The Subject in Discourse"
    (Clifford), 212–13
subjectivity. *See also* social
    construction
    analysis of, 195

and authority, 178n4, 212
construction of, 82–84,
    137n2, 158–67, 169–70,
    177
conversation impeded by, 246,
    256–60
of students, 246–56
Sutcliffe, Karen, 22, 23, 191, 281

"Taking Women Students
    Seriously" (Rich), 145
Tan, Amy, 239n5
Taylor (college student), 27–29,
    32–33, 46–47, 117–18
    agency of, 247, 248–49
teacher
    advocacy by, 262–68, 272
    authority of, 102–3, 147–48,
        172–73, 175, 178n4,
        233–34, 263–74
    role of, 7, 88–89, 95n3, 99,
        125, 246, 261–74, 280–82,
        286n3
teacher training, 133–36
Teaching to Transgress (hooks),
    178n1
theory, vs. practice, 5, 15–17,
    19–21, 54, 99, 122–29,
    130–33
Tuman, Myron, 48n2, 48n3, 83

University of Massachusetts at
    Amherst Writing Program, 97
"Untitled" (Miyamoto and
    Iijima), 196–97

Villanueva, Victor, 88, 118, 149,
    150
voice, 142–43

Weedon, Chris, 137n2, 169,
    178n3, 195

AUTHOR

Amy Lee is assistant professor and co-director of writing in the General College at the University of Minnesota, an open admissions program within the university that aims to promote access and success to postsecondary education. She teaches Basic Writing and Community Action Learning writing courses. She has been active in facilitating teacher and pedagogy development programs and has taught graduate courses in composition theory, critical theory, and pedagogy studies, as well as a range of undergraduate writing courses.

This book was typeset in Adobe Sabon by Electronic Imaging.
Typefaces used on the cover include Gill Sans and ITC Fenice.
The book was printed on 50-lb. Williamsburg Smooth by Versa Press.